American Football

The Records

Peter Rowe

GUINNESS BOOKS

Peter Rowe is one of Europe's leading authorities on American football.

He is a director and news editor of *First Down*, Britain's weekly newspaper on the sport, and a major contributor to *Quarterback*, the NFL's licensed monthly magazine.

Peter also covers the game for the *Daily Mail* and has contributed through commentary to many live US TV and radio broadcasts.

He has been a driving force in establishing the sport in Europe and is constantly in demand for advice on all aspects of the game both here in the UK and in the USA itself.

Acknowledgements

Numerous people, too many unfortunately to mention individually, should be thanked for their valuable assistance in compiling this book. Thank you to Beatrice Frei and all at Guinness Books, the staff at Mediawatch Ltd, especially Keith Webster, Ross Biddiscombe and Alan Lees, *Quarterback* magazine, the National Collegiate Athletic Association, the Canadian Football League, Don Smith at the Football Hall of Fame, Seymour Siwoff, President of the Elias Sports Bureau Inc., NY, and all the public relations directors of the NFL clubs and sports information directors of the major colleges in the USA.

Last but not least a big thank you to my wife Jane – the world's No 1 football widow.

Editor: Beatrice Frei
Design and Layout: Eric Drewery

© Peter Rowe and Guinness Superlatives Ltd, 1987

First published in 1985
Revised and updated in 1986
Third edition 1987

Published in Great Britain by Guinness Superlatives Ltd, 33 London Road, Enfield, Middlesex

Typeset in Palatino, Helvetica and Eras
by Input Typesetting Ltd, London
Printed and bound in Great Britain by
A. J. Acford, Chichester, Sussex

'Guinness' is a registered trade mark of Guinness Superlatives Ltd

British Library Cataloguing in Publication Data

Rowe, Peter
  Guinness American football: the records.
  —3rd ed.
  1. Football—History
  I. Title
  796.332'09   GV950

ISBN 0–85112–497–6

CONTENTS

1 History of American Football

1869–1960

The roots of American football, as all football games, can be traced back over 2000 years to 206 bc when the Chinese were known to have played a game called Tsu Chu. Although nothing like the ball games of today, Tsu Chu and its ancient equivalents, Harpastun from Rome, Episkylos from Greece, Kemari from Japan and the 11th century Norman game of La Soule were evidence of our ancestors' basic inclination to kick around an object for pleasure and perhaps sport.

During the next few centuries various types of unorganized games involving a ball that was kicked were developed and played all over Europe. There is evidence that a rudimentary game of football was played in the American colonies as early as 1700.

Naturally, when the European settlers flooded into the New World in the 19th century they brought their ball games with them.

As in England, at the turn of the century, the sport had a school-tie image and the north-eastern colleges of Princeton, Rutgers, Columbia, Yale and Harvard all played a game more akin to soccer than rugby.

The very first rules giving a semblance of order to the game were set down in 1867 and were known as the 'Princeton Rules'. Two years later on 6 November 1869 the first inter-collegiate game took place in New Brunswick, New Jersey, where Rutgers defeated Princeton 6–4. In a return match the following week Princeton won 8–0. Whilst the majority were playing a largely kicking game, Harvard had decided to allow a certain amount of running with the ball as in rugby. No one else in the north-east was interested in playing this style of game which is known to historians as 'The Boston Game', so a Canadian rugby team from McGill University in Montreal was invited to travel the 250 miles south to play in Cambridge, Massachusetts.

Unfortunately, four members of the McGill team fell ill before leaving and only 11 of the 15 playing members made the journey across the border on 15 May 1874. As a result the game went ahead with 11 instead of the normal 15 men per side. Had those four men been fit, American football might well be played with 15 men today.

The game was an enormous success and slowly the other northeastern schools took up the same style of play. On 13 November 1875 Yale met Harvard in the first game between two American universities under the new rules. A year later, on 23 November 1876 at Springfield, Massachusetts, the five colleges met and drew up the rules for the first intercollegiate league based largely on the rugby code and proclaiming itself the Intercollegiate Football Association.

The rugby style of heeling back the ball was played until 1880 when Walter Camp, the father of the modern game, introduced the scrimmage which allowed for more orderly possession of the ball.

Another founding father of the game was a gentleman with the unlikely name of Amos Alonzo Stagg. Stagg was a great innovator, designing and introducing the huddle in 1894, as well as the center snap, man-in-motion, reverses, diagrammed playbooks, backfield shifts, tackling dummies and various other refinements such as numbers on uniforms. Stagg was not only an inventor, he was also a brilliant coach. His 314 career victories was a record until Paul 'Bear' Bryant of Alabama University surpassed it in 1981.

The first rules were set down in 1867 and were known as the Princeton Rules.

Whilst Camp and Stagg were steadily moving the game away from its European roots other States in the nation were taking an interest in what they were doing.

In 1887 the Virginia Military Institute at Lexington introduced the game to the southern States. But it wasn't until 1898 that the north-eastern stranglehold was broken when Chicago University's halfback Clarence Herschberger was elected to an All-American team.

During this same period professional football had begun to take root. In 1892 Pudge Heffelfinger was paid the princely sum of $500 to play for the Allegheny Athletic Association. Travelling with three companions, who only received their return rail fare, Heffelfinger proved himself to be worth every penny of his fee. He won the game in one fell swoop by jarring the ball loose from an opposing half-back with a crunching tackle, then returning it and running across the goal line for the only score of the game in a 4–0 victory.

By 1895 professionalism had made rapid progress. During these stone age days of football, however, players received on average only $10 apiece for their efforts. Most of the teams in the new 'professional' leagues oper-ated in the steel belts of Pennsylvania and were sponsored by local steel companies. Of necessity games were played on Sundays and local businessmen found them worth backing in order to give their workers some recreation over the weekends. The better players on the teams were more often than not college men 'moonlighting' in the pro ranks, and the majority of colleges played their games on Saturdays. The game continued to grow and the very first night game was played in 1902 with makeshift floodlights set along the side-lines of a field in Elmira, New York.

Many of the teams were operated by baseball clubs who found it a useful occupation for their players during the winter months. One such player was the legendary turn-of-the-century pitcher Rube Waddell. Waddell however could not use his potent throwing arm since the forward pass was not to be legalized until 1906.

There were at this time no leagues, sched-ules, or league offices, and there was no Commissioner and very little money. As a result colourful episodes of ingenuity and rivalry were commonplace. Among the teams that flourished briefly during this period were the Duquesne Country and Athletic Club, the Homestead Library and Athletic Club and a team from Beloit, Wisconsin whose players had the nickname of the 'Fairies' because they were sponsored by the Fairbanks-Morse Company.

Since there was no overall governing body, eligibility rules were only conspicuous by their absence. Players would move from club to club

The University of Chicago, first team to use the T-formation.

The Massillon Tigers who were involved in the first gridiron betting scandal.

and many used more than six aliases in one season. In 1902 The Philadelphia Athletics claimed to be National Champions. A Pittsburgh team made the same claim and guaranteed the Athletics $3000 if they would settle the matter with a game. When the Athletics showed up at the football ground no money was forthcoming, so coach Connie Mack loaded his players into hansom cabs and headed back to the railway station. Fortunately for the fans who had turned up for the game a prosperous looking gentleman stopped them on the way. Mack explained to this gentleman that without the guarantee there would be no game, so the gentleman, who turned out to be William Lovey, the President of Carnegie Steel, saved the situation by signing one of his own personal cheques, whereupon the Athletics returned to win the game.

In 1906 the first major scandal in the history of professional football occurred. It centred on the fever-pitched inter-city rivalry of the Canton Bulldogs and the Massillon Tigers, both of the State of Ohio. In 1905 the Tigers, so called because of their striped jerseys, met the Bulldogs for the local championship.

The Tigers are to this day the only team in recorded history to be owned by a city editor, and it was he who thoughtfully provided a 10-ounce school ball for the game instead of the regulation 16-ounce one used by the professionals.

Needless to say, Massillon won the game 10–0. Blondy Wallace, the Canton coach, protested vigorously, but to no avail, so he retaliated by recruiting the whole Massillon starting backfield for the next season. At this stage in football's history there were no draft rules or restrictions against raiding other teams, so his action was perfectly legal.

The next year with his new backfield, Wallace beat Massillon 10–5 in the first game of a two-game series. The Bulldogs were naturally made favourites for the second, to be held in Massillon. They lost 12–6 and the day after the game the city editor of the *Massillon Independence* broke football's first betting scandal story. It is still the only substantiated story of a fix in pro football history.

Wallace, so the story went, had first tried to bribe several players on the Massillon team,

---

The five colleges of Yale, Princeton, Harvard, Rutgers and Columbia, formed the first football association, the Intercollegiate Football Association on 23 November 1876, at a meeting at Springfield, Massachusetts.

---

with no success. So he then persuaded one of his own players to throw the game. The player was allegedly chased out of Canton by irate citizens, but Wallace protested his innocence and even sued the newspaper. He later dropped the lawsuit when he was shown proof of his guilt. The scandal almost stopped the growth of professional football for good. It was 10 years before it began to thrive again.

Whilst the professional circuit was suffering its setbacks, college football was developing. Variations of the game were sprouting up in the far west and a version known as 'Kickball' was played as early as 1880. In this game a touchdown was worth only five points instead of the usual six.

The Universities of Stanford and California met in 1892 in what was the inaugural west coast collegiate game. Three years later the Western Athletic Conference (later to be called the Big Ten), was formed in the midwest. On 1 January 1902, 8000 fans turned out to watch the very first bowl game – the Rose Bowl. The game was the brainchild of the organizing committee of the Pasadena flower pageant, which the previous year had decided that this exciting new ball game would add to the attraction of its annual festival.

In the first game Michigan travelled the 2000 miles west to defeat stanford 49–9. For mainly financial reasons the game was then suspended for the next 14 years. College football was on the increase, but like its professional counterpart, the college game was heading for trouble. It experienced nothing as scandalous but there was still a serious enough problem to warrant the intervention of the President himself.

During the 1890s and early 1900s the game had become increasingly violent. In 1892 Harvard introduced their famous flying wedge, one of the most spectacular yet highly-dangerous moves ever seen in football. It was employed at a kick-off when a great wedge of the team's biggest and meanest players would form a 'V' shape and thunder towards the opposition's goal protecting the ball-carrier and inflicting as much damage as possible.

Stanford met California in 1892—the first inter-collegiate game on the west coast of America. The two teams have played each other every year since.

This violent style of play continued unchecked until it reached a peak in 1905 when 159 players were seriously injured and 18 actually died.

It was at this point that President Theodore Roosevelt stepped in and demanded to see the leaders of college football at the White House in Washington. He declared that if the league didn't make efforts to clean the game up he would ban it.

So it was that in 1906 the National Collegiate Athletic Association was set up to revise the rules, with the aim of ensuring safer, more open football without losing any of the game's character. Slugging, hurdling, mass turtleback attacking, and interlocked interference (which included the flying wedge) were all banned. The most important change, which broke the last major link with British rugby, was the introduction of the forward pass.

By 1912 American football had achieved its present form, which makes it quite distinct from any other kind of football.

The Indian Jim Thorpe was the biggest draw in the professional league until Red Grange came along in 1925, playing for Cleveland, Toledo, the Oorang Indians, the New York Giants, Toledo, Rock Island, and the Chicago Cardinals as well as Canton during his eight-year NFL career.

Whilst the Indian was helping to relaunch the professional game, another Indian settlement in Indiana was giving the college game an enormous lift. The former Indian fur trading post of South Bend had on its doorstep a university founded by French priests in the late 1800s. Notre Dame first came to prominence in 1913 when it unexpectedly beat the all-conquering Army team at West Point. After the First World War the university became part of football's folklore as its team was unbeaten for five seasons. A former chemistry graduate of Scandinavian parentage made the 'Fighting Irish' of Notre Dame into one of the country's most feared yet respected teams. Knute Rockne took over the reins at Notre Dame in 1918 and during his twelve-year tenure the Irish won 105 games and lost only 12. In 1920 halfback George Gipp set a record of 2341 yards on 369 carries, before being struck down with pneumonia in his senior year. On his death-bed he reportedly told coach Rockne, 'When things look bad, tell the boys to go in there and win one for the Gipper', a historic battle cry that was to make the football-crazy

Irish the team of the thirties and forties. Rockne waited eight years to relay this parting request. On 10 November 1928, after losing two of its first four games, an injury-riddled Notre Dame team travelled to Yankee Stadium to face the unbeaten Army. At half-time, Rockne made a passionate speech to his team relaying Gipp's request of 1920. He concluded, 'This is the day and you are the team'. Notre Dame went out and beat Army 12–6 in what many to this day describe as the finest demonstration of inspired football. Rockne was killed in a plane crash in 1931, but he still ranks as one of the best college coaches ever with his 105–12–5 record.

Three months before Gipp's untimely death a meeting took place at the Ralph E. Hay Motor Company at 122–134 McKinley Avenue North in Canton, Ohio. It was a hot Friday evening in September and the men who had gathered to discuss the formation of a stable professional football league sat on the running boards of the eight cars in the showroom in their shirt-sleeves. Ten teams were represented: Akron, Canton, Cleveland and Dayton, from Ohio; Chicago, Decatur and Rock Island from Illinois; Hammond and Muncie from Indiana; and Rochester from New York.

About the only thing the organizers decided on that day was the name—The American Professional Football Association. The fee to own a team (known as a franchise) was set at $100 and Jim Thorpe, who was representing Canton at the meeting, was elected as its first President. Thorpe is said to have known a great deal more about baseball than about

The great Jim Thorpe during his happy days playing gridiron.

running a football league and his tenure only lasted one year. In 1921 the new association was reorganized.

In that first season there was no official schedule of matches and the whole affair was rather haphazard, three teams eventually claiming the League Championship which was ultimately awarded to Akron. The next year George Halas's Chicago Staleys won the championship. There was again no official schedule, teams played each other on a catch-as-catch-can basis from week to week. Halas's club compiled a 10–1–1 record and despite protests from Buffalo that one of the Staleys' games was against non-league opposition they became the second champions of the APFA. In 1922 under the guidance of Halas the league changed its name to the National Football League, which it has been ever since.

Despite the new name and some reorganization the league continued to operate on a rather casual basis for the first few years. There was no constitution until 1921 when Joe Carr, a former sports writer who had taken over the presidency from Thorpe, drew up the first rules.

The rules were few and insubstantial. The number of players per team was established at 16, and the total payroll per game per team was limited to $1200 which was to include the coach or manager if either of them played. A team decimated by injury could, in an emergency, borrow a player or two from its opponents but had to pay his wages for that game.

The prize for winning the championship was a small engraved gold football for each player, which was not to cost more than $10, and the team was given a pennant. The one significant clause in the rules that had much to do with the subsequent success of professional football concerned the recruitment of players.

College 'moonlighting' was ended by a ruling that stated that no player who had performed on a Saturday could turn out in the same city for a professional team, or any other for that matter, on a Sunday. More importantly, the signing of a college player before his class had graduated was forbidden. An infringement of this rule carried a $1000 fine, no mean amount in those days, and could even result in a loss of franchise.

This ruling was put in to counteract the storm of protest that had surrounded the signing of Red Grange by the Chicago Bears

---

Goalposts of a sort were used in the Rutgers–Princeton game of 1869. They were 25 yards apart. The first proper goal posts were used in a game between Harvard and McGill University from Montreal, Canada, at Cambridge, Massachusetts in 1874. This game, coincidentally, was the first known game where an admission fee was charged.

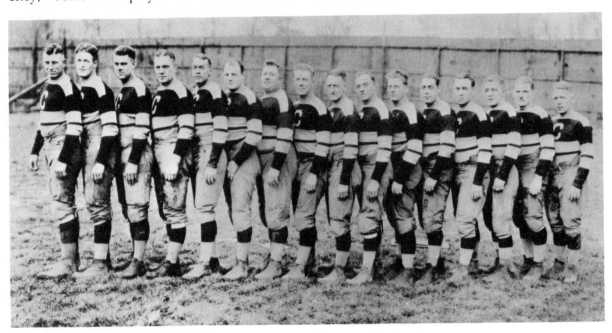

The Canton Buildings, considered to be the world's professional champions of 1922–23.

immediately after his final game for Illinois University in November 1925. The publicity that followed the signing of Grange was enormous and brought the professional ranks into the public eye at a national level for the first time.

Grange received a staggering $50 000 for playing 7 games in 11 days. Some thought it madness to pay such an amount but George Halas and the Chicago Bears were more than happy to hand it over. The Bears played before 36 000 fans in Chicago, 35 000 in Philadelphia and more than 65 000 in New York. Such huge crowds for professional football were unheard of in the mid 1920s.

After he had finished his first tour with the Bears, George departed on a hastily arranged trip to the South and West for which he earned another $75 000. No player, or owner, had ever earned $100 000 in a season before, and none would for many years to come. Grange, however, was a fine football player, and partly because of him professional football at last began to gain respectability on the sports pages of the national press.

The prosperity Grange brought to the Bears, though, was short-lived. Halas spent much of his time on street corners hawking tickets for the games and getting his share from an away gate was an even more hazardous affair. The Chicago boss would collect his percentage at half-time in a brown paper bag. He then assigned the task of escaping with the money to George Trafton, an All-American center from Notre Dame who he later described as 'meaner than a junkyard dog'. By the time the game was coming to an end most of the home fans were baying for Trafton's blood, since one of his favourite ploys was the use of the 'Notre Dame drop kick', a particularly nasty knee to a sensitive part of an opponent's anatomy. Halas would take Trafton out of the game with a minute or two left, give him the brown paper bag and dispatch him to the railway station at top speed. Such was 'Mean' Trafton's reputation that no one dared interrupt his flight and he was always at the station with the paper bag waiting for the arrival of his team-mates.

Professional football struggled through the 1920s. Twenty-two teams started the 1926 season, but by July 1927 ten of them had folded. In the late 1920s most of the franchises held by small towns died. The Depression that followed also had a damaging effect on pro football's status. Towns such as Providence

Rhode Island, Dayton Ohio, Hammond and Muncie of Indiana all lost teams. Providence actually won the championship in 1928, hit the Depression in 1929 and went out of business in 1932. Only eight teams survived the Depression and only six of them are still in business today: Chicago Bears, Chicago-St Louis Cardinals, the Detroit Lions (formerly the Portsmouth Spartans), the Green Bay Packers, the New York Giants and the Philadelphia Eagles, who began life as the Frankford Yellowjackets. It wasn't until 1932, that a new breed of owner enabled professional football to expand again.

College football, like its professional brother, was in difficulties but was beginning to attract growing crowds and during this period witnessed one of the greatest college games of all time.

In 1922 Notre Dame's genius of a coach Knute Rockne had devised a lineup of backfield players that for four seasons ran rampant

Harold 'The Galloping Ghost' Grange in action. (NFL Hall of Fame).

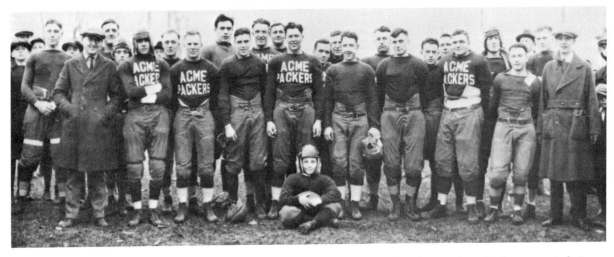

The Acme Packers, soon to be known as the Green Bay Packers. Note the player whose broken nose is being held in place by tape.

through their opponents' defenses. The Four Horsemen were quarterback Harry Stuhldreher, left halfback Jim Crowley, right halfback Don Miller and fullback Elmer Layden. In four seasons together Notre Dame only lost twice, both times to Nebraska. Their nickname, now one of the most famous in American sports history, arose after the Irish had defeated the Army 13–7 on 18 October 1924. A reporter wrote, 'Outlined against a blue-grey sky the four horsemen rode again'. A legend was born.

The four played their last game for the Indiana college in the 1925 Rose Bowl against Pop Warner's mighty Stanford. A crowd of 53 000 packed the Pasadena stadium that day in sweltering temperatures to witness a show of pure magic as Notre Dame's Elmer Layden scored three touchdowns to win the game 27–10. Included in Layden's tally was an interception of an Ernie Nevers pass when he ran 78 yards to give the Irish a 13–3 half-time lead. Stuhldreher broke an ankle early on in the game yet still returned to lead Rockne's team to a perfect 10–0 season and the National Championship.

The Rose Bowl game was reinstated in 1916 after a 14-year absence when Washington State beat Brown University 14–0. Many cities tried to copy the success of the Rose but mainly for

financial reasons none succeeded and it wasn't until 1935 that a serious contender in Miami, the Orange Bowl, was founded. Over the years the Rose Bowl had not been without its lighter moments. In the 1928 game California's center Roy Riegels picked up a fumble and ran 68 yards the wrong way with the ball before being tackled by his own quarterback!

Notre Dame, along with Stanford and Pittsburgh, continued to dominate college football until the early 1930s. But the untimely death of Rockne in 1931 created a vacuum at South Bend that was not to be filled until after the Second World War.

In 1932 two men entered the world of professional football and within a year their names were already imprinted in the pages of the game's history. George Preston Marshall was awarded a franchise for Boston on 9 July 1932. Bert Bell became a part-owner of the Philadelphia Eagles in 1933.

A year after joining the league Marshall suggested that it should be split into two divisions and that the two divisional champions should play for the World Title. In order to produce a believable championship for both the press and the public he insisted that each team should play the same number of games against the same opponents, an arrangement which, until then, had not been thought of.

At the spring 1935 owners' meeting, Bell, prompted by Marshall, made radical new proposals for a draft system. Until then it had been a dog-eat-dog affair with only a few of the top teams attracting the best of the graduating collegians. Bell's idea was simple: the last team

---

Amos Alonzo Stagg is widely credited with inventing the tackling dummy by sewing together two old gymnasium mats whilst coach at Yale in 1889.

Bert Bell, first commissioner of the NFL.

The first full uniform was worn by Leonidas P. Smock who turned out for Princeton in 1887 in a jersey on which was the letter P in orange, a canvas jacket and black knee breeches and socks.

Chicago All-Star Game took place between the Chicago Bears and an all-star college team. The collegians held the Bears to a 0–0 draw and the game marked a truce between the two factions. Until then many college administrators had openly declared war on the fledgling professional league. Now, with the inauguration of the all-star event, the colleges had more or less given the NFL the recognition it badly needed. The league had thus achieved respectability and at last established itself as a major element in American sport.

Despite the draft system the New York Giants and the Chicago Bears continued to dominate the league. The Bears were fuelled by a fullback from Minnesota who was to become a living legend. Bronko Nagurski stood 6ft 2in tall and weighed in at 230 lb— this being an extraordinary size for the 1930s. Nagurski played for the Bears from 1930 to 1937 and during that time was credited with 4031 yards in 872 carries, averaging a remarkable 4.6 yards per carry. Bronko Nagurski

in the league would get the first pick, and so on until the champions got the last selection in each round. The draft worked and some twenty years later Bell could say with justification, 'On any given Sunday, any team in this league can defeat any other'.

Coincidentally, the first draft in 1936 saw Bell's Philadelphia Eagles gain the first pick, as they had finished at the bottom of the league the previous season. The first player picked was Chicago University's tailback, Jay Berwanger. Berwanger could have become one of the greatest backs in professional football history, but because he wanted $1000 per game no team in the league could afford him, not even the rich Green Bay Packers or the Chicago Bears. So the very first draft pick in football history disappeared into oblivion.

In 1937 George Preston Marshall moved his Boston Redskins to Washington. Overnight the game of football took on a new perspective. Marshall introduced the first marching band and even had a team battle song specially written for the band to play. At half-time in all of his games he would have the band marching up and down the field and his showmanship gave football the broad appeal it has today.

The 1930s marked the coming of age of the National Football League. In 1934 the first

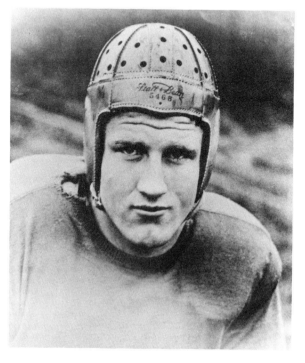

Bronko Nagurski.

could also pass and completed 38 of 80 passes during his career. His reputation was awesome, so much so that the owner of the Detroit franchise once offered him $10 000 to retire early.

Nagurski did retire in 1937 to concentrate on wrestling and farming back in his native Minnesota, but in 1943, when many of the top players were away fighting in the Second World War, he was persuaded to return to help the Bears to win the divisional title. In the championship game that year he scored a touchdown as Chicago defeated Washington 41–21.

In 1936 the only championship game to be played on a neutral field before the advent of the Super Bowls was staged at the New York Polo Grounds, when the Green Bay Packers met the Boston Redskins. The reason for the neutrality of the location was that Boston owner George Preston Marshall had become displeased with the lack of support afforded to his team, and in a final act of defiance to the city moved the game to New York. The Packers, with end Don Hutson dominant in their passing offense, won the game 21–6, but the remarkable thing about the game was that nearly 30 000 fans turned out in a neutral city to watch it. This gave a strong indication that professional football had at last arrived.

The 1940s began with what many experts reckoned to be one of the most influential games in the history of football: the championship final between the Washington Redskins and the Chicago Bears. The Bears completely swamped the Redskins to win the title 73–0. This became known as the game that changed the face of football.

The Chicago Bears used an updated version of the T-formation conceived by assistant coach Clark Shaughnessy, an eccentric genius who had previously coached at the Universities of Chicago and Stanford.

Before the advent of the T most teams had used a variety of formations, notably the single and double wing, and the Notre Dame Box.

George Musso – one of pro football's legends. (NFL Hall of Fame).

The Chicago T-formation included a man-in-motion, and they had gone through the regular season with an 8–3 record. Before the championship game with the Redskins, who had won the Eastern division, the Washington coach Ray Flaherty devised a defense to stop the Bears' offensive moves. But George Halas and Shaughnessy came up with a simple counter measure that caught the overshifting defense unawares.

Before the game ended 10 Bears had scored 11 touchdowns and the T-formation had captured the imagination of the football world.

The T-formation also had its effect on the college game. Shaughnessy had been head coach at the University of Stanford, and in 1940, after only one season, he had taken the Indians through the regular season unbeaten, ending the year as the nations' second best team with a Rose Bowl victory.

The war years also saw the emergence in college football of the military academies. The Army team and the mid 1940s, led superbly by

The first betting scandal took place at a game between the Canton Bulldogs and the Massillon Tigers in 1906.

Glen 'Mr Outside' Davis and Doc 'Mr Inside' Blanchard, became as legendary in college circles as Halas's Bears had become in the pro ranks. In one season Army averaged a record high of 56 points per game.

In 1946 a new professional league was born. The All-America Football Conference started life as a second rate league but within two years it had established itself as a serious contender for the NFL's crown. At various times there were franchises in Los Angeles, San Francisco, Cleveland, Buffalo, Baltimore, Chicago, New York and Miami, but only the Cleveland Browns, the San Francisco 49ers and the Buffalo Bills were successful.

After four years in which Cleveland had won each of the AAFC championships, the NFL announced a merger between the two football leagues. Only three teams—Cleveland, San Francisco and Baltimore—entered the enlarged National American Football League. However, its new name lasted only three months and it soon became known again as the NFL.

The most successful of the new teams from the AAFC had been Cleveland. In 1946 the NFL champions, the Cleveland Rams, had been given permission to move to Los Angeles, as the Rams, while the new Cleveland Browns, trained by one of the greatest coaches in pro football history, Paul Brown, moved in to continue their success albeit in the rival league.

In 1950 the first championship game of the two merged leagues threw up one of football's greatest contests: the Cleveland Browns against the Los Angeles Rams. The game was eventually won by a Lou Groza field goal with only 28 seconds left as the Browns, in their first season of NFL play, won 30–28. The strict disciplinarian tactics of Brown worked wonders at his namesake club and throughout the 1950s Cleveland was one of the dominant forces in the NFL.

The club beaten in that 1950 final game, the Los Angeles Rams, were also about to make an impact on the league. Clark Shaughnessy's pioneering tactics that had helped Chicago to the title in 1940 were now being used to change the face of football on the west coast.

In 1949, the Rams acquired Elroy Hirsch.

Hirsch had only just recovered from a fractured skull that had ended his career with the Chicago Rockets, and Shaughnessy was reluctant to place his new back in the backfield where relentless tackling might cause another injury. So the genius of a coach took Hirsch out of the backfield and flanked him wide, outside the end. The new offense was so explosive that Elroy 'Crazylegs' Hirsch never returned to the backfield and the pro-set as it was called became the new offensive formation for practically every team in the league.

The Rams' team of the early 1950s was a fearsome outfit. Leading the attack were quarterbacks Bob Waterfield and Norm Van Brocklin; Shaughnessy's air-orientated game with its variety of passing combinations to Hirsch, Tom Fears and Vitamin T. Smith broke almost every record in the book.

In the 1951 championship game an almost identical team met Cleveland in a replay of the 1950 game and this time reversed the result, winning 24–17.

Such was the ferocity of the Ram's offense that in one particular game against New York, Los Angeles gained a record-breaking 735

Bob Waterfield became a member of the NFL's Hall of Fame in 1965. (NFL Hall of Fame).

yards, Van Brocklin throwing for 554 yards (still a record in the NFL today).

The 1950s saw the emergence of a new force that was to help football establish itself as the national game – television. Over a period of eight years or so television had built up a healthy interest in the game and the televising of one particular game in 1958 caused that interest quite literally to explode. The championship between the Baltimore Colts and the New York Giants was so dramatic that it changed the football-loving American's perspective of the game. The hero of the day was Johnny Unitas, the Baltimore quarterback. Unitas had recovered from an injury to lead the Colts from behind to one of the most famous overtime victories ever. With barely two minutes left on the clock he engineered the drive that secured Baltimore's equalizing field

---

Makeshift floodlights were set along the sidelines for a game in Elmira, New York in 1902—the first floodlit game of football in the USA.

---

goal and then proceeded to march the Colts downfield in 14 plays to win the game with a delicate hand-off to Alan Ameche from the one yard line.

Whilst pro football's dynasties of the 1950s were forming, college football also had its star teams. One of the greatest schools of this era was undoubtedly Oklahoma. Under coach Bud Wilkinson the Sooners had developed into a devastating outfit. Such names as Billy Vessels, Heisman Trophy winning halfback of 1952, and the giant tackle Jim Weatherall, were the outstanding players in a team that brimmed with confidence.

In 1957 a fullback of average ability was drafted by Cleveland. If Unitas was the yardstick for quarterbacks then Jim Brown was to become the same for running backs. A giant of a man, a fine performer in both track events and basketball, Brown was also an All-America lacrosse player, but above all he was to become the most devastating running back who ever carried a football. Standing 6ft 2in and weighing 228lb, Jim Brown was said to have run with the speed of a sprinter, and to have hit with the impact of an express train. During

Detroit Lions Bobby Layne in action in 1951.

Sam Huff – a feared linebacker. (NFL Hall of Fame).

George Halas gives advice to Raymond Berry in the 1964 Pro Bowl. (NFL Hall of Fame).

his nine-year career Brown broke almost every record in the book. He averaged an astounding 5.2 yards per carry against defenses whose sole purpose was to stop him, and was an awesome sight with his long low gliding stride, and his way of keeping both feet firmly planted on the ground when tackled.

It is quite a surprise to learn that in spite of his position and size he was only injured a couple of times in his career, a career that saw him gain 12 312 yards and carry the ball 2359 times.

Brown would glide down the line of scrimmage looking for a gap, and when finding it would blast his way clear of grasping arms, to set up record-breaking runs. When collision became inevitable, he would lower his arm and shoulder and bring his thick muscular arm up into the tackler's head or chest with such ferocity that it would lift the defender off his feet.

Once when asked why Cleveland used Brown so much, coach Paul Brown replied,

'When you have the big gun, you pull the trigger'. Brown's influence on the growth in popularity of the league was probably greater than that of any player before him. At last the new breed of television fans had a figure to admire and attempt to copy.

The decade of the 1960s saw the beginnings of the game as we know it today, with the formation of the AFL and the appointment of Pete Rozelle as the league's third commissioner.

The first professional player was Pudge Heffelfinger who was paid $500 to play for the Allegheny Athletic Association in 1892.

FRANCO HARRIS

The Pittsburgh Steelers, the club that owner Art Rooney bought for $2500 in 1933, had waited a long time for a championship win.

But in 1974 time and talent (in the shape of Franco Harris) all came together to give Steelers fans, and perhaps their biggest, Rooney himself, the time of their life.

In the locker room after the Super Bowl IX game, Rooney gave a cigar to Harris, an obvious endorsement of the player's selection as the game's MVP. Harris had just done a demolition job on the Minnesota Vikings.

But it was two years earlier that Harris and the Steelers came together. And 'Mean' Joe Greene reckons that Harris and success was no coincidence. 'Franco was the key man on our ball club,' the Steelers defensive captain said. 'We're coming on every year, getting better and better. All we needed was the catalyst and Franco was it. He could have come here four years earlier and not made any difference at all, but that year, he was just what we needed.'

Franco Harris came to the Steelers from Penn State University. One of nine children, the son of a wartime marriage between an American army sergeant and an Italian woman, he was their first-round draft choice, and a controversial one at that. Many scouts questioned his desire. Some even said that he was a part-time player, drifting in and out of a game whenever he felt like it. That sort of attitude in American football is not tolerated.

He got off to a slow start, and backfield coach Dick Hoak later admitted, 'We thought we had a real dud on our hands'. In his first professional game, Harris gained a miserly 35 yards and fumbled twice in a loss to Cincinnati. But midway through his rookie season, Franco turned it on. He rushed for over 100 yards in six straight games, equalling Jim Brown's NFL record. The Steelers won nine of

their next ten games en route to the first play-off berth in their 40-year history.

His finest hour came in the playoffs when Franco made the play that will never be forgotten, catching a deflected pass and thundering 42 yards to the game-winning touchdown against Oakland. The play was instantly dubbed as 'The Immaculate Reception'.

Super Bowl IX was Harris's finest hour. He came into the game as the major threat to Minnesota coach Bud Grant's plans. But Franco had only trained lightly that week and was suffering from a heavy cold.

He shook it off and shook off the Vikings challenge. Carrying the ball six times on the Steelers' final touchdown drive and 11 times during that fourth quarter, Harris's rushing production for the day increased to 158 yards and broke the record of 145 yards set by Larry Csonka in Super Bowl VIII.

Harris went on to become one of the most durable, most productive runners in NFL history. He went over the 1000-yard mark seven times. His thirteen year total of 12 120 yards left him fourth on the all-time list.

But what was even more impressive was his record in playoff competition.

He was at the time the NFL's post-season leading rusher with 1482 yards. Holding the single-game records for yards gained in both AFC play-off competition and in Super Bowl (158), a record that has since been broken by first John Riggins and then Marcus Allen.

Franco Harris appeared in eight straight Pro Bowls, the only AFC player to do so before he retired in 1984. He spent an unhappy season at Seattle before the injuries took their toll and Franco Harris bowed out of football for good.

But, despite being one of the best backs in the business, from a statistical viewpoint, during his tenure in Pittsburgh, the Steelers never missed a playoff season.

A Chronological History of Professional Football

1892 Rutgers and Princeton had played a college soccer football game, the first ever, in 1869. Rugby had gained favour over soccer, however, and from it rugby football, then football, had evolved among American colleges. It was also played by athletic clubs. Intensive competition existed between two Pittsburgh clubs, Allegheny Athletic Association and Pittsburgh Athletic Club. William (Pudge) Heffelfinger, former star at Yale, brought in by AAA, paid $500 to play in game against PAC, becoming first person known to have been paid openly to play football, 12 November, AAA won 4–0 when Heffelfinger picked up PAC fumble and ran for touchdown, which then counted four points.

1898 Morgan AC founded on Chicago's South Side, later became Chicago Normals, Racine (a Chicago street) Cardinals, Chicago Cardinals, and St Louis Cardinals, oldest continuing operation in pro football.

1899 Duquesne Country and Athletic Club, or Pittsburgh Duquesnes, included large payroll signing players returning from Spanish-American War, sought help from Pittsburgh sportsman William C. Temple. He bought football team from athletic club, became first known individual club owner.

1901 Temple and Barney Dreyfuss of baseball Pirates formed new team and urged cross-state rivalry with Philadelphia.

1902 Philadelphia Athletics, managed by Connie Mack, and Nationals or Phillies formed football teams. Athletics won first night football game, 39–0 over Kanaweola AC at Elmira, NY, 21 November.

Athletics claimed pro championship after winning two, losing one against Phillies and going 1–1–1 against Pittsburgh Pros. Pitcher Rube Waddell played for Athletics, pitcher Christy Matthewson was fullback for Pittsburgh in one game.

'World Series', actually four-team tournament, played among Athletics, New York Knickerbockers, Watertown, NY, Red and Blacks, and Syracuse AC, was played in Madison Square Garden. Philadelphia and Syracuse played first indoor football game before 3000, 28 December. Syracuse, with Pop Warner at guard, won game 6–0, went on to win tournament.

1903 Franklin (Pa.) AC won second and last 'World Series' of pro football over Philadelphia, Watertown, and Orange, NJ, AC.

Pro football declined in Pittsburgh area. Some PAC players hired by Massillon, Ohio, Tigers, making Massillon first openly professional team in Ohio.

1904 Ohio had at least eight pro teams. Attempt failed to form league to end cut-throat bidding for players, write rules for all.

1905 Canton Bulldogs turned professional.

1906 Archrivals Massillon and Canton played twice. Massillon won both. Because of betting scandal, Canton manager Blondy Wallace left in disgrace, interest in pro football in two cities declined.

1913 Jim Thorpe, former football star for Carlisle Indian School and hero of 1912 Olympics, played season for Pine Village Pros in Indiana.

1915 Canton revived name 'Bulldogs' and signed Thorpe for $250 a game.

1916 With Thorpe starring, Canton won 10 straight, most by lopsided scores, was acclaimed pro football champion of world.

1919 George Calhoun, Curly Lambeau organized Green Bay Packers. Indian Packing Company provided equipment, name 'Packers'. They had 10–1 record against other company teams.

1920 Pro football was in state of confusion, teams were loosely organized, players moved freely among teams, there was no system for recruiting players. A league in which all followed the same rules was needed. Meeting was held among interested teams in August, second meeting was held in Canton and American Professional Football Association, forerunner of National Football League, formed 17 September. Teams were from four states—Akron Pros, Canton Bulldogs, Cleveland Indians, Dayton Triangles from Ohio; Hammond Pros, Muncie Flyers from Indiana; Racine (Chicago) Cardinals, Rock Island Independents, Decatur Staleys, represented by George Hallas, from Illinois; Rochester, NY, Jeffersons.

Capitalizing on his fame, Thorpe was chosen league president, Stan Cofall of Cleveland vice president. Membership fee of $100 arrived at to give aura of respectability. No team ever paid it. Buffalo All-Americans, Chicago Tigers, Columbus, Ohio, Panhandles, and Detroit Tigers joined league later in year. League operated sporadically, teams played as many non-members as members, either no standings kept or have since been lost. Akron, Buffalo, Canton all claimed championship, hastily arranged series of games, one of them between Buffalo and Canton at Polo Grounds, New York City, failed to settle issue of championship.

First recorded player deal sale of Bob Nash, tackle and end for Akron, to Buffalo for $300, 5 per cent of gate receipts.

1921 APFA reorganized at Akron, Joe Carr of Panhandles named president, 30 April. Carl Storck of Dayton named secretary-treasurer. Carr established league headquarters at Columbus. Carr's first order was to declare Akron 1920 league champions.

J. E. Clair of Acme Packing Company granted franchise for Green Bay Packers, 27 August. Cincinnati Celts also joined league.

A. E. Staley turned Decatur Staleys over to George Halas, who moved them to Cubs Park in Chicago, promising to keep the name 'Staleys' one more year.

Chicago Staleys claimed league championship with 10–1–1 record. Buffalo, 9–1–2, claimed Chicago included non-league games in record, but Carr ruled for Staleys.

1922 Packers disciplined for using college players under assumed names.

APFA changed name to National Football League, 24 June. Staleys became Chicago Bears.

The Green Bay Packers were thrown out of the NFL in 1922 for using college players under assumed names. The club returned to the league later in the same year.

Thorpe, other Indian players formed Oorang Indians in Marion, Ohio, sponsored by Oorang dog kennels.
1923 Oorang folded with 1–10 record, Thorpe moved to Toledo Maroons. Player-coach Halas of Chicago recovered fumble by Thorpe in game against Oorang, ran 98 yards for touchdown.
1924 Frankford Yellowjackets of Philadelphia awarded franchise, that city entered league for first time. League champion Canton moved to Cleveland to play before larger crowds to meet rising payroll.
1925 Tim Mara and Billy Gibson awarded franchise for New York City for $500. Detroit Panthers, Pottsville Maroons, Providence Steam Roller also entered league. New team in Canton took name 'Bulldogs.'

University of Illinois season ended and Red Grange signed contract to play for Chicago Bears immediately, 22 November. Crowd of 38 000 watched Grange and Bears in traditional Thanksgiving game against Cardinals. Chicago Cardinals, with best record, were the 1925 champions.
1926 Grange's manager, C. C. Pyle, asked Bears for five-figure salary for Grange, one-third ownership of team. Bears refused, lost Grange. AFL champion Philadelphia Quakers played post-season game against NFL New York Giants, lost 31–0.

NFL membership swelled to 22, frustrating AFL growth. Paddy Driscoll of Cardinals moved to rival Bears.
1927 AFL folded, NFL shrank to 12 teams. Akron, Canton, Columbus left NFL. New York Yankees and Grange joined NFL. New York Giants won first NFL championship, scoring five consecutive shutouts at one point.
1928 Grange left football, appeared in movie and on vaudeville circuit.
1929 NFL added fourth official, field judge, 28 July. Cardinals became first pro team to go to out-of-town training camp, Coldwater, Michigan, 21 August. Dayton played final season, last of original Ohio teams to leave league.

Packers signed back Johnny Blood (McNally), tackle Cal Hubbard, guard Mike Michalske, and won first NFL championship.
1930 Portsmouth, Ohio, Spartans joined NFL. Defunct Dayton franchise became Brooklyn Dodgers. Bears and Cardinals played exhibition for unemployment relief funds, indoors at Chicago Stadium, layer of dirt covering arena floor. New York Giants, 'Notre Dame All-Stars' coached by Knute Rockne, played charity exhibition before 55 000 at Polo Grounds.

Packers won second straight NFL championship.
1931 Pro football shrank to 10 teams. Carr fined Bears, Packers, Portsmouth $1000 each for using players whose college classes had not graduated.

Green Bay won third straight NFL championship
1932 George P. Marshall awarded franchise for Boston. Named team 'Braves' after baseball team using same park.

NFL membership dropped to eight, lowest in history. First playoff in NFL history arranged between Bears and Spartans. Moved indoors to Chicago Stadium because of blizzard conditions in city. Arena allowed only 80-yard field that came right to walls. For safety, goal posts moved from end to goal lines, inbounds lines or hashmarks drawn 10 yards from side-lines for ball to be put in play. Bears won 9–0, 18

Gerritt Smith Miller, a student at the Dixwell School in Peterborough, New York, organized the Oneida football club of Boston in 1862. The first known football organization in the USA.

December, scoring touchdown disputed by Spartans who claimed Bronko Nagurski threw jump pass to Red Grange from point less than five yards behind the line of scrimmage, violating existing passing rule.
1933 NFL made significant changes in rules of football first time. Innovations of 1932 indoor playoffs—inbounds lines or hashmarks 10 yards from side-lines, goal posts on goal lines—became rules. Also, the forward pass legalized anywhere behind line of scrimmage.

Franchise was awarded to Art Rooney and A. McCool of Pittsburgh, team was named 'Pirates'. In Philadelphia franchise awarded to Bert Bell, Lud Wray; named team 'Eagles'. Boston changed name to 'Redskins'. George Halas bought out Ed (Dutch) Sternamen, became sole owner of Chicago Bears, reinstated himself as head coach.

Eastern Division champion New York Giants met Western Division champion Bears at Wrigley Field in first NFL championship game, 17 December. Bears won 23–21.
1934 Bears played scoreless tie against collegians in first Chicago All-Star Game before 79 432 at Soldier Field, 31 August.
1935 Bell of Philadelphia proposed, NFL adopted annual draft of college players, to begin in 1936, with team finishing last in standings having first choice each round of draft.
1936 Last place previous year, Philadelphia Eagles made Jay Berwanger, University of Chicago back, first choice in first NFL draft. Eagles later traded negotiation rights to him to Bears. He never played pro football.

Rival league was formed, became second to call itself American Football League. It included six teams, Boston Shamrocks won championship.
1937 Cleveland returned to NFL. Homer Marshman was granted a franchise, he named new team 'Rams'. Marshall moved Redskins to Washington.
1938 Los Angeles newspaper officials established Pro Bowl game between NFL champion, team of all-stars.
1939 New York Giants defeated Pro All-Stars 13–10 in first Pro Bowl game at Wrigley Field, Los Angeles.

Carr, NFL president since 1921, died in Columbus, 20 May. Carl Storck named successor, 25 May.

National Broadcasting Company camera beamed Brooklyn Dodgers—Philadelphia Eagles game from Ebbets Field back to studios of network, handful of sets then in New York City, first NFL game to be televised.
1940 Clipping penalty reduced from 25 to 15 yards, all distance penalties enforced from spot on field of play limited to half distance to goal.

Pittsburgh changed nickname from Pirates to Steelers.

Art Rooney sold Pittsburgh to Alexis Thompson, 9

December, and later purchased part-interest in Philadelphia.

Bears, playing T-formation with man-in-motion, defeated Washington 73–0 in NFL championship, 8 December. It was first championship carried on network radio, broadcast by Red Barber to 120 stations of Mutual Broadcasting System, which paid $2500 for rights.

1941 Elmer Layden, head coach, athletic director at Notre Dame, named first commissioner of NFL, 1 March. Moved league headquarters to Chicago. Carl Storck resigned as president-secretary, 5 April.

Co-owners Bell, Rooney of Eagles transferred ownership to Alexis Thompson in exchange for Pittsburgh franchise.

Playoffs were provided for in case of ties in division races. Sudden-death overtime provided for in case playoff was tied after four quarters.

Bears defeated Green Bay 33–14 in first divisional playoff in NFL history, winning Western Division championship, 14 December.

1942 Players departing for service in Second World War reduced rosters of NFL teams.

1943 Cleveland Rams granted permission to suspend operations for one season.

NFL adopted free substitution, 7 April. Abbreviated wartime rosters, however, prevented its effects from taking place immediately. Also made helmets mandatory and approved 10-game schedule.

Philadelphia, Pittsburgh granted permission to merge, became Phil-Pitt. They divided home games between two cities. Merger automatically dissolved last day of season.

Ted Collins granted franchise for Boston to become active in 1944.

1944 Collins, who had wanted franchise in Yankee Stadium in New York, named new team in Boston 'Yanks'. Cleveland resumed operations. Brooklyn Dodgers changed name to 'Tigers'.

Cardinals, Pittsburgh requested by league to merge for one year under name, Card-Pit. Merger automatically dissolved last day of season.

Coaching from bench legalized.

1945 Players required to wear long stockings.

Boston Yanks, Brooklyn Tigers merged as 'Yanks'.

Halas rejoined Bears after service with US Navy in Pacific. Returned to head coaching.

After Japanese surrender ending Second World War, count showed NFL service roster, limited to men who played in league games, totalled 638, 21 of whom had died.

1946 Layden resigned as commissioner, replaced by Bell, co-owner of Pittsburgh Steelers. Bell moved

---

In New Jersey the Orange Athletic Club awarded trophies and watches to its players at the end of each season. Some clubs said that this was a form of paying as many players later pawned their rewards. But once again the governing body, the American Amateur Athletic Union, decreed that this was all right.

---

league headquarters from Chicago to Philadelphia suburb of Bala Cynwyd.

Free substituion withdrawn, substitutions limited to no more than three men at time. Forward passes made automatically incomplete upon striking goal posts.

NFL champion Cleveland given permission to transfer to Los Angeles. NFL became coast-to-coast league for first time.

Rival league, All-America Football Conference, formed. Four of its eight teams were in same population centres as NFL teams—Brooklyn Dodgers, New York Yankees, Chicago Rockets, Los Angeles Dons. Cleveland Browns won AAFC championship.

Backs Frank Filchock and Merle Hapes of the Giants questioned about attempt by New York man to fix championship game vs. Chicago; Commissioner Bell suspended Hapes, permitted Filchock to play. He played well but Chicago won 24–14.

1947 Bell's contract as commissioner was renewed for five years.

NFL added fifth official, back judge. Sudden death readopted for championship games.

Halfback Fred Gehrke of Los Angeles Rams painted horns on Rams helmets, first helmet emblems in pro football.

AAFC again had eight teams. Cleveland Browns won second championship.

1948 Plastic head protectors prohibited. Flexible artificial tee permitted at kickoff. Officials besides referee equipped with whistles, not horns.

Cleveland Browns won third straight championship of eight-team AAFC.

1949 Thompson sold NFL champion Philadelphia Eagles to syndicate headed by James P. Clark.

Commissioner Bell, vice president and treasurer Dennis Shea, given 10-year contracts.

Free substitution adapted for one year.

Boston Yanks became New York Bulldogs, shared Polo Grounds with Giants.

Cleveland won fourth straight championship of AAFC, reduced to seven teams. Bell announced merger agreement 9 December in which three AAFC teams—Cleveland, San Francisco 49ers, Baltimore Colts—would enter NFL in 1950.

1950 Free substitution restored, way opened for two-platoon era, specialization in pro football.

Name 'National Football League' returned after about three months as 'National-American Football League'. American, National conferences replaced Eastern, Western divisions.

New York Bulldogs became 'Yanks', divided players of former AAFC Yankees with Giants.

Los Angeles Rams became first NFL team to contract to have all its games televised. Arrangement covered both home and away games, sponsor agreed to make up difference in home game income if lower than year before (cost sponsor $307 000). Washington also arranged to televise games, other teams made deals to put selected games on television.

For first time in history deadlocks occurred, playoffs were necessary in both conferences (divisions). Cleveland defeated Giants in American, Los Angeles defeated Bears in National. In one of the most exciting championship games, Cleveland defeated Los Angeles 30–28, 24 December.

1951 Pro Bowl game, dormant since 1942, revived

In 1932 the NFL's membership shrank to only eight teams. The smallest in its 67-year history.

under new format matching all-stars of each conference at Los Angeles Memorial Coliseum. American Conference defeated National 28–27.

Rule passed that no tackle, guard, or center eligible for forward pass.

DuMont Network paid $75 000 for rights to championship game, televised coast-to-coast for first time, Los Angeles defeated Cleveland 24–17.

1952 Ted Collins sold New York Yanks' franchise to NFL. New franchise awarded to Dallas Texans, first NFL team in Texas. Yanks had been, in order, Boston Yanks, New York Bulldogs, New York Yanks. Texans, won 1, lost 11, folded, last NFL team to become extinct.

1953 Baltimore re-entered NFL. League awarded holdings of defunct Dallas franchise to group headed by Carroll Rosenbloom that formed team with name 'Colts', same as former franchise.

Names of American, National Conferences changed to Eastern, Western Conferences.

1954 Bell given new 12-year contract.

1955 Sudden death overtime rule used for first time, on experimental basis in pre-season game between Los Angeles, New York at Portland, Oregon, 28 August. Los Angeles won 23–17 three minutes into overtime.

Quarterback Otto Graham played last game for Cleveland, 38–14 victory over Los Angeles for NFL championship.

NBC replaced DuMont as network for title game, paying rights fee of $100 000.

1956 Halas retired as coach of Bears, replaced by Paddy Driscoll. Giants moved from Polo Grounds to Yankee Stadium.

Grabbing opponent's facemask made illegal, with exception of ball carrier's.

CBS became first to broadcast some NFL regular season games to selected television markets across nation.

Then NFL-record crowd, 102 368, saw 49ers–Rams game at Los Angeles Memorial Coliseum, 10 November. Detroit Lions came from 20 points down for playoff victory over 49ers 31–27, 22 December.

1958 Halas reinstated himself as Bears coach for third time; others were in 1933, 1946.

Jim Brown of Cleveland gained NFL-record 1527 yards rushing.

Baltimore, coached by Weeb Ewbank, defeated New York 23–17 in first sudden death NFL championship game, Alan Ameche scoring for Colts after 8 minutes, 15 seconds of overtime.

1959 Tim Mara, co-founder of Giants, died.

Lamar Hunt announced intentions to form second pro football league. Hunt representing Dallas, others representing Denver, Houston, Los Angeles, Minneapolis-St. Paul, New York City. Held first meeting of league at Chicago, 14 August. Made plans to begin play in 1960. Eight days later at second meeting announced name of organization would be 'American Football League'. Buffalo became seventh AFL team, Boston eighth. First AFL draft held, 22 November. Joe Foss named AFL commissioner.

NFL commissioner Bell died of heart attack suffered at Franklin Field, Philadelphia, during last two minutes of game between Eagles–Pittsburgh, 11 October. Treasurer Austin Gunsel named President in office of commissioner until January 1960, annual meeting.

1960 Pete Rozelle elected NFL commissioner on twenty-third ballot, succeeding Bell.

Hunt, founder of AFL, elected president for 1960, Oakland became eighth AFL team, 30 January. Eastern, Western divisions set up. Five-year contract signed with American Broadcasting Company for network television of selected games.

NFL awarded Dallas 1960 franchise, Minnesota 1961 franchise, expanding to 14 teams. They took nicknames 'Cowboys', 'Vikings'.

Chicago Cardinals transferred to St Louis.

Boston Patriots defeated Bills 28–7 at Buffalo in first AFL pre-season game before 16 000. Denver Broncos defeated Patriots 13–10 at Boston in first AFL regular season game before 21 597.

1961 Houston Oilers defeated Los Angeles Chargers 24–16 for first AFL championship before 32 183 at Houston.

End Willard Dewveall of Bears played out his option, joined Houston of AFL, first player deliberately to move from one league to other.

NBC awarded two-year contract for radio and tele-

In 1962 the Lions 'Fearsome Foursome' defense of Alex Karras, Roger Brown, Darris McGord and Sam Williams sacked Green Bay quarterback Bart Starr 11 times.

1939 marked the year when football found itself on TV for the first time. On 30 September 1939 Fordham's 34–7 victory over Waynesburg College was televised in New York. A month later the NBC company showed the game between the Brooklyn Dodgers and the Philadelphia Eagles.

vision rights to NFL championship game for $615 000 annually, $300 000 of which was to go directly into NFL Player Benefit Plan.

Canton, where league that became NFL had been formed in 1920, chosen site of Pro Football Hall of Fame.

Green Bay won first NFL championship since 1944, defeating New York 37–0.

1962 West defeated East 47–27 in first AFL All-Star Game before 20 973 in San Diego.

NFL prohibited grabbing any player's facemask.

Commissioners Rozelle of NFL, Foss of AFL given new five-year contracts.

NFL entered into single network agreement with CBS for telecasting all regular season games for $4 650 000 annually, 10 January.

Judge Roszel Thompson of US District Court, Baltimore, ruled against AFL in anti-trust suit against NFL, 21 May. AFL had charged monopoly, conspiracy in areas of expansion, television, player-signings. Case lasted two and a half years, trial lasted two months.

Dallas defeated Oilers 20–17 for AFL championship at Houston after 17 minutes, 54 seconds of sudden death overtime on 25-yard field goal by Tommy Brooker, 23 December. Game lasted record 77 minutes, 54 seconds.

1963 AFL's guarantee for visiting teams during regular season increased from $20 000 to $30 000.

Hunt's Dallas Texans transferred to Kansas City, becoming 'Chiefs'. New York Titans sold to five-member syndicate headed by David (Sonny) Werblin, name changed to 'Jets'.

Commissioner Rozelle suspended indefinitely Paul Hornung, Green Bay halfback, Alex Karras, Detroit defensive tackle, for placing bets on their own teams and on other games; also fined five other Detroit players $2000 each for betting on one game in which they did not participate, and the Detroit Lions Football Co. $2000 on each of two counts for failure to report promptly information and for lack of side-line supervision.

NBC awarded exclusive network broadcasting rights for 1963 AFL championship game for $926 000, 23 May.

Boston defeated Buffalo 26–8 in first divisional play-off in AFL history before 33 044 in Buffalo.

Chicago defeated New York 14–10 for NFL championship, record sixth and last title for Halas in his thirty-sixth season as Bears' coach.

1964 Paul Hornung of Green Bay, Alex Karras of Detroit, reinstated by Rozelle.

Paul Brown departed Cleveland after 17 years as their head coach Blanton Collier replaced him.

AFL commissioner Foss given new three-year contract commencing in 1965.

New York defeated Denver 30–6 before then AFL-record crowd of 46 665 in first game at Shea Stadium.

Peter Gogolak of Cornell signed contract with Buffalo, becoming first soccer-style kicker in pro football.

1965 NFL teams pledged not to sign college seniors until completion of all their games, including bowl games, empowered commissioner to discipline clubs up to as much as loss of entire draft list for violation of pledge, 15 February.

NFL added sixth official, line judge. Colour of officials' penalty flags changed from white to bright gold.

Atlanta awarded NFL franchise for 1966, with Rankin Smith as owner. Miami awarded AFL franchise for 1966, with Joe Robbie, Danny Thomas as owners.

Green Bay defeated Baltimore 13–10 in sudden death Western Conference playoff game. Don Chandler kicking 25-yard field goal for Packers after 13 minutes, 39 seconds of overtime.

CBS acquired rights to NFL regular season games in 1966, 1967, plus option for 1968, for $18.8 million per year.

1966 AFL–NFL war reached its peak, leagues spent combined total of $7 million to sign 1966 draft choices. NFL signed 75 per cent of its 232 draftees, AFL 46 per cent of its 181. Of 111 common draft choices, 79 joined NFL, 28 joined AFL, four went unsigned.

Joe Foss resigned as AFL commissioner, 7 April. Al Davis, head coach, general manager of Oakland Raiders, named to replace him.

Goal posts offset from goal line, coloured bright gold, with uprights 20 feet above crossbar made standard in NFL.

Merger announced; NFL, AFL entered into agreement to form combined league of 24 teams, expanding to 26 in 1968, 8 June. Rozelle named commissioner. Leagues agreed to play separate schedules until 1970, but would meet, starting in 1967, in world championship game (Super Bowl) and play each other in pre-season games.

Davis rejoined Oakland Raiders. Milt Woodard named president of AFL.

New Orleans awarded NFL franchise to begin play in 1967.

NFL realigned for 1967–69 seasons into Capitol, Century divisions in Eastern Conference, Central, Coastal divisions in Western Conference. New Orleans, New York agreed to switch divisions in 1968, return to 1967 alignment in 1969.

Rights to Super Bowl for four years sold to CBS and NBC for $9.5 million.

1967 Green Bay Packers of NFL defeated Kansas City of AFL 35–10 at Los Angeles in first Super Bowl, 15 January. Winning share for Packers was $15 000 each, losing share for Chiefs $7500 each.

'Sling-shot' goal post, six-foot-wide border around field made standard in NFL.

Baltimore made Bubba Smith, Michigan State defensive lineman, first choice in first combined AFL–NFL draft.

AFL awarded franchise to Cincinnati, to begin play in 1968, with Paul Brown as part-owner, general manager, head coach.

AFL team defeated NFL team for first time, Denver beat Detroit 13–7 in pre-season game, 5 August.

Until 1956 coaches were permitted to coach from the side-lines with the help of a loudspeaker.

Green Bay defeated Dallas 21–17 for NFL championship on last-minute one-yard quarterback sneak by Bart Starr in 13-below temperature at Green Bay.

George Halas retired fourth and last time as head coach of Chicago Bears at age 73.

1968 Green Bay defeated Oakland 33–14 in Super Bowl II at Miami, game had first $3 million gate in pro football history, 14 January.

Lombardi resigned as head coach of Packers, remained as general manager.

'Heidi' became a part of the nation's vocabulary when last 1:05 of key Jets–Raiders game was cut off the air to permit children's special to begin on time. Raiders scored two touchdowns in last 42 seconds to win 43–32.

Ewbank became first coach to win titles in both NFL, AFL, his Jets defeated Oakland 27–23 for AFL championship.

1969 AFL team won Super Bowl for first time; Jets defeated Baltimore 16–7 at Miami, 12 January.

Lombardi became part-owner, executive vice president, head coach of Washington Redskins.

Baltimore, Cleveland, Pittsburgh agreed to join AFL teams to form 13-team American Football Conference, remaining NFL teams to form National Football Conference in NFL in 1970. AFC teams voted to realign in Eastern, Central, Western divisions.

Monday night football set for 1970; ABC acquired rights to televise 13 NFL regular season Monday night games in 1970, 1971, 1972.

George P. Marshall, president emeritus of Redskins, died at 72.

1970 Kansas City defeated Minnesota 23–7 in Super Bowl IV at New Orleans, 11 January. Gross receipts of approximately $3.8 million largest ever for one-day team sports event, television audience largest ever for one-day sports event.

NFC realigned into Eastern, Central, Western divisions.

Lombardi, part-owner, executive vice president, head coach of Redskins, died at 57.

Tom Dempsey of New Orleans Saints kicked game-winning NFL-record 63-yard field goal against Detroit Lions.

1971 Baltimore defeated Dallas 16–13 on Jim O'Brien's 32-yard field goal with five seconds to go in Super Bowl V at Miami, 17 January. NBC telecast was viewed in estimated 23 980 000 homes, largest audience ever for one-day sports event.

NFC defeated AFC 27–6 in first AFC–NFC Pro Bowl at Los Angeles.

Boston Patriots changed name to New England Patriots.

Miami defeated Kansas City 27–24 in sudden death in AFC divisional play-off game, Garo Yepremian kicking 37-yard field goal for Dolphins after 22 minutes, 40 seconds of overtime, game lasting 82 minutes, 40 seconds in all, longest in history, 25 December.

1972 Dallas defeated Miami 24–3 in Super Bowl VI at Miami, 16 January. CBS telecast was viewed in estimated 27 450 000 homes, top-rated one-day telecast ever.

Robert Irsay purchased Los Angeles, transferred ownership to Carroll Rosenbloom in exchange for Baltimore.

William V. Bidwill purchased stock of brother Charles (Stormy) Bidwill, became sole owner, president of St Louis Cardinals.

Franco Harris's 'Immaculate Reception' gave Steelers first post-season win in franchise's 40-year history, 13–7 over the Raiders.

1973 Rozelle announced all Super Bowl VII tickets sold, game would be telecast in Los Angeles, site of game, on experimental basis.

Miami defeated Washington 14–7 in Super Bowl VII at Los Angeles, completing undefeated 17–0 record for 1972 season, 14 January. NBC telecast viewed by approximately 75 000 000 people. Although all 90 182 tickets had been sold and temperatures reached 84 degrees on clear, sunny day, 8476 ticket buyers did not attend game that was first ever televised locally.

AFC defeated NFC 33–28 in Pro Bowl in Dallas, first time since 1951 game played outside Los Angeles.

Jersey numbering system adopted, 1–19 for quarterbacks, specialists; 20–49, running, defensive backs; 50–59, centers, linebackers; 60–79, defensive linemen, interior offensive linemen except centers; 80–89, wide receivers, tight ends, 5 April. Players who had been in NFL in 1972 could continue to use old numbers.

NFL Charities non-profit organization created to derive income from monies generated by licensing of NFL trademarks and names, 26 June; would support education, charitable activities, supply economic support to persons formerly associated with professional football no longer able to support themselves.

Joe Perry – 1969 Hall of Fame inductee. (NFL Hall of Fame).

1974 Miami defeated Minnesota 24–7 in Super Bowl VIII at Houston, second straight Super Bowl championship for Miami.

Rival league formed; World Football League held organizational meeting.

Tampa awarded franchise to begin play in 1976. NFL announced one more franchise would be awarded to become operative in 1976.

Sweeping rule changes adopted as recommended by Competition Committee to add action, tempo to game: sudden death for pre-season, regular season games, limited to one 15-minute overtime; goal posts moved from goal line to end lines; kick-offs to be made from 35- not 40-yard line; after missed field goals ball to be returned to line of scrimmage or 20-yard line, whichever is furthest from goal line; restrictions placed on members of punting team to open up return possibilities; roll-blocking, cutting of wide receivers eliminated, extent of downfield contact defender can have with eligible receivers restricted; penalty for offensive holding, illegal use of hands, tripping reduced from 15 yards to 10 yards when occurs within three yards of line of scrimmage; wide receivers blocking back toward ball within three yards of line of scrimmage prevented from blocking below the waist, 25 April.

Seattle awarded NFL franchise to begin play in 1976.

Birmingham Americans defeated Florida Blazers 22–21 in WFL World Bowl, winning championship of the 12-team league.

1975 Pittsburgh defeated Minnesota 16–6 in Supebowl IX at New Orleans, Steelers' first championship since entering NFL in 1933. NBC telecast was viewed by approximately 78 million people.

Rules changed making incomplete pass into end zone on fourth down with line of scrimmage inside 20 returned to line of scrimmage instead of 20; double shift on or inside opponent's 20 permitted provided it has been shown three times in game instead of three times in quarter; penalty for ineligible receiver downfield reduced from 15 to 10 yards; goal post uprights raised to 30 feet above crossbar, 19 March. Also voted to equip referees with wireless microphones in pre-season experiment. Test results positive; microphone adopted for all pre-season, regular season and post-season games.

Divisional winners with highest won-lost percentage made home teams for play offs, surviving winners with highest percentage made home teams for championship games, 26 June.

World Football League folded.

1976 Pittsburgh defeated Dallas 21–17 in Super Bowl X in Miami; Steelers joined Green Bay, Miami as two-time winners of Super Bowl, CBS telecast viewed by estimated 80 million people, largest television audience in history.

Super Bowl XII awarded to New Orleans.

Steelers defeated College All-Stars 24–0 in storm-shortened final Chicago All-Star Game. St Louis defeated San Diego 20–10 in pre-season game before 38 000 in Korakuen Stadium, Tokyo, in first NFL game outside North America, 16 August.

1977 Oakland defeated Minnesota 32–14 before record crowd of 100 421 in Super Bowl XI at Pasadena, 9 January. Paid attendance was pro-record 103 438. NBC telecast was viewed by 81.9 million people, largest ever to view sports event. Victory was fifth straight for AFC.

NFL regular season paid attendance was record 11 070 543.

San Francisco 49ers sold to Edward J. DeBartolo, Jr.

Sixteen-game regular season, four-game pre-season adopted to begin in 1978, 29 March. Second wild card team adopted for playoffs beginning in 1978, wild card teams to play each other with winners advancing to round of eight post-season series along with six division winners.

Defender permitted to contact eligible receiver either in three-yard zone at or beyond line of scrimmage or once beyond that zone, but not both. Wide receivers prohibited from clipping anywhere, even in legal clipping zone. Penalty of loss of coin toss option in addition to 15-yard penalty provided if team does not arrive on field for warm-up at least 15 minutes prior to scheduled kick-off.

Seattle Seahawks permanently aligned in AFC Western Division, Tampa Bay in NFC Central Division.

NFL decided to experiment with seventh official in selected pre-season games.

Rules changes made it illegal to strike an opponent above shoulders (head slap) during initial charge of a defensive lineman; made it illegal for an offensive lineman to thrust his hands to an opponent's neck, face, or head; made it illegal for a back who lines up inside the tight end to break to the outside and then cut back inside to deliver a block below the waist of an opponent. Also, if a punting team commits a foul before its opponent takes possession and the receiving team subsequently commits a foul, the penalties offset each other and the down is replayed.

Chicago's Walter Payton set a single-game rushing record with 275 yards (49 carries) against Minnesota, 20 November.

Cincinnati defeated Kansas City 27–7 at Arrowhead Stadium in the NFL's 5000th game in recorded history.

1978 Dallas defeated Denver 27–10 in Super Bowl XII, held indoors for the first time, at the Louisiana Superdome in New Orleans, 15 January. Dallas's win was first NFC victory in last six Super Bowls. Added a seventh official, side judge.

The NFL played for the first time in Mexico City with the Saints defeating the Eagles, 14–7, in a pre-season game before a sellout crowd.

1979 Pittsburgh defeated Dallas 35–31 in Super Bowl XIII to become the first team ever to win three Super Bowls, 21 January. Super Bowl XIII was the top-ranked TV sporting event of all time, according to figures compiled by A. C. Nielsen Co. The NBC telecast was viewed in 35 090 000 homes, which bettered the previous record of Super Bowl XII with 34 410 000.

Rule changes emphasized additional player safety: officials instructed to blow play dead as soon as quarterback is in grasp of a defender; prohibited players on the receiving team from blocking below the waist during kickoffs, punts, and field goal attempts;

Washington Redskins originally played their home games at Griffith Stadium. It wasn't until 1961 that they moved to the more fashionable and new District of Columbia Stadium.

28

prohibited wearing of torn or altered equipment and exposed pads that may be hazardous; extended the zone in which there can be no crackback blocks from three yards on either side of the line of scrimmage to five yards in order to provide a greater measure of protection; permitted free activation of three players from the injured reserve list after the final cutdown to 45 players.

Commissioner Pete Rozelle announced that the 1980 AFC–NFC Pro Bowl Game would be played at Aloha Stadium in Honolulu, Hawaii. This would mark the first time in the 30-year history of the Pro Bowl that the game would be played in a non-NFL city.

1980 Nielsen figures showed that the CBS telecast of Super Bowl XIV between Pittsburgh and Los Angeles was the most watched sports event of all time. It was viewed in 35 330 000 homes.

CBS, with a record bid of $12 million, won the national radio rights to 26 National Football League regular season games and all 10 post-season games for the 1980 through 1983 seasons.

NFL regular season attendance of nearly 13.4 million set a record for the second year in a row; total for 1979 was 13.2 million. Average paid attendance for the 224-game 1980 regular season was 59 787, highest in the league's 61-year history. The previous high was 58 961 for 182 games in 1973. NFL games in 1980 were played before 92.4 per cent of total stadium capacity.

Television ratings in 1980 were the second-best in NFL history, trailing only the combined ratings of the 1976 season.

1981 The Oakland Raiders became the first wild card team to win the Super Bowl by defeating Philadelphia 27–10 at the Louisiana Superdome in New Orleans.

Jim Ringo joined pro football's Hall of Fame in 1981. (NFL Hall of Fame).

The Raiders finished second to San Diego in the AFC Western Division. In the playoffs they beat Houston at Oakland and Cleveland and San Diego on the road to advance to the Super Bowl.

The 1980 season concluded with a record Aloha Stadium crowd viewing the NFC's win over the AFC in the annual AFC–NFC Pro Bowl game in Honolulu, 1 February. It was the second straight sellout of the game in Honolulu.

NFL paid attendance reached record levels for the second year in a row. The 1980 figure of 13.4 million was 1.5 per cent above last year's record 13.2 million. NFL games in 1980 were played before 92.4 per cent of total stadium capacity.

1982 The 1981 NFL regular season paid attendance of 13 606 990 for an average of 60 745 was the highest in the league's 62-year history. It also was the first time the season average exceeded 60 000. NFL games in 1981 were played before 93.8 per cent of total stadium capacity.

The San Francisco-Cincinnati Super Bowl XVI game on 24 January achieved the highest rating of any televised sports event. The game was watched by a record 110 230 000 viewers in this country for a rating of 49.1. CBS Radio reported 14 million listeners for the game.

The 1982 season was reduced from a 16-game schedule to 9 as the result of the 57-day players' strike. The strike was called at 12:00 midnight on Monday, 20 September following the Green Bay at NY Giants game. Play resumed the weekend of 21–22 November following ratification of the agreement by NFL owners, 17 November in New York.

The Collective Bargaining Agreement, which expired after the 1986 season, set a salary minimum for each year of experience for players; doubled post-season play-off shares; and set up a severance pay schedule to aid career transition, the first of its kind in professional sports.

Miami defeated Minnesota 22–14 at the Orange Bowl in the NFL's 6 000th regular season game in recorded history.

1983 Because of the shortened season, the league adopted for the 1982 playoffs a format of 16 teams competing in a Super Bowl Tournament. NFC number-one seed Washington eventually defeated AFC number-two seed Miami, 27–17, in Super Bowl XVII at the Rose Bowl to mark only the second time the NFC had won consecutive Super Bowls.

Despite the players' strike, the average paid attendance in 1982 was 58 472, the fifth highest in league history, compared to record average of 60 745 in 1981.

Rule changes permitted any player on the field to call a team time out; stipulated that there is no pass interference if there is incidental contact while moving to the ball that does not materially affect the route of a receiver or defender to the ball; and provided for automatic disqualification of a player who uses a helmet he is not wearing as a weapon, 22 March.

1984 The Los Angeles Raiders–Washington Redskins Super Bowl XVIII game on 22 January achieved a 46.4 television rating to become the eleventh highest rated TV programme of all time and the fifth highest Superbowl.

Businessman Patrick Bowlen purchased a majority interest in the Denver Broncos from Edgar Kaiser.

Colts relocated to Indianapolis.

Frank Gatski – 1985 Hall of Fame member. (NFL Hall of Fame).

Real estate developer Alex G. Spanos purchased a majority interest in the San Diego Chargers from Eugene V. Klein.

Houston defeated Pittsburgh 23–20 to mark the 100th overtime game in regular season play since the rule was adopted in 1974.

According to a CBS Sports/*New York Times* survey, 53 per cent of the nation's sports fans said they most enjoy watching football, compared to 18 per cent for baseball.

1985 Super Bowl XIX, in which San Francisco defeated Miami 38–16, was viewed on television by more people than any other live event in history. President Ronald Reagan, who took his second oath of office before tossing the coin for Super Bowl XIX, was one of 115 936 000 viewers who watched a portion of the 20 January game. The game drew a 46.4 rating and a 63 per cent share. In addition, six million viewed the game live in the UK and close to that figure in Italy. Super Bowl XIX had a direct economic impact of $113.5 million on the San Francisco Bay Area.

Norman Braman, in partnership with Edward Leibowitz, bought the Philadelphia Eagles from Leonard Tose.

Bruce Smith, Virginia Tech defensive lineman, selected by Buffalo, was the first player chosen in the fiftieth NFL draft.

NFL announced that a voice amplification experiment, designed to combat excessive sound levels in noisy stadiums, would be tested with equipment furnished by the Telex Corporation during the pre-season.

Owners adopted resolution calling for a series of overseas pre-season games, beginning in 1986, with one game to be played in England/Europe, and/or one game in Japan each year. Game would be fifth pre-season game for involved clubs and all arrangements and selection of clubs will be under the control of the Commissioner.

NFL sets single weekend paid attendance record when 902 657 tickets were sold for the weekend of 27–28 October.

The Chicago–Miami Monday night game on 2 December produced the highest rating, 29.6, and share, 46.0 of any prime-time game in NFL history. It was viewed in over 25 million homes.

1986 The NFC Chicago Bears captured their first NFL title since 1963 by defeating AFC Wild Card entrant New England Patriots, 46–10 in Super Bowl XX, played in the Louisiana Superdome on 26 January. The game was also crowned the champion of television by drawing an audience of 127 million, the largest in television history, replacing the final episode of *M*A*S*H*, according to A. C. Nielsen figures. Of the six shows in TV history to attract audiences of over 100 million, five are Super Bowls.

In addition to drawing a 48.3 rating and 70 per cent share in the United States, Super Bowl XX was televised in 59 foreign countries and beamed via satellite to the *QE II*. An estimated 300 million Chinese viewed a tape delay of the game in March. NBC Radio figures indicated an audience of 10 million for the game.

Super Bowl XX injected over $1000 million into the local New Orleans economy and fans spent $250 per day and a record $17.69 per person on game day.

Paid attendance exceeded 13 million for the sixth consecutive season when the per-game average was 59 567, the fourth highest in history. NFL teams played before 88.45 per cent of stadium capacity in 1985.

Owners adopted limited use of instant replay as an officiating aid, prohibited players from wearing or otherwise displaying equipment, apparel, or other items which carry commercial names, names of organizations, or personal messages of any type, 11 May.

Commissioner Rozelle announced that the series of international pre-season games would begin on Sunday, 3 August 1986, when the Super Bowl XX champions Chicago Bears play the Dallas Cowboys at Wembley Stadium in London in the first American Bowl, 12 March.

NFL COMMISSIONERS AND PRESIDENTS

1920	Jim Thorpe,	President
1921–39	Joe Carr,	President
1939–41	Carl Storck,	President
1941–46	Elmer Layden,	Commissioner
1946–59	Bert Bell,	Commissioner
1960–present	Pete Rozelle,	Commissioner

2 The National Football League

1960–Present day

Although the history of the National Football League goes back to 1920, 1960 marks its coming of age. In that year Alvin (Pete) Rozelle was appointed as the league's new commissioner and the American Football League was born. This eventually merged with the NFL and took on its present-day form.

In 1959 there were only 12 professional football teams in operation in the NFL. Football desperately needed a new spark of initiative and the two events of the following year certainly gave it that.

Pete Rozelle was given the commissioner's job almost by accident. Since 1957 Rozelle had been general manager of the Los Angeles Rams, and when votes were cast at the NFL meeting in Miami on 26 January, his name was nowhere to be seen. The league's former commissioner Bert Bell had died suddenly the previous October of a heart attack whilst watching his beloved Philadelphia Eagles playing Pittsburgh. On Bell's death the NFL's treasurer Austin Gunsel had been appointed as interim commissioner, and it was Gunsel and Marshall Leahy the attorney for the San Francisco 49ers, who were the main contenders. After the first 22 ballots the voting was at a deadlock. The old guard favoured Gunsel whilst the new members were casting their votes for Leahy.

Leahy then made a calculated gamble that backfired. He proposed that if elected he would move the league's office from Philadelphia to his home town of San Francisco. Time was running out and a clear winner was yet to be found. As a compromise Cleveland's Paul Brown was suggested, but Brown did not really want the job and, like Leahy before him, stated that he too, if elected, would move the office, this time to Cleveland. He in turn suggested Pete Rozelle, and on the 23rd ballot

Rozelle became the third commissioner of the NFL.

In his first two years of office, Pete Rozelle became a powerful voice in American sport. He negotiated lucrative television contracts which eventually put the clubs on a sound financial footing; successfully lobbied Congress to allow the NFL to negotiate TV contracts as a league rather than individually; upheld the league's name in the 1962 anti-trust suit brought before the courts by the AFL in which the NFL won the battle; and managed to get the US district court of New York to uphold the legality of the NFL's television blackout within 75 miles of a home game. Because of his work Rozelle was given a new five-year contract in 1962.

As well as the election of Pete Rozelle, 1960 saw the emergence of another league to challenge the NFL monopoly of professional football. The American Football League was the brainchild of one Lamar Hunt, the son of a Texas oil millionaire who had always harboured a great desire to own a football team.

In the summer of 1959, after months of flying thousands of miles, Hunt announced the formation of the league. To start with there were only six teams but within six months the number had increased to eight.

On 30 July 1960 the AFL was put to the test when the first pre-season game between the Boston Patriots and the Buffalo Bills was staged. The Patriots defeated the Bills 28–7 in

Giants head coach Bill Parcells was a seventh round draft pick for Detroit Lions in 1964 but declined a pro career, opting to coach at smalltime Hastings College, Nebraska.

front of 16 000 fans. The dream that Hunt had carried for many years was at last a reality. The first regular season game in the two-conference league happened in Boston on 9 September 1960. A crowd of 21 597 turned out in New England to see the Denver Broncos defeat their home team 13–10.

By the time the first championship game arrived the following January, football in AFL territory had begun to take hold. Houston Oilers won the first final game over the Los Angeles Chargers by a 24–16 score in Houston on New Year's Day 1961. A pleasing crowd of 32 000 turned out for the event.

The 1962 Championship game, again held in Houston, turned out to be a real heartstopper. Hunt's Dallas Texans eventually defeated the reigning champions, Houston, by 20 to 17 after 17 minutes and 54 seconds of overtime. A Tommy Brooker 25-yard field goal decided the outcome. This game was the longest game played in pro football history at the time.

Despite their fine win, the Dallas Texans were in deep trouble. In 1960 the NFL had opened their own franchise in the city and it was their Cowboys who were getting the attendances.

It was said that Hunt was losing something in the region of over $1 million a year, and when his multi-millionaire father was informed of this he said, 'At that rate he will be out of business in about 150 years'.

But Hunt was a wise football club owner, and rather than stay and fight it out to the death, he decided in 1963 to cut his losses and move the team to Kansas City where they became the Chiefs.

Another team in deep trouble was the New York Titans. Owned by a newspaperman they had literally run out of money and couldn't even afford to heat their offices. Luckily, a month after Hunt's move the Titans were bought out by Sonny Werblin and renamed the Jets.

In the first two or three years of the AFL's existence, teams made do with NFL rejects or players who had extended their careers by moving into the new league. But slowly, with the help of television contracts, more money became available and they soon began to offer a serious challenge for the year's best college talent.

The battle between the two leagues proved to be a long and costly one. The war reached its peak in 1966 when the two leagues spent a

Alex Karras, now a Hollywood film star, began his career with the Detroit Lions.

combined total of $7 million signing their draft choices. It is arguable that if an agreement had not been found, and the open hostility had persisted, certainly one, and maybe both leagues would have gone out of business. Thankfully, common sense prevailed and both leagues eventually got round a table in the spring of 1966 for merger talks. On 8 June the historic announcement of an agreement was made, and everyone breathed a huge sigh of relief. The two leagues agreed to play in separate schedules until 1970, but would meet the following year in a World Championship game, and play each other in pre-season games. The World Championship game was the brainchild of two men: the then AFL commissioner Al Davis thought of the idea and Lamar Hunt is credited with the title of 'Super Bowl'.

Davis and Rozelle, who was named commissioner of the new league, never saw eye to eye. Their open dislike of each other is remembered to this day, but for the good of football, it seems, they agreed to buy their differences. Davis returned to Oakland and Rozelle carried on at the NFL.

The year 1966 also saw the NFL expand. Atlanta and Miami were awarded franchises and in 1967 New Orleans became the sixteenth club in the league.

Football's long awaited battle of the giants came on 15 January 1967 when Vince Lombardi's Green Bay Packers proved their NFL supremacy over the AFL's Kansas City Chiefs in Super Bowl I. The Packers won the game 35–10 in the Los Angeles Coliseum, and although the match brought together the two previously warring factions it did little to encourage the idea of equality.

The AFL did get their first taste of victory over the NFL, however, in a pre-season game on 5 August of that year when Denver beat Detroit 13–7, but it wasn't until Super Bowl III that people really began to take any serious notice of this young upstart.

Two teams dominated the year 1968—Green Bay and Cincinnati. Green Bay, because they won the Super Bowl for a second successive year, beating Oakland 33–14 in Miami, and Cincinnati, because this was their first season in the AFL, although a disastrous 3–11 record did little to help their cause. By now the AFL had 10 members and the NFL had 16, a total of 26 teams playing professional football under

one banner the length and breadth of the USA.

In 1969 the AFL came of age, for Super Bowl III was the year of the jets, and in particular their star quarterback Joe Namath. The Jets, the pre-game underdogs, defeated the favourites, Baltimore, 16–7 in a tense ground battle in Miami on 12 January.

The year 1970 saw not only the dawning of a new decade, but the dawning of a new NFL. The 1970 season was the first under the combined banner. Baltimore, Cleveland and Pittsburgh agreed to join the AFL teams to form a 13-team American Football Conference. The remaining NFL clubs formed the National Football Conference with both conferences adopting Eastern, Central and Western Divisions.

The season's Super Bowl was played once again in Miami and Baltimore snatched a last minute victory over Dallas when Jim O'Brien kicked a 32-yard field goal with only five seconds left on the clock.

A week later the NFC gained its revenge as the first AFC–NFC Pro Bowl was held in Los

O.J. drafted by the Buffalo Bills went on to play brilliantly in the NFL.

Larry Csonka, Miami's bullish running back of the 1970s.

Angeles, the National Football Conference winning 27–6.

The merging of the two leagues also brought about another change. At their meeting on 18 March 1970 the league agreed to print players' names on the backs of jerseys. The move was generally welcomed as it then became a lot easier not only for officials and commentators to identify players but for spectators as well.

Two months later the Boston Patriots changed their name to the New England Patriots, a decision which created some unrest in Boston itself, but after a while the locals got used to the name and it has become a proud symbol of professional football in America's north-east corner.

The 1971 season came and went with very little to talk about, except for the AFC divisional playoff game between Miami and Kansas City on Christmas Day. The Dolphins' kicker Gary Yepremian placed a 37-yard field goal for Miami after a record-breaking 22 minutes and 40 seconds of overtime. The game lasted 82 minutes and 40 seconds in all and still holds the record for the longest played game in the history of the NFL.

After all their work in the playoffs, Miami stayed at home for Super Bowl VI, but any home advantage they thought they might have had was quickly swept away by Dallas as the Cowboys ran up 24 points to the Dolphins' solitary field goal. It is interesting to note that the CBS television coverage of the game was viewed in as many as 27 450 000 homes across the American continent.

The 1973 Super Bowl just had to go one better, and of course it did. All 90 182 tickets were sold for the game to be held in Los Angeles. For the first time as well as being televised across the nation, the game was screened locally. Maybe because of this, 8476 ticket holders didn't turn up. The TV audience was huge as usual. A massive 75 000 000 people watched Super Bowl VII, yet another record.

The year 1973 was significant for the NFL for many reasons. A new system of jersey numbering was adopted, although players who had been in the league before 1972 were allowed to keep their old numbers. For a while the mixture of old and new numbers was a little confusing, but as a lot of these players gradually drifted from the league the problem decreased. There are literally only a handful of the old players still remaining in the NFL today, and one of the best known is San Francisco's linebacker Jack Reynolds whose number is 64, when linebackers under the new rules of 1973 should be between 50–59.

On 6 June 1973 another milestone in the NFL's history was reached. The NFL set up a charitable organization to derive income from money generated by the licensing of NFL trademarks, logos and names. The NFL Charity was set up to help other worthy charities across the country. Today this part of the vast NFL network gives millions and millions of dollars to charities each year.

The NFL has always been very aware of the product it puts in front of the spectators in the stadiums and the armchair fans. It is one of the only sports in the world which consistently updates its rules if it thinks that public support is waning. In 1974, for instance, sweeping rule changes were recommended by the Competition Committee to bring about a more offensive-oriented game. There comes a time every now and then when the defense catches up tactically with the offense and the game itself becomes a defensive bore. The rule changes approved were designed to add action and quicken the tempo of the game. Sudden-death overtime was introduced for pre-season games and one 15-minute period of extra time was added for regular season fixtures. The goal-posts, which for a long time had been positioned on the goal line itself, were moved back to the end lines. This was done mainly for safety reasons. Countless numbers of players had injured themselves running into the upright which is four inches in diameter. Kicking, like running, is something that an athlete can improve dramatically over the course of a number of seasons. The kick off spot had been sited on the 40-yard line and nearly every week there would be an embarrassing occasion when a kicker would kick the ball straight out of the end zone. To combat this, the kick off spot was moved 5 yards back to the 35-yard line. Various other rules to open up the game were introduced; roll-blocking, or cutting out wide receivers, was made illegal; penalties for tripping within a certain distance were reduced and penalties were introduced for offensive holding and the illegal use of hands on the line of scrimmage. The results were immediate, the game once again became a feast of offensive play and the NFL's intention of keeping the game of football at the top of the sports listing was achieved.

The year 1974 also saw the formation of yet another new league, the World Football League. The original intention of the new league was to have franchises in cities all over the world, hence its name. But no sooner had it begun, than it was beset with all sorts of problems. Finance was the main cause of the fast decline of the WFL. The league only played one season, that of 1974, when the Birmingham Americans defeated the Florida Blazers in the only championship game of the 12-team league. The WLF folded on 22 September 1975.

The middle seventies belonged to Pittsburgh. The team won both Super Bowls IX and X and continued its remarkable streak of success in 1979 winning Super Bowl XIII to become the first team in NFL history to win three world championships. In 1980, of course, the Steelers put their name firmly in the record books, having been led on the field by Terry Bradshaw and off it by coach Chuck Noll after chalking up their fourth victory in six years.

Every decade has its outstanding team. The sixties provided Green Bay, but the seventies gave football the Pittsburgh Steelers, one of the most efficient professional teams ever seen. With Bradshaw orchestrating the offense which included such stars as Lynn Swann and John Stallworth, and a defense known by all as the 'Steel Curtain', the Steelers swept all before them as they broke record after record.

Whilst the Steelers were notching up one victory after another, two new teams joined the NFL in 1976 bringing the league to its present day strength of 28 teams. The west coast city of Seattle, high up on the Washington border, was chosen, as was the fast-growing area in central Florida known as Tampa Bay.

Seattle, with its home state, Washington, has had a long history of producing good foot-

Pittsburgh Steelers' Chuck Nolls is the only coach to win the Super Bowl four times. (Pittsburgh Steelers).

ballers from its two main universities, so there was no surprise when its membership was announced. The inclusion of Tampa on the other hand was a strange decision, but under its president Hugh H. Culverhouse the 'Buccanneers' quickly found their feet, albeit getting them wet in the process. Tampa has consistently provided one of the league's hard-luck stories always finishing at or very near the bottom of their division.

On 16 August 1976 the NFL went oriental. The first NFL game to be played outside the USA was staged in the Korakuen Stadium in Tokyo, Japan. Some 38 000 Japanese fans turned out to see the St Louis Cardinals defeat San Diego 20–10.

The late 1970s saw many rule changes affecting almost every part of the game. Passing, receiving, rushing, kicking, punts and returns were all subjected to sweeping changes which even the hardest cynic would say were for the better.

A sports survey was conducted amongst America's fans in 1978 which threw up some startling results. According to the Harris Sports survey, 70 per cent of the nation's sports fans followed football compared with only 54 per cent who had an interest in baseball.

After their success in Japan, two teams from the NFL, the New Orleans Saints and the Philadelphia Eagles, travelled to Mexico City on 5 August 1978 to play an exhibition match 'South of the Border'. A capacity crowd greeted their arrival and the Saints went on to win 14–7. Due to its proximity to America it is no real surprise that in Mexico football is big business. Millions listen every week to play-by-play reports in Spanish on the radio. At the time of one Super Bowl, which was televised live, only a handful of spectators turned up for the biggest bullfight of the year, and it had to be postponed. Soccer is still the Mexicans' national sport, but football is rapidly catching up.

Bolstered by the expansion of the regular season from 14 games to 16 in 1978, the league announced record attendances for the 1978 season. Over 12 million fans had paid to watch NFL football. The average attendance of 57 071 was the third highest in the NFL's history and the best since 1973. Football was indeed on a high.

The league under Rozelle's expert guidance had negotiated in 1977 what some sources considered to be the largest single TV package ever, and both the television companies and the leagues itself were highly delighted with the viewing figures.

According to CBS television the Super Bowl XII game in Louisiana between Dallas and Denver attracted a record 102 010 000 viewers throughout the world, which meant that the game was watched by more people than any other show in the history of television. That record has since been broken by the *M*A*S*H* series.

The 1979 season began with the addition of a seventh official, a side judge, and ended with Pittsburgh defeating the Los Angeles Rams in Super Bowl XIV on 20 January 1980. A record 103 985 fans packed into the Pasadena Rose

Dallas' star Bob Lilly joined the Hall of Fame in 1980. (NFL Hall of Fame).

Bowl to witness the event, and the end of another era.

Until 1980 the rules covering the use of hands around the helmet were fairly lax, but this was to change. Several medical inquiries had produced evidence that players were suffering serious neck and head injuries as a result of unfair play. Under the heading of 'personal foul', players were now prohibited from directly striking, swinging, or clubbing around the head, neck or face of an opponent. If only for safety's sake, this new rule was badly needed, and almost overnight it cut down the number of serious head injuries.

In 1981 the Oakland Raiders became the first and only team in NFL history to go all the way as the wild card entry and actually win the Super Bowl defeating Philadelphia in Louisiana's Superdome 27–10. The Raiders had finished second to San Diego in the AFC Western Division, widely regarded as the league's toughest. In the playoffs they beat Houston at Oakland and Cleveland and San Diego on the way to the championship game.

The following year, 1982, began on a bright note. The Super Bowl game between San Francisco and Cincinnati at the Pontiac Silverdome attracted more than 110 000 000 TV viewers. But within eight months the league and the sport were in turmoil.

After only two games of the regular season the players' association announced a players' strike on 20 September. The effect was catastrophic, and there are still repercussions today. The strike, which was about basic salaries and earnings deriving from the clubs' huge television receipts, lasted 57 days. It wasn't the first time that the players had exercised their right to withdraw their labour. In 1974 the veterans held out for most of the pre-season training period and many clubs were forced to play only rookies (new players) in their warm-up games. Luckily, a settlement was reached before the season began and the veterans returned to their clubs two weeks before the regular games were due to start.

Pete Rozelle's qualities as a negotiator were tested to the full, and the ever-smiling commissioner eventually came through with flying colours. So did the players as their demands were met, or nearly, and the season began again on 16 November. Because of the stoppage a new schedule had to be hastily arranged. For the playoffs the league adopted a 16-team Super Bowl Tournament which was

Denver's home—Mile High Stadium—was until 14 December 1968 known as Bears Stadium. The stadium was originally built in 1948 for the Denver Bears of the Western baseball league.

operated on a sort of knock-out basis. The NFC's No 1 seed, Washington, eventually defeated the AFC's No 2 seed Miami in the Super Bowl final itself, coming from behind to win 27–17 after a 'superman' performance in the second half.

The game marked the first Super Bowl to be televised live in the homes of British fans. Some 4 million stayed up to the early hours glued to their sets with excitement. Their season had also suffered from the strike, since the new television Channel 4 had originally scheduled the start of their new sport's coverage for October. Despite its late arrival, American football in Britain then took off.

The 1983 season gave British fans their first taste of live football action when the Minnesota Vikings played the St Louis Cardinals before some 35 000 fans at Wembley Stadium.

The new season also gave the sport its latest pretenders. The United States Football League was formed and began playing in the spring of 1983. The league folded after three years.

The 1984 season came to a climax in Stanford Stadium, California when the home team, San Francisco 49ers, whipped the Miami Dolphins 38–16. Again record TV attendances were announced and after the problems of the early 1980s, the National Football League is consolidating its position for another push in two or three years' time.

Super Bowl XX confirmed the popularity of

The Louisiana Superdome.

the sport worldwide as hundreds of millions watched on television. It was hardly surprising that a one-minute advertisement during the telecast cost $1.1 million. The actual game was a one-sided affair as the Chicago Bears ran out 46–10 winners against the New England Patriots in a game that saw no fewer than 12 Super Bowl records broken.

Records were also broken at Wembley Stadium in August 1986 when Chicago and Dallas met in the first-ever American Bowl. Some 83 699 packed into the grand old stadium on a wet and windy Sunday night to see the brash Bears trounce the Cowboys 20–3. Football, NFL style had at last arrived in Europe and, more specifically, Britain.

American Bowl seems to be with us for a long, long time. Talk is now rife amongst the ever-growing band of gridiron followers in the UK of a London franchise in the not too distant future. Who knows, perhaps that's the next step. For the time being though the NFL is content with its lot in the USA. It won a moral victory over its rival, the USFL in an anti-trust suit court battle. The USFL won the case but was awarded only $1 in damages, which under US law is automatically tripled.

The NFL is likely to expand in the next few years but Arizona and Memphis seem to be further up the list of priorities than London at present.

The future, despite many drug related prob-

Jim Kelly moved to Buffalo in 1986 from the USFL.

The Giants first-ever game, in the New York Polo Grounds on 18 October 1925, was an unmitigated disaster. They lost 14–0 to the now defunct Frankford Yellowjackets in front of a crowd of only 200.

lems and some infighting amongst team owners, is good. Entering its 68th year the National Football League is going to be around for many years yet.

The Draft

Every spring the National Football League concludes its search for talented new stars from the college ranks with its annual draft. The draft was the brainchild of the league's second commissioner Bert Bell who, in 1935, was the co-owner of the Philadelphia Eagles. It was noticeable at this period in the league's history that only the teams with financial muscle were getting the best players. Chicago and the New York Giants, who had the most money, were able to sign the best players the colleges had to offer each year and thus continued to dominate the league.

Bell, with the help of George Preston Marshall, proposed that a draft system be inaugurated that would allow the worst team in the league to have first pick of the season's graduating collegians. The scheme was more advantageous to these two astute businessmen than to most, as their teams were suffering from a lack of success. On 19 May 1935 the draft proposal was adopted and put into effect the following year.

The first player selected in the first draft was Chicago University's talented halfback Jay Berwanger. Coincidentally it was Bell's Eagles who had finished last the previous year who selected him. But the very first player to be selected by this new process priced himself out of the market by apparently asking for $1000 per game, a figure which neither Philadelphia nor the rich Chicago or New York clubs could afford. But the system had been set in motion and over the years has developed almost into a piece of showbusiness. Today, the draft is normally held late in April at a hotel in New York City.

If a college player has graduated, that is to say, has completed four years of college education, he is eligible to be drafted. On draft, day, an occasion which is covered by the news media by the hundreds, each team has representatives at the draft headquarters. A telephone link is established between each team's representatives and their coaches, staff and scouts in their home town.

The 28 clubs select their choices in reverse order to their positions at the end of the previous season. Hence the team with the worst record picks first and the Super Bowl champions last. There are 12 rounds in the draft, and in every round each team makes a selection. Some teams might have more than one selection or none at all in certain rounds; this is because many teams will trade draft selections for current players. But in mathematical terms, since there are 12 rounds at which 28 selections are being made, a total of 336 players are drafted.

There is a specific amount of time allowed for teams to make their selections. In rounds 1 and 2 each team is allowed a maximum of 15 minutes to make their choice. There will often be frantic telephone calls between representatives and their home bases, relaying information about who has already been chosen and who is left. For rounds 3 to 12 only five minutes is allowed, so everybody must be on their toes. If a team hasn't made its choice in the allotted time, they must wait and try to jump into the order when they can—not an easy thing to do when everybody is frantically trying to snap up the best players.

Back home in the team's draft room, huge boards are placed on the walls listing many hundreds of players. As players are chosen, they are taken off the board and others are moved up, so when it is a particular team's turn to make a selection, the staff in the draft room can inform their representative over the telephone who they want, and the choice is then made. The selected players are then informed by the clubs that they have been selected, and, subject to agreements, they will turn up at the team's summer camp in July.

Those players not selected are called 'free agents,' and will often travel around trying to sell their talents to individual clubs. There is no limit to the number of free agents a club can sign. Once a player has agreed to sign with a certain club, the next item on the agenda is of course the size of his salary.

In 1984 the minimum allowed under an agreement between the NFL and the players' union was $40 000 a year. For the 1985 season this minimum increased to $50 000. Depending on the round in which they were drafted, players can then negotiate a figure above this. The earlier the player is drafted then of course the more he is likely to get. Salaries are then augmented by substantial signing-on bonuses and other inducements that can earn a round 1 draft choice well over $250 000 per annum.

The Babysitters

The nickname of 'babysitters' was first given to scouts in the mid-1960s during the NFL–AFL war.

Such was the fierceness of the competition to sign top quality players, that clubs' scouts were employed to take their prized catches into hiding and literally to 'babysit' them.

Of course when the AFL and the NFL eventually forgot their differences and merged, the need for babysitters disappeared. With the emergence of the USFL in 1982 the babysitting ploy again came into use as the two rival leagues battled to get their hands on the best of the year's college graduates.

All professional teams employ a team of scouts and most of them also belong to a scouting consortium to which they pay fees for certain player information. A scout will attend practices and games and look at miles and miles of film, evaluating each player from all angles. Not only will his playing ability be taken into account but his academic qualifications and his general attitude toward life and to other people will also be noted on his report file.

Scouts will then grade the players on a 1–10 scale and the player will be filed away with hundreds of others until draft day.

For obvious reasons the highest-graded players will almost certainly be first-round draft choices, and so on down the scale.

Human nature being what it is, many scouts will mark a player as a certainty, where others might grade him as a reject, and another might report that he has scope for improvement, all of which makes the scout's job one of the hardest yet most crucial to any team's success.

ROGER STAUBACH

The year 1969 was a time for long hair and way-out parties. In comparison, Roger Staubach was the complete opposite. His hair was clipped Annapolis short, his values were sturdy and old fashioned and when he joined the Dallas Cowboys as a 27-year-old rookie quarterback, everyone asked whether a commitment to the defense of his country had taken its toll.

It hadn't, but it took Roger Staubach two years to gain the confidence of coach Tom Landry and grab the starting quarterback's job – the beginning of a brilliant career.

Staubach spent his first two years on the bench behind Craig Morton, but the morning following the Cowboys' defeat by the Baltimore Colts in Super Bowl V, Staubach was back at work at the Dallas practice grounds throwing a football at a passing board—he was determined that the job was going to be his, but it was not easy.

Midway through the 1971 season, the Cowboys were struggling along at 4–3 when coach Tom Landry installed Staubach at quarterback. They never looked back. The Cowboys won their ten remaining games, including the playoffs and a superb 24–3 romp over the Miami Dolphins in Super Bowl VI.

It was the first world championship for the Cowboys, a team that had always been labelled as the club who never wins the big one. With Roger Staubach at the helm, the Cowboys were clearly sailing into a new era.

The Cowboys dominated the NFC during the 1970s and Staubach was there directing the offense with coolness and control.

Roger led Dallas almost singlehandedly, say some, to four NFC titles, and became famous throughout the USA for dragging his team mates off death row nearly every week.

Staubach was one of those come-from-behind experts who are rarely seen in professional football. He brought the Cowboys back from the jaws of defeat during 24 games in his illustrious career in Texas, and many of those comebacks were nothing short of miraculous. He threw two touchdown passes in the final two minutes to beat the San Francisco 49ers 30–28 in the 1972 playoffs, but he will always be remembered for his last minute touchdown pass to Drew Pearson that beat Minnesota 17–14 in 1975.

Staubach was the master of the two-minute drill. It was as if he thrived on the last-gasp big play, the one that would make everything else pale into insignificance.

The Navy Academy man was drafted by the Cowboys in 1964. The Dallas club knew that he was in the arms of Uncle Sam for four years, but their patience and foresight paid off in the end. 'We had Dandy Don Meredith at the time', recalled Tex Schramm. 'We knew that we wouldn't need Roger for a while and he was the best quarterback to come out of college in years. He was well worth waiting for.'

Following the 1979 season, Roger Staubach aged 38, announced his retirement from football. His decision, although not unexpected, saddened the pro football world and probably the whole nation, for here was a player who was respected, liked and admired by everyone on and off the field.

Fittingly, Roger Staubach went out on top. He was the NFC's leading passer in 1979, throwing for a career high 3568 yards and 27 touchdowns and his lifetime efficiency is the fourth highest in the NFL today.

At his final press conference, Staubach was asked how he would like to be remembered. 'As a pretty darn consistent quarterback', was his reply, understating to the very end, for Roger Staubach was not only a pretty consistent quarterback, he was one of the best that there has ever been.

Number One Draft Choices

Season	Team	Player	Position	College
1987	Tampa Bay	Vinny Testaverde	QB	Miama
1986	Tampa Bay	Bo Jackson	RB	Auburn
1985	Buffalo	Bruce Smith	DT	Virginia Tech.
1984	New England	Irving Fryar	RB	Nebraska
1983	Baltimore (traded to Denver)	John Elway	QB	Stanford
1982	New England	Ken Sims	DT	Texas
1981	New Orleans	George Rogers	RB	S. Carolina
1980	Detroit	Billy Sims	RB	Oklahoma
1979	Buffalo	Tom Cousineau	LB	Ohio State
1978	Houston	Earl Campbell	RB	Texas
1977	Tampa Bay	Ricky Bell	RB	S. California
1976	Tampa Bay	Lee Roy Selmon	DE	Oklahoma
1975	Atlanta	Steve Bartkowski	QB	California
1974	Dallas	Ed Jones	DE	Tennessee St.
1973	Houston	John Matuszak	DE	Tampa
1972	Buffalo	Walt Patulski	DE	Notre Dame
1971	New England	Jim Plunkett	QB	Stanford
1970	Pittsburgh	Terry Bradshaw	QB	Louisiana Tech.
1969	Buffalo	O. J. Simpson	RB	S. California
1968	Minnesota	Ron Yary	T	S. California
1967	Baltimore	Bubba Smith	DT	Michigan St.
1966	Atlanta (NFL)	Tommy Nobis	LB	Texas
	Miami (AFL)	Jim Grabowski	RB	Illinois
1965	NY Giants (NFL)	Tucker Frederickson	RB	Auburn
	Houston (AFL)	Lawrence Elkins	E	Baylor
1964	San Francisco (NFL)	Dave Parks	E	Texas Tech.
	Boston (AFL)	Jack Concannon	QB	Boston College
1963	Los Angeles (NFL)	Terry Baker	QB	Oregon State
	Kansas City (AFL)	Buck Buchanan	DT	Grambling
1962	Washington (NFL)	Ernie Davis	RB	Syracuse
	Oakland (AFL)	Roman Gabriel	QB	N. Carolina St.
1961	Minnesota (NFL)	Tommy Mason	RB	Tulane
	Buffalo (AFL)	Ken Rice	G	Auburn
1960	Los Angeles	Billy Cannon	RB	Louisiana State University
	(AFL had no formal pick in their first year of operation)			
1959	Green Bay	Randy Duncan	QB	Iowa
1958	Chicago Cardinals	King Hill	QB	Rice
1957	Green Bay	Paul Hornung	HB	Notre Dame
1956	Pittsburgh	Gary Glick	DB	Colorado A & M
1955	Baltimore	George Shaw	QB	Oregon
1954	Cleveland	Bobby Garrett	QB	Stanford
1953	San Francisco	Harry Babcock	E	Georgia
1952	Los Angeles	Bill Wade	QB	Vanderbilt
1951	NY Giants	Kyle Rote	HB	Southern Methodist University
1950	Detroit	Leon Hart	E	Notre Dame
1949	Philadelphia	Chuck Bednarik	C	Pennsylvania
1948	Washington	Harry Gilmer	QB	Alabama
1947	Chicago Bears	Bob Fenimore	HB	Oklahoma A & M
1946	Boston	Frank Dancewicz	QB	Notre Dame
1945	Chicago Cardinals	Charley Trippi	HB	Georgia
1944	Boston	Angelo Bertelli	QB	Notre Dame
1943	Detroit	Frank Sinkwich	QB	Georgia
1942	Pittsburgh	Bill Dudley	HB	Virginia
1941	Chicago Bears	Tom Harmon	HB	Michigan
1940	Chicago Cardinals	George Cafego	HB	Tennessee
1939	Chicago Cardinals	Ki Aldrich	C	TCU
1938	Cleveland	Corbett Davis	FB	Indiana
1937	Philadelphia	Sam Francis	FB	Nebraska
1936	Philadelphia	Jay Berwanger	HB	Chicago

The Super Bowls

The name 'Super Bowl' was devised by Kansas City Chiefs' owner Lamar Hunt in 1966. At the meeting in that year of the NFL and the rival AFL (of which Hunt was a member and leading figure), it was decided to hold an inter-league championship game, to be called the 'World Championship of Professional Football', the following year.

The Memorial Coliseum at Los Angeles was chosen as the site of the sporting showdown for which the whole of America had been waiting. On 15 January 1967, Vince Lombardi and his Green Bay Packers, representing the NFL confronted Hunts' Chiefs, who held the AFL title, before a crowd of 61 946 fans.

But the opening round in a long series of inter-league rivalries went to the NFL as the Packers stormed to a memorable 35–10 victory.

The hero of the day was a seventeenth-round draft choice called Bart Starr. Most players selected in such a late round do not survive the rigours of professional football, and Starr recalled after the game that had he followed the usual path, he too would have decided upon a different career in the US Air Force. Instead, Starr served as a 'General' guiding the Packer attack to two consecutive Super Bowl victories. In that first game Starr completed 16 of 23 passes for 250 yards and two touchdowns to reserve wide receiver Max McGee.

Starr was the master tactician, carrying out coach Lombardi's gameplan to near perfection and he was the deserved winner of the very first Super Bowl's MVP (most valuable player) award.

Starr continued to dominate in Super Bowl II in Miami, Florida. The Packers had just won their third consecutive NFL title and were worthy representatives against the Oakland Raiders. Over 75 000 people provided football

with its first $3 million dollar gate. The Packers wore down a very strong Raiders team to win the game and the title by 33 points to 14. Starr was again awarded the MVP award for his superb control of a game in which he connected on 13 of 24 passes for 202 yards including a massive 62-yard pass to Boyd Dowler. Kicker Don Chandler was another Green Machine hero, scoring four field goals, while corner back Herb Adderley capped a victorious day for the Wisconsin outfit with a

Green Bay Packers' quarterback Bart Starr was the MVP in both Super Bowls I and II. (Green Bay Packers).

Green Bay Packers' quarterback Bart Starr was the first Super Bowl MVP, leading the Packers to 35–10 victory over the Kansas City Chiefs in Super Bowl I.

Dallas Cowboys' linebacker Chuck Howley became the first and only player on a losing side to win the Super Bowl MVP award in game V.

Super Bowl V was the first championship game to be played on artificial turf in Miami's Orange Bowl.

Dallas Cowboys in Super Bowl VI, became the first team to prevent the opposition from scoring a touchdown in a Super Bowl.

Super Bowl XII produced the first dual MVP award when Dallas' Randy White and Harvey Martin were awarded the trophy.

60-yard score on an interception late in the fourth quarter.

It wasn't until Super Bowl III that the AFL gained credibility in the eyes of most football supporters. The New York Jets came to Miami as the underdogs for their championship game against the all-conquering Baltimore Colts. On the Thursday before the game the Jets' quarterback Joe Namath 'guaranteed' to the world's press that the New York team would win. Namath put his words into action on the day of the game as he led the Jets to a thrilling 16–7 victory. The Colts' star quarterback Johnny Unitas, who had been injured for most of the season, came off the bench late in the fourth quarter to lead the Baltimore team to its only touchdown as the AFL celebrated their coming of age.

The AFL dominance continued the following year in Super Bowl IV. A crowd in excess of 80 000 turned out in the New Orleans' Tulane Stadium to watch Hank Stram grab a famous 23–7 win. It is customary for presidents of the United States to telephone the winning team after the game, but President Richard Nixon broke the rule by calling the Chiefs before the event. His main purpose was to assure the Kansas City quarterback Len Dawson that he had been cleared of any involvement in a federal gambling investigation. Relieved of this pressure, Dawson threw for 122 yards and a touchdown to lead the Chiefs to victory, against a tame Minnesota Vikings team.

Super Bowl V created yet another piece of history. Dallas Cowboys' linebacker Chuck Howley became the only player on the losing side to win the prestigious MVP award.

Super Bowl V marked the first championship game to be played on artificial turf, in Miami's Orange Bowl. The game was finely balanced until the final seconds as Dallas and Baltimore had scored 13 apiece. Although Howley won the MVP for outstanding work on the Cowboy's defense, the real hero of the day was the Colts' kicker Jim O'Brien. O'Brien, who had dreamt the night before that he would kick the winning field goal, kicked a 32-yard attempt between the posts with only five seconds remaining.

The Cowboys returned to the Super Bowl the next year in New Orleans to regain their pride and record a victory over the Miami Dolphins 24–3. The Cowboys' defense under the charge of Howley kept the Dolphins' offense at bay and they became the first team to stop the opposition from scoring a touchdown in a Super Bowl. The player voted MVP, Roger Staubach, had not competed in the previous year's game, but in Super Bowl VI he controlled a potent offense that rushed for a record 252 yards and personally threw for 119 yards and two touchdowns to take the title back to the Lone Star State.

After the Dolphins had finished as bridesmaids in Super Bowls III and VI, Don Shula became the second coach to win consecutive titles in games VII and VIII. In Super Bowl VII the Dolphins created football history by completing the 'perfect season', that is, going through the whole season unbeaten. Miami's 'no-name' defense suddenly found it had a star worth naming in Jake Scott, who was the free safety and played the whole game, intercepting two passes, including a critical sneak midway through the fourth quarter when a Washington offense had really begun to roll. Miami had marched into a 14–0 lead, but with Scott's help the Dolphins kept the Redskins down to only one touchdown to seal a famous win.

The Dolphins marched proudly into their third consecutive Super Bowl appearance in Rice Stadium, Houston on 13 January 1974 for a showdown with the Minnesota Vikings. The game saw the emergency of a new all-American hero, Larry Csonka. Csonka slammed into the Vikings time and time again for a record-breaking total of 145 yards, as the Dolphins, led by quarterback Bob Griese, swamped Minnesota 24–7. Csonka, who carried the football 33 times and scored two touchdowns, was so effective that Griese only had to throw the ball seven times.

The Vikings returned to the fray in Super Bowl IX, once again staged in New Orleans' Tulane Stadium. But as had happened in their two previous outings, they had to play second fiddle. The victory this time went to a team in its first Super Bowl. Dallas, always in the lead, kept its cool and won 27–10. The key to its success was, without doubt, their twin blitz threat of defensive end Harvey Martin and defensive tackle Randy White who gave Denver's quarterback Craig Morton so much trouble that his passing became very, very erratic. So erratic in fact that the Cowboys' defense picked off four interceptions and recovered four fumbles. Martin and White became the first co-owners of the game's MVP trophy.

Super Bowl XIII in Miami in 1979 was a victory for the 'Steel Curtain' and the 'Steel Arm'. The Steel Curtain belonged to Pittsburgh's marauding defensive unit consisting of 'Mean' Joe Greene, Jack Ham and Jack Lambert. The Steel Arm belonged to quarterback Terry Bradshaw who threw for four touchdowns and a total of 318 yards to win the MVP award. The game was one of the most exciting seen in Super Bowl history, as the Steelers rushed into a 35–17 lead with only 7 minutes left on the clock, during which they scored two touchdowns in 19 seconds. Dallas, superbly led by the unflappable Roger Staubach, came back to score two themselves before time ran out.

The Steelers' supremacy continued in 1980 as they defeated the Los Angeles Rams by 31 points to 19. In Pasadena's Rose Bowl another record breaking crowd of 103 985 witnessed Terry Bradshaw retain the team title as well as the MVP trophy. Bradshaw completed 14 of 21 passes for 309 yards and two touchdowns, and set Super Bowl records for most yards gained in Super Bowls (932), most yards gained in a single final (318), highest average gain in a career (11.10 yards per pass), highest average gain per game (14.17), most touchdown passes (9), and most touchdown passes in a single final game (4). Jim Plunkett almost came back from the dead to rise to fame in the Super Bowl XV game. Plunkett had been discarded by near neighbours San Francisco after a couple of injury riddled years. The 1970 Heisman Trophy winner had been the toast of all football when he was drafted by the New England Patriots in 1971, but five troubled years there, and two with the 49ers, had given him a sound education in the hardships of football life. The Raiders became the first team in NFL history to reach a Super Bowl as the wild card entrants. The game, in the New Orleans Superdome against the Philadelphia Eagles, eventually proved to be a one-sided affair as Plunkett threw three touchdown passes, including an amazing 80-yard bomb to Kenny King.

The World Championship stayed in California in 1982 when across the bay the San Francisco 49ers under the leadership of another great quarterback, Joe Montana, eclipsed the Cincinnati Bengals 26–21 in Detroit's Pontiac Silverdome. Freezing weather outside the domed stadium did not stop the Californian sunshine boys from victory as Montana scored himself on a one-yard sneak and later connected on an 11-yard pass to Earl Cooper. In spite of all their efforts, the Bengals, who rushed 356 yards compared to the 49ers' 275 yards, could not prevent the title going back west as the well organized and effectively simple game plan of San Francisco paid handsome dividends.

Washington Redskins' remarkable victory in Super Bowl XVII was their first NFL championship since 1942. Opponents Miami had amassed a 7–0 lead at the end of the first quarter, and nobody expected the Redskins to return from the brink of disaster. Statistics, amongst other things, proved the difficulty of this, but Washington, with second-year head coach Joe Gibbs on the sidelines, quarterback Joe Theismann controlling the offense and a certain John Riggins rushing behind the powerful blocking of the offensive line's aptly named Hogs, rallied in the second half to score 14 unanswered points in the fourth quarter to win the game. Riggins ran in on a 43-yard rush and Charlie Brown caught a 6-yard pass from Theismann with one minute fifty five seconds

Denver owner Patrick Bowlen is an outstanding athlete in his own right. Bowlen has completed the Ironman Triathlon—an event in which he had to swim 2.4 miles, ride a bicycle 112 miles and then run a marathon—consecutively.

left to complete the scoring. Miami's Fulton Walker made Super Bowl history just before the break with a 98-yard kick off return, and the MVP award went to John Riggins who rushed for a second 166 yards on 38 carries, an achievement which did much to spark the Washington team to victory.

After winning the previous year's final in such style Washington returned in 1984 to play the Los Angeles Raiders, in what many termed as the toughest final yet. The game turned out to be the most lop-sided victory for the Raiders as their defense snuffed out the potent Washington pass and rush. The Raiders, always in control, took a 21–3 half-time lead and continued to dominate totally on both offense and defense. Marcus Allen typified their domination with a superb 74-yard touchdown run in the third quarter, first going one way, finding the path blocked and magnificently changing direction to find a massive hole in the Redskin's defense. Allen rushed for a record 191 yards and two touchdowns to win the coveted MVP award.

The pre-game talk of a showdown between the two offensive giants of the 1984 season, San Francisco 49ers and Miami Dolphins, proved sadly to be a total miscalculation of events. Both teams had arrived at Super Bowl XIX in Stanford's Stadium with high hopes. Both had outstanding quarterbacks in Joe Montana and the record-breaking Dan Marino. For Marino the game turned into a real nightmare as the 49ers defense upset his plan of play. Montana on the other hand was Mr. Cool, as he cajoled his team to a 38–16 victory almost with ease. Montana completed 24 of 35 passes for a Super Bowl record of 331 yards and three touchdowns. Running back Roger Craig was a close second for the MVP award when he became the first player to score three touchdowns in a final. In another one-sided game San Francisco operating a superb double and sometimes triple coverage plan gave Marino nothing to pass to and for the second year running the World Championship stayed on the west coast.

Giants scout Chris Mara likes keeping things in the family. He is the great grandson of founder Tim. And Chris has also married into another great football family—the Rooneys of Pittsburgh.

Super Bowl Winners

I	Green Bay Packers 35 Kansas City Chiefs 10
II	Green Bay Packers 33 Oakland Raiders 14
III	New York Jets 16 Baltimore Colts 7
IV	Kansas City Chiefs 23 Minnesota Vikings 7
V	Baltimore Colts 16 Dallas Cowboys 13
VI	Dallas Cowboys 24 Miami Dolphins 3
VII	Miami Dolphins 14 Washington Redskins 7
VIII	Miami Dolphins 24 Minnesota Vikings 7
IX	Pittsburgh Steelers 16 Minnesota Vikings 6
X	Pittsburgh Steelers 21 Dallas Cowboys 17
XI	Oakland Raiders 32 Minnesota Vikings 14
XII	Dallas Cowboys 27 Denver Broncos 10
XIII	Pittsburgh Steelers 35 Dallas Cowboys 31
XIV	Pittsburgh Steelers 31 Los Angeles Rams 19
XV	Oakland Raiders 27 Philadelphia Eagles 10
XVI	San Francisco 49ers 26 Cincinnati Bengals 21
XVII	Washington Redskins 27 Miami Dolphins 17
XVIII	Los Angeles Raiders 28 Washington Redskins 9
XIX	San Francisco 49ers 38 Miami Dolphins 16
XX	Chicago Bears 46 New England Patriots 10
XXI	New York Giants 39 Denver Broncos 20

Forthcoming Super Bowl
XXII 24 January 1988, Jack Murphy Stadium, San Diego, California

The much publicized battle had become a massacre as the Super Bowl left one decade and entered another.

The Chicago Bears and New England Patriots both appeared in their first Super Bowl in 1986 and the Bears won yet another one-sided final in which 12 Super Bowl records were broken. Their score of 46 bettered the old record by eight and their winning margin was seven more than the Raiders' winning margin of 29 over the Redskins in Super Bowl XVIII.

For the all conquering New York Giants, Super Bowl XXI was the culmination of a brilliant season.

The Giants had dominated the NFL all season. In their two play off games they had only conceded three points in victories over the San Francisco 49ers and the Washington Redskins.

Their opponents in Pasadena were the AFC champion Denver Broncos who had reached their second final with a brilliant come-from-behind victory over the Cleveland Browns. Their hero was quarterback John Elway, a brash young man who had the ability to cause the unexpected upset.

The Giants were a massive ten-point favourite, but at half-time they trailed 10–9. The Giants' defense, which had been solid all season, was beginning to falter.

But a second-half performance from MVP winning quarterback Phil Simms was enough

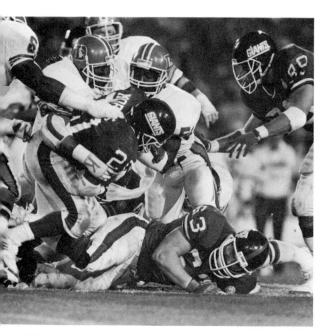

Diminutive Joe Morris proved a handful for Denver's defense in Super Bowl XXI.

Phil Sims – Super Bowl XXI MVP.

to ensure victory. Simms completed a new Super Bowl record for pass completions—88 per cent, during a third quarter that saw Mark Bavaro and fellow receiver Phil McConkey break the back of a stubborn Broncos' defense.

New York had won its first Super Bowl since Joe Namath's Jets in game III, and the Giants had won their first NFL championship in 30 years.

Super Bowl XXI Records

This is the rundown on records set or tied in Super Bowl XXI.

New Records
Most consecutive completions, game — 10, Phil Simms, NY Giants (old record: 8, Len Dawson, Kansas City, Super Bowl I; Joe Theismann, Washington, XVIII).
Highest completion percentage, game (minimum 15 completions) — 88.0 Phil Simms, NY Giants (old record: 73.9 Ken Anderson, Cincinnati, XVI).
Shortest field goal missed — 23 yards, Rich Karlis, Denver (old record: 27 yards, Lou Michaels, Baltimore, III).
Narrowest half-time margin — 1 point, Denver 10, NY Giants 9 (old record: 2 points, Pittsburgh 2, Minnesota 0, IX).
Most points, one half, team — 30, NY Giants, second half (old record: 28, San Francisco, first half, XIX).
Most points, second half, both teams — 40, NY Giants 30, Denver 10 (old record: 31, Dallas 17, Pittsburgh 14, XIII).
Highest completion percentage, game, team — 88.0, NY Giants (old record: 73.9 Cincinnati XVI).
Fewest punts, game, both teams — 5, Denver 2, NY Giants 3 (old record: 6, Oakland 3, Philadelphia 3, XV).

Tied
Longest field goal — 48 yards, Rich Karlis, Denver (tied record of Jan Stenerud, Kansas City, IV).
Most safeties, game — 1, George Martin, NY Giants (tied record of Dwight White, Pittsburgh, IX; Reggie Harrison, Pittsburgh, X; Henry Waechter, Chicago, XX).
Most touchdowns, game, team — 5, NY Giants (tied record of Green Bay, 1; Pittsburgh, XIII; L.A. Raiders, XVIII; San Francisco, XIX; Chicago, XX).
Most points, first quarter, both teams — 17, Denver 10, NY Giants 7 (tied record of Miami 10, San Francisco 7, XIX).
Fewest punts, game, team — 2, Denver (tied record of Pittsburgh, XIV).
Fewest punt returns, game, both teams – 2, Denver 1, NY Giants 1 (tied record of Dallas 1, Miami 1, VI).

Super Bowl Bonus

As well as their normal salaries the players, coaches and administration staff of the competing teams collect massive bonuses for their appearance in a Super Bowl.

In Super Bowl XVII, between the Washington Redskins and the Miami Dolphins, the winning players collected $36 000 each, whilst the losers received $18 000. As well as the players' pay, the coaching staff and all the backroom staff at both clubs receive a hefty paycheque. A figure in excess of $2.6 million was paid to the two competing clubs in Super Bowl XVII.

The Broncos wore vertically striped socks early in their history. But the socks were considered so ugly that all of them (bar one which is in the Hall of Fame in Canton, Ohio) were burned at a ceremonial bonfire in July 1962. Local TV carried pictures of the burn-in on their early-evening bulletins.

Attendance History

A total of 1 628 864 people have attended the first 21 Super Bowls. The largest crowd was 103 985 at Super Bowl XIV, which was played in the Pasadena Rose Bowl, California.

Rings of War

Unlike most other major sporting finals, the winners of each Super Bowl collect not a medal but a ring for their efforts. This is no ordinary ring though; for instance the one made for the victorious Super Bowl XVI team, the San Francisco 49ers, contained more than two carats of diamonds and were valued at over $5000. Each winning club chooses a manufacturer and from various designs submitted the final choice, usually very complex, will be made. Rings are also given to those elected to the Hall of Fame. The rings will be designed and made during the off season, and those returning to the team for pre-season training in July will collect them then. But such is the mystique of these precious objects that many players have been known to fly in from various parts of the USA to collect them as soon as they are ready. Approximately 75 rings are produced for each winning club.

The biggest ring ever produced was for the Green Bay Packers' victory in Super Bowl II. The ring cost $1900 to produce in 1968 and weighs 30 pennyweight—a real knuckleduster.

The largest sized ring produced for an individual was a size 20 ring made for San Francisco 49ers defensive end Lawrence Pillers in 1982. Previously the record was held by Bronko Nagurski for his size 19 Pro Football Hall of Fame ring.

The winning club is presented immediately after the game with the Vince Lombardi Trophy. Symbolizing the Championship of Professional Football the trophy is made of sterling silver, stands 20 inches high and weighs approximately 7 pounds. It depicts a regulation size football on an elongated base with three concave sides. On the front surface

---

Giants running back Joe Morris' younger brother Jamie is a star halfback for the University of Michigan and rookie defensive end Eric Dorsey is a cousin of Houston Oilers tailback Allen Pinkett.

The National Football League Super Bowls Most Valuable Player Awards

I	Bart Starr, Quarterback, Green Bay Packers
II	Bart Starr, Quarterback, Green Bay Packers
III	Joe Namath, Quarterback, New York Jets
IV	Len Dawson, Quarterback, Kansas City Chiefs
V	Chuck Howley, Linebacker, Dallas Cowboys
VI	Roger Staubach, Quarterback, Dallas Cowboys
VII	Jake Scott, Safety, Miami Dolphins
VIII	Larry Csonka, Running Back, Miami Dolphins
IX	Franco Harris, Running Back, Pittsburgh Steelers
X	Lynn Swann, Wide Receiver, Pittsburgh Steelers
XI	Fred Biletnikoff, Wide Receiver, Oakland Raiders
XII	Harvey Martin, Defensive End and Randy White, Defensive Tackle, Dallas Cowboys
XIII	Terry Bradshaw, Quarterback, Pittsburgh Steelers
XIV	Terry Bradshaw, Quarterback, Pittsburgh Steelers
XV	Jim Plunkett, Quarterback, Oakland Raiders
XVI	Joe Montana, Quarterback, San Francisco 49ers
XVII	John Riggins, Running Back, Washington Redskins
XVIII	Marcus Allen, Running Back, Los Angeles Raiders
XIX	Joe Montana, Quarterback, San Francisco 49ers
XX	Richard Dent, Defensive End, Chicago Bears
XXI	Phil Simms, Quarterback, New York Giants

Choice of colours
The AFC and NFC Champions alternate as the home team. The home team always has the choice of wearing coloured or white jerseys.

---

is engraved, *Vince Lombardi Trophy*. Below that appears the NFL shield, and the words, *Super Bowl* and *AFC vs NFC*. Each year a new trophy is cast, as the winning team gains permanent possession of this supreme professional football award.

The Pro Bowls

The first Pro Bowl of sorts took place at Los Angeles's Wrigley Field on 15 January 1939.

That day the NFL champions, the New York Giants, met an all-star team and won 13–10.

The idea for such a game came from Washington Redskins' owner George Preston Marshall who teamed up with a Los Angeles newspaper to launch it. In 1942, largely because of the war, the game was sidelined, and it wasn't until 1951 that it returned in a new format.

The 1951 Bowl matched the all-stars of the National Conference against the American. The AFC won on that day 28–27 in the Los Angeles Coliseum. The Pro Bowl was played for in various ways until 1971, when, after the merger of the two rival leagues (the American Football League and the National Football League), the AFC–NFC end of season game acquired a new significance.

Results

Year	Date	Winner	Loser	Place	Attendance
1987	1 Feb	AFC 10	NFC 6	Honolulu	52 340
1986	2 Feb	NFC 28	AFC 24	Honolulu	50 101
1985	27 Jan	AFC 22	NFC 14	Honolulu	46 200
1984	29 Jan	NFC 45	AFC 3	Honolulu	50 445
1983	6 Feb	NFC 20	AFC 19	Honolulu	47 201
1982	31 Jan	AFC 16	NFC 13	Honolulu	49 521
1981	1 Feb	NFC 21	AFC 7	Honolulu	47 879
1980	27 Jan	NFC 37	AFC 27	Honolulu	48 060
1979	29 Jan	NFC 13	AFC 7	Los Angeles	46 281
1979	23 Jan	AFC 14	NFC 13	Tampa	51 337
1977	17 Jan	AFC 24	NFC 14	Seattle	64 151
1976	26 Jan	NFC 23	AFC 20	New Orleans	30 546
1975	20 Jan	NFC 17	AFC 10	Miami	26 484
1974	20 Jan	AFC 15	NFC 13	Kansas City	66 918
1973	21 Jan	AFC 33	NFC 28	Dallas	37 091
1972	23 Jan	AFC 26	NFC 13	Los Angeles	53 647
1971	24 Jan	NFC 27	AFC 6	Los Angeles	48 222

The first game, held in Los Angeles on 24 January 1971, was a victory for the traditional NFC who beat the new AFC 27–6. In 1973 the event moved to the Texas Stadium, the home of the Dallas Cowboys, where the AFC erased a first half deficit of 14 points to win 32–28, thanks largely to the powerful running of one O. J. Simpson. The Pro Bowl then went on a sort of walkabout across the USA as it moved from Texas to Kansas, Miami, New Orleans, Seattle, Tampa and back to Los Angeles in 1979 before it took up residence in Honolulu the following year.

In the history of the modern day Pro Bowl the NFC has won the game ten times compared to the AFC's seven.

The players for the Pro Bowl are selected because of their record during the previous season and each conference will also select a coach for each team. In the 1986 game Miami's Don Shula coached the AFC whilst L.A. Rams coach John Robinson had the honour of coaching the NFC.

The National Football League's Hall of Fame

The National Football League decided on 27 April 1961 to set up a professional football Hall of Fame in Canton, Ohio. Canton was chosen because the original meeting to found the league had been held there in 1920.

Individuals, foundations and companies in and around the Canton area donated nearly $400 000 in cash and services to help fund the project and the Hall of Fame was opened on 7 September 1963.

The original complex was almost doubled in size in 1971 when a $620 000 expansion project was completed. A second expansion was finished in 1978, which included three extra exhibition areas and a theatre twice the size of the original one.

The Hall of Fame caters for every aspect of professional football. There are three large and colourful exhibition galleries built around two halls enshrining football greats, a theatre, a research library, and an NFL gift shop. In

The NFL's pro football Hall of Fame in Canton, Ohio. Note the white football-shaped dome rising from the centre of the building. (NFL Hall of Fame).

recent years the Hall of Fame has become an extremely popular tourist attraction.

Members of the pro football Hall of Fame are elected annually by the 29 members of a national board of selectors, made up of media writers from every league city and the president of the pro football writers' association. Between four and seven new members are elected each year, and to get voted into the hall a nominee must gain the votes of approximately 80 per cent of the board.

Anybody may nominate a player or contributor for election, simply by writing to the Hall of Fame. Nominated players, however, must have been retired for at least five years to be eligible, but a coach can be elected immediately on retirement, and others, such as administrators and owners, may be elected whilst still in office.

At the first election in 1963, 17 members were elected into what has become known as the 'charter' class. Amongst the elected members in that inaugural year were Jim Thorpe, the NFL's first president in 1920; Joe Carr, who was president from 1921–39; commissioner Bert Bell; Chicago Bears' owner and coach George Halas; veteran players Sammy Baugh, Don Hutson, Bronko Nagurski and the all-star fullback of the 1920s and 1930s, Ernie Nevers.

By 1987, when Larry Gouka, Len Dawson, Joe Greene, John Johnson, Jim Langer, Don Maynard and Gene Upshaw were chosen, the membership of this elite club stood at 140.

The Jim Thorpe display at the Hall of Fame. (NFL Hall of Fame).

1963 Charter Membership of the Hall of Fame

Sammy Baugh Quarterback, Washington Redskins, 1937–52
Bert Bell Team owner and Commissioner of NFL, 1946–59
Joe Carr President of the NFL, 1921–39
Earl (Dutch) Clark Quarterback, Portsmouth Spartans, 1931–32; Detroit Lions, 1934–38
Red Grange Halfback, Chicago Bears and New York Yankees, 1925–34
George Halas Coach, 1920–67, and team owner of Chicago Bears until death in 1983
Mel Hein Center, New York Giants, 1931–45
Wilbur (Pete) Henry Tackle, Canton Bulldogs, 1920–23; Canton Bulldogs, 1925–26; New York Giants, 1927; Pottsville Maroons, 1927–28
Cal Hubbard Tackle, New York Giants, Green Bay Packers and Pittsburgh Pirates, 1927–36
Don Hutson End, Green Bay Packers, 1935–45

Earl (Curly) Lambeau Coach, Green Bay Packers, 1919–49; Chicago Cardinals, 1950–51; Washington Redskins, 1952–53
Johnny (Blood) McNally Halfback, Milwaukee Badgers, Duluth Eskimos, Pottsville Maroons, Green Bay Packers, Pittsburgh Pirates, 1925–39
Tim Mara Team Owner, New York Giants, 1925–59
George Preston Marshall Team Owner, Boston Braves, 1932; Boston Redskins, 1933–36; Washington Redskins, 1936–69
Bronko Nagurski Fullback, Chicago Bears, 1930–37 and 1943
Ernie Nevers Fullback, Duluth Eskimos, 1926–27; Chicago Cardinals, 1929–31
Jim Thorpe Halfback, Canton Bulldogs, Cleveland Indians, Oorang Indians, Toledo Maroons, Rock Island Independents, New York Giants, Chicago Cardinals. First President of the American Professional Football Association, forerunner of the NFL, 1920–28

Pro Football Hall of Fame
Roster of Members (excluding 1987 elections)

Herb Adderley
Defensive back. 6-1, 200. Born in Philadelphia, Pennsylvania 8 June 1939. Michigan State. Inducted in 1980. 1961–69 Green Bay Packers, 1970–72 Dallas Cowboys.

Lance Alworth
Wide receiver. 6-0, 184. Born in Houston, Texas, 3 August 1940. Arkansas. Inducted in 1978. 1962–70 San Diego Chargers, 1971–72 Dallas Cowboys.

Doug Atkins
Defensive end. 6-8, 275. Born in Humboldt, Tennessee, 8 May 1930. Tennessee. Inducted in 1982. 1953–54 Cleveland Browns, 1955–66 Chicago Bears, 1967–69 New Orleans Saints.

Morris (Red) Badgro
End. 6-0, 190. Born in Orilla, Washington, 1 December 1902. Southern California. Inducted in 1981. 1927 New York Yankees, 1930–35 New York Giants, 1936 Brooklyn Dodgers.

Cliff Battles
Halfback. 6-1, 201. Born in Akron, Ohio, 1 May 1910. Died 27 April 1981. West Virginia Wesleyan. Inducted in 1968. 1932 Boston Braves, 1933–36 Boston Redskins, 1937 Washington Redskins.

Sammy Baugh
Quarterback, 6-2, 180. Born in Temple, Texas, 17 March 1914. Texas Christian. Inducted in 1963. 1937–52 Washington Redskins.

Chuck Bednarik
Center-linebacker. 6-3, 230. Born in Bethlehem, Pennsylvania, 1 May 1925. Pennsylvania. Inducted in 1967. 1949–62 Philadelphia Eagles.

Bert Bell
Commissioner. Team owner. Born in Philadelphia, Pennsylvania, 25 February 1895. Died 11 October 1959. Pennsylvania. Inducted in 1963. 1933–40 Philadelphia Eagles, 1941–42 Pittsburgh Steelers, 1943 Phil-Pitt, 1944–46 Pittsburgh Steelers. Commissioner, 1946–59.

Bobby Bell
Linebacker. 6-4, 225. Born in Shelby, North Carolina, 17 June 1940. Minnesota. Inducted in 1983. 1963–74 Kansas City Chiefs.

Raymond Berry
End. 6-2, 187. Born in Corpus Christi, Texas, 27 February 1933. Southern Methodist. Inducted in 1973. 1955–67 Baltimore Colts.

Charles W. Bidwill, Sen.
Team owner. Born in Chicago, Illinois, 16 September 1895. Died 19 April 1947. Loyola of Chicago. Inducted in 1967. 1933–43 Chicago Cardinals, 1944 Card-Pitt, 1945–47 Chicago Cardinals.

George Blanda
Quarterback-kicker. 6-2, 215. Born in Youngwood, Pennsylvania, 17 September 1927. Kentucky. Inducted in 1981. 1949–58 Chicago Bears, 1950 Baltimore Colts, 1960–66 Houston Oilers, 1967–75 Oakland Raiders.

Jim Brown
Fullback, 6-2, 232. Born in St Simons, George, 17 February 1936. Syracuse. Inducted in 1971. 1957–65 Cleveland Browns.

Paul Brown
Coach. Born in Norwalk, Ohio, 7 September 1908. Miami, Oho. Inducted in 1967. 1946–49 Cleveland Browns (AAFC), 1950–62 Cleveland Browns, 1968–75 Cincinatti Bengals.

Roosevelt Brown
Offensive tackle. 6-3, 255. Born in Charlottesville, Virginia, 20 October 1932. Morgan State. Inducted in 1975. 1953–65 New York Giants.

Willie Brown
Defensive back. 6-1, 210. Born in Yazoo City, Mississippi, 2 December 1940. Grambling. Inducted in 1984. 1963–66 Denver Broncos, 1967–78 Oakland Raiders.

Dick Butkus
Linebacker. 6-3, 245. Born in Chicago, Illinois, 9 December 1942. Illinois. Inducted in 1979. 1965–73 Chicago Bears.

Tony Canadeo
Halfback. 5-11, 195. Born in Chicago, Illinois, 5 May 1919. Gonzaga. Inducted in 1974. 1941–44, 1946–52 Green Bay Packers.

Joe Carr
NFL president. Born in Columbus, Ohio, 22 October 1880. Died 20 May 1939. Did not attend college. Inducted in 1963. President, 1921–39 NFL.

Guy Chamberlin
End. Coach. 6-2, 210. Born in Blue Springs, Nebraska, 16 January 1894. Died 4 April 1967. Nebraska. Inducted in 1965. 1920 Decatur Staleys, 1921 Chicago Staleys, player-coach 1922–23 Canton Bulldogs, 1924 Cleveland Bulldogs, 1925–26 Frankford Yellow Jackets, 1927 Chicago Cardinals.

Jack Christiansen
Defensive back. 6-1, 185. Born in Sublette, Kansas, 20 December 1928. Colordo State. Inducted in 1970. 1951–58 Detroit Lions.

Earl (Dutch) Clark
Quarterback. 6-0, 185. Born in Fowler, Colorado, 11 October 1906. Died 5 August 1978. Colorado College. Inducted in 1963. 1931-32 Portsmouth Spartans, 1934–38 Detroit Lions.

George Connor
Tackle-linebacker. 6-3, 240. Born in Chicago, Illinois, 1 January 1925. Holy Cross, Notre Dame. Inducted in 1975. 1948–55 Chicago Bears.

Jimmy Conzelman
Quarterback. Coach. Team owner. 6-0, 180. Born in St. Louis, Missouri, 6 March 1898. Died 31 July 1970. Washington, Missouri. Inducted in 1964. 1920 Decatur Staleys, 1921–22 Rock Island, Ill., Independents, 1923–24 Milwaukee Badgers; owner-coach, 1925–26 Detroit Panthers; player-coach 1927–29, coach 1930 Providence Steamroller; coach, 1940–42 Chicago Cardinals, 1946–48 Chicago Cardinals.

Willie Davis
Defensive end. 6-3, 245. Born in Lisbon, Louisiana, 24 July 1934. Grambling. Inducted in 1981. 1958–59 Cleveland Browns, 1960–69 Green Bay Packers.

Denver's Keith Bishop, a Pro-Bowl bound center, appeared in the 1981 World's Strongest Man competition. After finishing sixth in that he went on to become the sumo wrestling champion of the USA.

Art Donovan
Defensive tackle. 6-3, 265. Born in Bronx, New York, 5 June 1925. Boston College. Inducted in 1968. 1950 Baltimore Colts, 1951 New York Yanks, 1952 Dallas Texans, 1953–61 Baltimore Colts.

John (Paddy) Driscoll
Quarterback. 5-11, 160. Born in Evanston, Illinois, 11 January 1896. Died 29 June 1968. Northwestern. Inducted in 1965. 1920 Decatur Staleys, 1920–25 Chicago Cardinals, 1926–29 Chicago Bears. Head coach, 1956–57 Chicago Bears.

Bili Dudley
Halfback. 5-10, 176. Born in Bluefield, Virginia, 24 December 1921. Virginia. Inducted in 1966. 1942 Pittsburgh Steelers. 1945–46 Pittsburgh Steelers, 1947–49 Detroit Lions, 1950–51, 1953 Washington Redskins.

Glen (Turk) Edwards
Tackle. 6-2, 260. Born in Mold, Washington, 28 September 1907. Died 10 January 1973. Washington State. Inducted in 1969. 1932 Boston Braves, 1933–36 Boston Redskins, 1937–40 Washington Redskins.

Weeb Ewbank
Coach. Born in Richmond, Indiana, 6 May 1907. Miami. Ohio. Inducted in 1978. 1954–62 Baltimore Colts, 1963–73 New York Jets.

Tom Fears
End. 6-2, 215. Born in Los Angeles, California, 3 December 1923. Santa Clara, UCLA. Inducted in 1970. 1948–56 Los Angeles Rams.

Ray Flaherty
End. Coach. Born in Spokane, Washington, 1 September 1904. Gonzaga. Inducted in 1976. 1926 Los Angeles Wildcats (AFL), 1927–28 New York Yankees, 1928–29, 1931–35 New York Giants. Coach, 1936 Boston Redskins, 1937–42 Washington Redskins, 1946–48 New York Yankees (AAFC), 1949 Chicago Hornets (AAFC).

Len Ford
End. 6-5, 260. Born in Washington, DC, 18 February 1926. Died 14 March 1972. Michigan. Inducted in 1976. 1948–49 Los Angeles Dons (AAFC), 1950–57 Cleveland Browns, 1958 Green Bay Packers.

Dan Fortmann
Guard. 6-0, 207. Born in Pearl River, New York, 11 April 1916. Colgate. Inducted in 1965. 1936–43 Chicago Bears.

Frank Gatski
Center. 6-3, 240. Born in Farmington, West Virginia, 13 March 1922. Marshall, Auburn. Inducted in 1985. 1946–49 Cleveland Browns (AAFC), 1950–56 Cleveland Browns, 1957 Detroit Lions.

Bill George
Linebacker. 6-2, 230. Born in Waynesburg, Pennsylvania, 27 October 1930. Wake Forest. Inducted in 1974. 1952–65 Chicago Bears, 1966 Los Angeles Rams.

When the New York Giants lost to the Chicago Bears in the championship game in 1933 each player received a paltry $140.22 for his efforts. The Giants players of today each picked up $18 000 for winning the 1987 NFC championship.

Frank Gifford
Halfback. 6-1, 195. Born in Santa Monica, California, 16 August 1930. Southern California. Inducted in 1977. 1952–60, 1962–64 New York Giants.

Sid Gillman
Coach. Born in Minneapolis, Minnesota, 26 October 1911. Ohio State. Inducted in 1983. 1955–59 Los Angeles Rams, 1960 Los Angeles Chargers, 1961–69 San Diego Chargers, 1973–74 Houston Oilers.

Otto Graham
Quarterback, 6-1, 195. Born in Waukegan, Illinois, 6 December 1921. Northwestern. Inducted in 1965. 1945–49 Cleveland Browns (AAFC), 1950–55 Cleveland Browns.

Harold (Red) Grange
Halfback, 6-0, 185. Born in Forksville, Pennsylvania, 13 June 1903. Illinois. Inducted in 1963. 1925 Chicago Bears, 1926 New York Yankees (AFL), 1927 New York Yankees, 1929–34 Chicago Bears.

Forrest Gregg
Tackle. 6-4, 250. Born in Sulphur Springs, Texas, 18 October 1933. Southern Methodist. Inducted in 1977. 1956, 1958–70 Green Bay Packers, 1971 Dallas Cowboys.

Lou Groza
Tackle-kicker. 6-3, 250. Born in Martin's Ferry, Ohio, 25 January 1924. Ohio State. Inducted in 1974. 1946–49 Cleveland Browns (AAFC), 1950–59, 1961–67 Cleveland Browns.

Joe Guyon
Halfback. 6-1, 180. Born in Mahnomen, Minnesota, 26 November 1892. Died 27 November 1971. Carlisle, Georgia Tech. Inducted in 1966. 1920 Canton Bulldogs, 1921 Cleveland Indians, 1922–23 Oorang Indians, 1924 Rock Island, Ill., Independents, 1924–25 Kansas City Cowboys, 1927 New York Giants.

George Halas
End. Coach. Team owner. Born in Chicago, Illinois, 2 February 1895. Died 31 October 1983. Illinois. Inducted in 1963. 1920 Decatur Staleys, 1921 Chicago Staleys, 1922–29 Chicago Bears; coach, 1933–42, 1946–55, 1958–67 Chicago Bears.

Ed Healey
Tackle. 6-3, 220. Born in Indian Orchard, Massachusetts, 28 December 1894. Died 9 December 1978. Dartmouth. Inducted in 1964. 1920–22 Rock Island, Ill., Independents, 1922–27 Chicago Bears.

Mel Hein
Center, 6-2, 225. Born in Redding, California, August 22, 1909. Washington State. Inducted in 1963. 1931–45 New York Giants.

Wilbur (Pete) Henry
Tackle. 6-0, 250. Born in Mansfield, Ohio, 31 October 1897. Died 7 February 1952. Washington & Jefferson. Inducted in 1963. 1920–23 Canton Bulldogs, 1925–26 Canton Bulldogs, 1927 New York Giants, 1927–28 Pottsville Maroons.

Arnie Herber
Quarterback. 6-1, 200. Born in Green Bay, Wisconsin, 2 April 1910. Died 14 October 1969. Wisconsin, Regis College. Inducted in 1966. 1930–40 Green Bay Packers, 1944–45 New York Giants.

Bill Hewitt
End. 5-11, 191. Born in Bay City, Michigan, 8 October 1909. Died 14 January 1947. Michigan. Inducted in 1971. 1932–36 Chicago Bears, 1937–39 Philadelphia

Eagles, 1943 Phil-Pitt.

Clarke Hinkle
Fullback, 5-11, 201. Born in Toronto, Ohio, 10 April 1912. Bucknell. Inducted in 1964. 1932–41 Green Bay Packers.

Elroy (Crazylegs) Hirsch
Halfback-end. 6-2, 190. Born in Wausau, Wisconsin, 17 June 1923. Wisconsin, Michigan. Inducted in 1968. 1946–48 Chicago Rockets (AAFC), 1949–57 Los Angeles Rams.

Paul Hornung
Halfback. 6-2, 220. Born in Louisville, Kentucky, 23 December 1935. Notre Dame. Inducted in 1986. 1957–62, 1964–66 Green Bay Packers.

Ken Houston
Safety. 6-3, 198. Born in Lufkin, Texas, 12 November 1944. Prairie View A&M. Inducted in 1986. 1967–72 Houston Oilers, 1973–80 Washington Redskins.

Cal Hubbard
Tackle. 6-5, 250. Born in Keytesville, Missouri, 11 October 1900. Died 17 October 1977. Centenary, Geneva. Inducted in 1963. 1927–28 New York Giants, 1929–33, 1935 Green Bay Packers, 1936 New York Giants, 1936 Pittsburgh Pirates.

Sam Huff
Linebacker. 6-1, 230. Born in Morgantown, West Virginia, 4 October 1934. West Virginia. Inducted in 1982. 1956–63 New York Giants, 1964–67, 1969 Washington Redskins.

Lamar Hunt
Team owner. Born in El Dorado, Arkansas, 2 August 1932. Southern Methodist. Inducted in 1972. 1960–62 Dallas Texans, 1963–86 Kansas City Chiefs.

Don Hutson
End. 6-1, 180. Born in Pine Bluff, Arkansas, 31 January 1913. Alabama. Inducted in 1963. 1935–45 Green Bay Packers.

David (Deacon) Jones
Defensive end. 6-5, 250. Born in Eatonville, Florida, 9 December 1938. South Carolina State. Inducted 1980. 1961–71 Los Angeles Rams, 1972–73 San Diego Chargers, 1974 Washington Redskins.

Sonny Jurgensen
Quarterback. 6-0, 203. Born in Wilmington, North Carolina, 23 August 1934. Duke. Inducted in 1983. 1957–63 Philadelphia Eagles. 1964–74 Washington Redskins.

Walt Kiesling
Guard. Coach, 6-2, 245. Born in St Paul, Minnesota, 27 March 1903. Died 2 March 1962. St Thomas (Minnesota). Inducted in 1966. 1926–27 Duluth Eskimos, 1928 Pottsville Maroons, 1929–33 Chicago Cardinals, 1934 Chicago Bears, 1935–36 Green Bay Packers, 1937–38 Pittsburgh Pirates; coach, 1939–42 Pittsburgh Steelers; co-coach, 1943 Phil-Pitt, 1944 Card-Pitt; coach, 1954–56 Pittsburgh Steelers.

Frank (Bruiser) Kinard
Tackle. 6-1, 210. Born in Pelahatchie, Mississippi, 23 October 1914. Mississippi. Inducted in 1971. 1938–44 Brooklyn Dodgers-Tigers, 1946–47 New York Yankees (AAFC).

Earl (Curly) Lambeau
Coach. Born in Green Bay, Wisconsin, 9 April 1898. Died 1 June 1965. Notre Dame. Inducted in 1963. 1919–49 Green Bay Packers, 1950–51 Chicago Cardinals, 1952–53 Washington Redskins.

Dick (Night Train) Lane
Defensive back. 6-2, 210. Born in Austin, Texas, 16 April 1928. Scottsbluff Junior College. Inducted in 1974. 1952–53 Los Angeles Rams, 1954–59 Chicago Cardinals, 1960–65 Detroit Lions.

William Lanier
Linebacker. 6-1, 245. Born in Clover, Virginia, 8 August 1945. Morgan State. Inducted in 1966. 1967–77 Kansas City Chiefs.

Yale Lary
Defensive back-punter. 5–11, 189. Born in Fort Worth, Texas, 24 November 1930. Texas A&M. Inducted in 1979. 1952–53, 1956–64 Detroit Lions.

Dante Lavelli
End. 6-0, 199. Born in Hudson, Ohio, 23 February 1923. Ohio State. Inducted in 1975. 1946–49 Cleveland Browns (AAFC), 1950–56 Cleveland Browns.

Bobby Layne
Quarterback. 6-2, 190. Born in Santa Anna, Texas, 19 December 1926. Texas. Inducted in 1967. 1948 Chicago Bears, 1949 New York Bulldogs, 1950–58 Detroit Lions, 1958–62 Pittsburgh Steelers.

Alphonse (Tuffy) Leemans
Fullback. 6-0, 200. Born in Superior, Wisconsin, 12 November 1912. Died 19 January 1979. George Washington. Inducted in 1978. 1936–43 New York Giants.

Bob Lilly
Defensive tackle. 6-5, 260. Born in Olney, Texas, 24 July 1939. Texas Christian. Inducted in 1980. 1961–74 Dallas Cowboys.

Vince Lombardi
Coach. Born in Brooklyn, New York, 11 June 1913. Died 3 September 1970. Fordham. Inducted in 1971. 1959–67 Green Bay Packers, 1969 Washington Redskins.

Sid Luckman
Quarterback. 6-0, 195. Born in Brooklyn, New York, 21 November, 1916. Columbia. Inducted in 1965. 1939–50 Chicago Bears.

Roy (Link) Lyman
Tackle. 6-2, 252. Born in Table Rock, Nebraska, 30 November 1898. Died 28 December 1972. Nebraska. Inducted in 1964. 1922–23, 1925 Canton Bulldogs, 1924 Cleveland Bulldogs, 1925 Frankford Yellow Jackets, 1926–28, 1930–31, 1933–34 Chicago Bears.

George McAfee
Halfback. 6-0, 177. Born in Ironton, Ohio, 13 March 1918. Duke. Inducted in 1966. 1940–41, 1945–50 Chicago Bears.

Mike McCormack
Offensive tackle. 6-4, 248. Born in Chicago, Illinois, 21 June 1930. Kansas. Inducted in 1984. 1951 New York Yanks, 1954–62 Cleveland Browns.

Hugh McElhenny
Halfback. 6-1, 198. Born in Los Angeles, California, 31 December 1928. Washington. Inducted in 1970. 1952–60 San Francisco 49ers, 1961–62 Minnesota Vikings, 1963 New York Giants, 1964 Detroit Lions.

Johnny Blood (McNally)
Halfback. 6-0, 185. Born in New Richmond, Wisconsin, 27 November 1903. Died 28 November 1985. St John's (Minnesota). Inducted in 1963. 1925–26 Milwaukee Badgers, 1926–27 Duluth Eskimos, 1928 Pottsville Maroons, 1929–33 Green Bay Packers, 1934 Pittsburgh Pirates, 1935–36 Green Bay Packers; player-coach, 1937–39 Pittsburgh Pirates.

The Broncos are the most bumbling team in Super Bowl history. They turned the ball over eight times (four interceptions, four fumbles) in the 27–10 loss to Dallas in Super Bowl XII.

Tim Mara
Team owner. Born in New York, New York, 29 July 1887. Died 17 February 1959. Did not attend college. Inducted in 1963. 1925–59 New York Giants.

Gino Marchetti
Defensive end. 6-4, 245. Born in Antioch, California, 2 January 1927. San Francisco. Inducted in 1972. 1952 Dallas Texans, 1953–64, 1966 Baltimore Colts.

George Preston Marshall
Team owner. Born in Grafton, West Virginia, 11 October 1897. Died 9 August 1969. Randolph-Macon. Inducted in 1963. 1932 Boston Braves, 1933–36 Boston Redskins, 1937–69 Washington Redskins.

Ollie Matson
Halfback. 6-2, 220. Born in Trinity, Texas, 1 May 1930. San Francisco. Inducted in 1972. 1952, 1954–58 Chicago Cardinals, 1959–62 Los Angeles Rams, 1963 Detroit Lions, 1964–66 Philadelphia Eagles.

Mike Michalske
Guard. 6-9, 209. Born in Cleveland, Ohio, 24 April 1903. Penn State. Inducted in 1964. 1926 New York Yankees (AFL), 1927–28 New York Yankees, 1929–35, 1937 Green Bay Packers.

Wayne Millner
End. 6-0, 191. Born in Roxbury, Massachusetts, 31 January 1913. Died 19 November 1976. Notre Dame. Inducted in 1968. 1936 Boston Redskins, 1937–41, 1945 Washington Redskins.

Bobby Mitchell
Running back-wide receiver. 6-0, 195. Born in Hot Springs, Arkansas, 6 June 1935. Illinois. Inducted in 1983. 1958–61 Cleveland Browns, 1962–68 Washington Redskins.

Ron Mix
Tackle. 6-4, 250. Born in Los Angeles, California, 10 March 1938. Southern California. Inducted in 1979. 1960 Los Angeles Chargers, 1961–69 San Diego Chargers, 1971 Oakland Raiders.

Lenny Moore
Halfback. 6-1, 198. Born in Reading, Pennsylvania, 25 November 1933. Penn State. Inducted in 1975. 1956–67 Baltimore Colts.

Marion Motley
Fullback. 6-1, 238. Born in Leesburg, Georgia, 5 June 1920. South Carolina State, Nevada. Inducted in 1968. 1946–49 Cleveland Browns (AAFC), 1950–53 Cleveland Browns, 1955 Pittsburgh Steelers.

George Musso
Guard-tackle. 6-2, 270. Born in Collinsville, Illinois, 8 April 1910. Millikin. Inducted in 1982. 1933–44 Chicago Bears.

Bronko Nagurski
Fullback. 6-2, 225. Born in Rainy River, Ontario, Canada, 3 November 1908. Minnesota. Inducted in 1963. 1930–37, 1943 Chicago Bears.

Joe Namath
Quarterback, 6-2, 200. Born in Beaver Falls, Pennsylvania, 31 May 1943. Alabama. Inducted in 1985. 1965–76 New York Jets, 1977 Los Angeles Rams.

Earle (Greasy) Neale
Coach. Born in Parkersburg, West Virginia, 5 November 1891. Died 2 November 1973. West Virginia Wesleyan. Inducted in 1969. 1941–42, 1944–50 Philadelphia Eagles; co-coach, Phil-Pitt 1943.

Ernie Nevers
Fullback. 6-1, 205. Born in Willow River, Minnesota, 11 June 1903. Died 3 May 1976. Stanford. Inducted in 1963. 1926–27 Duluth Eskimos, 1929–31 Chicago Cardinals.

Ray Nitschke
Linebacker. 6-3, 235. Born in Elmwood Park, Illinois, 29 December 1936. Illinois. Inducted in 1978. 1958–72 Green Bay Packers.

Leo Nomellini
Defensive tackle. 6-3, 264. Born in Lucca, Italy, 19 June 1924. Minnesota. Inducted in 1969. 1950–63 San Francisco 49ers.

Merlin Olsen
Defensive tackle. 6-5, 270. Born in Logan, Utah, 14 September, 1940. Utah State. Inducted in 1982. 1962–76 Los Angeles Rams.

Jim Otto
Center. 6-2, 255. Born in Wausau, Wisconsin, 5 January 1938. Miami. Inducted in 1980. 1960–74 Oakland Raiders.

Steve Owen
Tackle. Coach. 6-0, 235. Born in Cleo Springs, Oklahoma, 21 April 1898. Died 17 May 1964. Phillips. Inducted in 1966. 1924–25 Kansas City Cowboys, 1926–30 New York Giants; coach, 1931–53 New York Giants.

Clarence (Ace) Parker
Quarterback, 5-11, 168. Born in Portsmouth, Virginia, 17 May 1912. Duke. Inducted in 1972. 1937–41 Brooklyn Dodgers, 1945 Boston Yanks, 1946 New York Yankees (AAFC).

Jim Parker
Guard-tackle. 6-3, 273. Born in Macon, Georgia, 3 April 1934. Ohio State. Inducted in 1973. 1957–67 Baltimore Colts.

Joe Perry
Fullback. 6-0, 200. Born in Stevens, Arkansas, 27 January 1927. Compton Junior College. Inducted in 1969. 1948–49 San Francisco 49ers (AAFC), 1950–60, 1963 San Francisco 49ers, 1961–62 Baltimore Colts.

Pete Pihos
End. 6-1, 210. Born in Orlando, Florida, 22 October 1923. Indiana. Inducted in 1970. 1947–55 Philadelphia Eagles.

Hugh (Shorty) Ray
Supervisor of officials 1938–56. Born in Highland Park, Illinois, 21 September 1884. Died 16 September 1956. Illinois. Inducted in 1966.

Dan Reeves
Team owner. Born in New York, New York, 30 June 1912. Died 15 April 1971. Georgetown. Inducted in 1967. 1941–45 Cleveland Rams, 1946–71 Los Angeles Rams.

Jim Ringo
Center, 6-1, 235. Born in Orange, New Jersey, 21 November 1932. Syracuse. Inducted in 1981. 1953–63 Green Bay Packers, 1964–67 Philadelphia Eagles.

Andy Robustelli
Defensive end. 6-0, 230. Born in Stamford, Connecticut, 6 December 1925. Arnold College. Inducted in 1971. 1951–55 Los Angeles Rams, 1956–65 New York Giants.

Art Rooney
Team owner. Born in Coulterville, Pennsylvania, 27 January 1901. Georgetown, Duquesne. Inducted in 1964. 1933–40 Pittsburgh Pirates, 1941–42, 1949–86 Pittsburgh Steelers, 1943 Phil-Pitt, 1944 Card-Pitt.

Pete Rozelle
Commissioner. Born in South Gate, California, 1 March 1926. San Francisco. Inducted in 1985. Commissioner 1960–86.

Gale Sayers
Running back. 6-0, 200. Born in Wichita, Kansas, 30 May 1943. Kansas. Inducted in 1977. 1965–71 Chicago Bears.

Joe Schmidt
Linebacker. 6-0, 222. Born in Pittsburgh, Pennsylvania, 19 January 1932. Pittsburgh. Inducted in 1973. 1953–65 Detroit Lions.

O. J. Simpson
Running back. 6-1, 212. Born in San Francisco, California, 9 July 1947. Southern California. Inducted in 1985. 1969–77 Buffalo Bills, 1978–79 San Francisco 49ers.

Bart Starr
Quarterback. 6-1, 200. Born in Montgomery, Alabama, 9 January 1934. Alabama. Inducted in 1977. 1956–71 Green Bay Packers; coach, 1975–83 Green Bay Packers.

Roger Staubach
Quarterback, 6-3, 202. Born in Cincinnati, Ohio, 5 February 1942. Navy. Inducted in 1985. 1969–79 Dallas Cowboys.

Ernie Stautner
Defensive tackle. 6-2, 235. Born in Cham, Bavaria, Germany, 20 April 1925. Boston College. Inducted in 1969. 1950–63 Pittsburgh Steelers.

Ken Strong
Halfback. 5-11, 210. Born in New Haven, Connecticut, 6 August 1906. Died 5 October 1979. New York University. Inducted in 1967. 1929–32 Staten Island Stapletons, 1936–37 New York Yanks (AF), 1933–35, 1939, 1944–47 New York Giants.

Joe Stydahar
Tackle. 6-4, 230. Born in Kaylor, Pennsylvania, 3 March 1912. Died 23 March 1977. West Virginia. Inducted in 1967. 1936–42, 1945–56 Chicago Bears.

Fran Tarkenton
Quarterback. 6-0, 185. Born in Richmond, Virginia, 3 February, 1940. George. Inducted in 1986. 1961–66, 1972–78 Minnesota Vikings, 1967–71 New York Giants.

Charley Taylor
Wide receiver-running back. 6-3, 210. Born in Grand Prairie, Texas. 28 September 1941. Arizona State. Inducted in 1984. 1964–75. 1977 Washington Redskins.

Jim Taylor
Fullback, 6-0, 216. Born in Baton Rouge, Louisiana, 20 September 1935. Louisiana State. Inducted in 1976. 1958–66 Green Bay Packers, 1967 New Orleans Saints.

Jim Thorpe
Halfback. 6-1. Born in Prague, Oklahoma, 28 May 1888. Died 28 March 1953. Carlisle. Inducted in 1963. 1920 Canton Bulldogs, 1921 Cleveland Indians, 1922–23 Oorang Indians, 1923 Toledo Maroons, 1924 Rock Island, Ill. Independents, 1925 New York Giants, 1926 Canton Bulldogs, 1928 Chicago Cardinals.

Y. A. Tittle
Quarterback. 6-0, 200. Born in Marshall, Texas, 24 October 1926. Lousiana State. Inducted in 1971. 1948–49 Baltimore Colts (AAFC), 1950 Baltimore Colts. 1951–60 San Francisco 49ers, 1961–64 New York Giants.

George Trafton
Center. 6-2, 235. Born in Chicago. Illinois, 6 December 1896. Died 5 September 1971. Notre Dame. Inducted in 1964. 1920 Decatur Staleys, 1921 Chicago Staleys, 1922–32 Chicago Bears.

Charley Trippi
Halfback. 6-0, 185. Born in Pittston, Pennsylvania, 14 December 1922. George. Inducted in 1968. 1947–55 Chicago Cardinals.

Emlen Tunnell
Safety. 6-1, 200. Born in Pennsylvania, 29 March 1925. Died 23 July 1975. Toledo, Iowa. Inducted in 1967. 1948–59 New York Giants, 1959–81 Green Bay Packers.

Clyde (Bulldog) Turner
Center. 6-2, 235. Born in Sweetwater, Texas, 10 November 1919. Hardin-Simmons. Inducted in 1966, 1940–52 Chicago Bears.

Johnny Unitas
Quarterback. 6-1, 195. Born in Pittsburgh, Pennsylvania, 7 May 1933. Louisville. Inducted in 1979. 1956–72 Baltimore Colts, 1973 San Diego Chargers.

Norm Van Brocklin
Quarterback. 6-1, 190. Born in Eagle Butte, South Dakota, 15 March 1926. Died 1 May 1983. Oregon. Inducted in 1971, 1949–57 Los Angeles Rams, 1958–60 Philadelphia Eagles.

Steve Van Buren
Halfback. 6-1, 200. Born in La Ceiba, Honduras, 28 December 1920. Louisiana State. Inducted in 1965. 1944–51 Philadelphia Eagles.

Doak Walker
Halfback. 5-10, 172. Born in Dallas, Texas, 1 January 1927. Southern Methodist. Inducted in 1986. 1950–55 Detroit Lions.

Paul Warfield
Wide receiver. 6-0, 188. Born in Warren, Ohio, 28 November 1942. Ohio State. Inducted in 1983. 1964–69, 1976–77 Cleveland Browns, 1970–74 Miami Dolphins, 1975 Memphis Grizzlies (WFL).

Bob Waterfield
Quarterback. 6-2. 200. Born in Elmira, New York, 26 July 1920. Died 25 April 1983. UCLA. Inducted in 1965. 1945 Cleveland Rams, 1946–52 Los Angeles Rams.

Arnie Weinmeister
Defensive tackle. 6-4, 235. Born in Rhein, Saskatchewan, Canada. 23 March 1923. Washington. Inducted in 1984. 1948–49 New York Yankees (AAFC), 1950–53 New York Giants.

Bill Willis
Guard. 6-2, 215. Born in Columbus, Ohio, 5 October 1921. Ohio State. Inducted in 1977. 1946–49 Cleveland Browns (AAFC). 1950–53 Cleveland Browns.

Larry Wilson
Defensive back. 6-0. 190. Born in Idaho, 24 March 1938. Utah. Inducted in 1978. 1960–72 St. Louis Cardinals.

Alex Wojciechowicz
Center. 6-0, 235. Born in South River, New Jersey, 12 August 1915. Fordham. Inducted in 1968. 1938–48 Detroit Lions, 1946–50 Philadelphia Eagles.

NORM VAN BROCKLIN

Before the start of the 1958 season, the Philadelphia Eagles acquired quarterback Norm Van Brocklin from the Los Angeles Rams for a tackle, a defensive back and a No 1 draft choice.

It was one of the sharpest deals ever made in football history because in just three years, the Flying Dutchman led the Eagles into the NFL championship game.

Van Brocklin's career had already reached unsurpassed heights—he was a standout for nine years with the Rams, but most football commentators believe that his generalship of the Eagles in 1960 was his most sterling accomplishment.

One of the most colourful and competitive of individuals, both as a player and later as a coach, Van Brocklin blazed a sometimes stormy, but always eventful, path in his 12 active seasons as a player.

His difficulties, if one can call them that, started on almost the day he was selected No. 4 by the Rams in the 1949 draft. He had a year's eligibility left at the University of Oregon, but the Rams, aware of his decision to forego a final college season, surprised the whole of football by taking the 1948 All-American.

Van Brocklin's rookie season was a quiet one. The Rams already had the brilliant Bob Waterfield, another gridiron giant, and as a result the Dutchman only saw brief action until the final game of the season against Washington, which the Rams needed to win to clinch the divisional title. Van Brocklin responded with a four-touchdown performance as Clark Shaughnessy's team charged a memorable win.

In 1950 the Rams had a new coach, Joe Stydahar, who decided to alternate his two great passers. Waterfield played in the first and third quarters, Van Brocklin in the second and fourth. The tactics worked. Van Brocklin won the NFL passing title and the Rams won their second straight division title.

A year later, Waterfield edged out his rival for the passing crown by less than one-hundredth of a yard per attempt, the criterion for naming passing leaders in those days. But in 1952 it was Van Brocklin again with the second of his three NFL titles.

Even though he missed out on the title in 1951, Van Brocklin's greatest day as a passer came early in that season when he threw for 554 yards against the New York Yanks. That mark is still an all-time NFL record.

In the NFL title game of that year, Van Brocklin sat on the bench for 3½ quarters while the Rams and the Cleveland Browns (who had taken over the city's franchise when the Rams moved west in the late 1940s), fought out a 17–17 stalemate.

Called on to the park late in the game, Van Brocklin connected with Tom Fears on a 73-yard pass-run play that ended the Browns' stubborn resistance.

When Waterfield retired at the end of the 1952 season, Van Brocklin had to contend with another challenger—Billy Wade.

The Rams won their division in 1955 under coach Sid Gillman but they then slumped badly and Van Brocklin openly talked of retirement.

The move to Philadelphia rekindled the spirit and Van Brocklin was also given a player-coach role, one which he enjoyed immensely. 'If it's the game plan you want, see Dutch', an Eagles' player once told a reporter seeking out head coach Buck Shaw.

But success didn't come instantly in Philadelphia. In 1958 they finished seven places worse than the previous year, but with the Flying Dutchman in superb form, the Eagles finished second in 1959 and won it all in 1960. By defeating Green Bay in that finale, Van

Brocklin became the only man to beat Vince Lombardi in a championship game during his years at the Packers.

The 1960 performance earned Van Brocklin a unanimous all-NFL selection and several MVP trophies including the Bert Bell Award and the Jim Thorpe Trophy. A month later, in the annual Pro Bowl (his eighth) he bowed out of active football.

Coaching positions at the Minnesota Vikings and at Atlanta followed but his role in the resurgence of the Eagles is legendary.

Norm Van Brocklin had passed his NFL examination with flying colours.

Training Camp

Professional football nowadays is an all-year sport. The season may well end in January, but for the league's players it is necessary for them to keep in trim.

During April and May, NFL teams hold a series of minicamps, checking on the fitness of their veteran players and looking at the college graduates who they hope to take in the season's draft.

If a team has a new head coach it is permitted to have an extra spring camp, so that the new coach has a chance to evaluate the players.

For the majority of players, July marks the traditional start to the season. Each team has a small college near its home town, or in the case of some clubs its own training complex where it gets down to some serious fitness training. Dallas, for instance, holds its camp in California because it is too hot in Texas in July. Atlanta Falcons have their own complex at Suwannee, in the beautiful Georgia countryside. Some of the northern clubs will move south to Florida for their summer camps.

The first two weeks at training camp are reserved for newcomers, those players who were drafted by the club in the spring, and free agents—players without club contracts who are trying to get into a team. The new boys are dubiously named 'rookies' while their more senior counterparts are called 'veterans' or more commonly, 'vets'. The veterans will return after the first two weeks, although many of the key players will actually turn up earlier to help out in the evaluation of the new players.

Training camp for many players resembles Colditz—being a tough regime where only the fittest survive. Players have already been assessed as to their speed and ability but they will have to go through it all again as the coaching staff push them to breaking point. Everything they do is recorded as the coaches keep an individual record of every player. The rookies are expected to learn the club's play-book from cover to cover and they are penalized if mistakes on the practice field occur. Extra laps of the field in full equipment as a scorching sun shines down is not to be treated lightly.

For some the gruelling pace is too much and many will fall by the wayside. Dallas coach, Tom Landry, once said that of the 50 or so rookies and free agents in the training camp, only four or five get a spot on the team. The most the Cowboys have ever retained is six.

At any time during camp the coaches can decide to cut a player. The most feared man in camp is a person called the Turk. He is the man who has to tell a player to return his kit and playbook. If a player is requested to report to the coach's office early the following morning, it is almost certain that he will be cut. Most players, though, almost instinctively know when they are going to be cut. But being dropped doesn't automatically mean that a player's career is over. He then becomes a free agent and may try to join another team.

Training camp is not fun. But it was never designed to be. The players live in dormitories and all meals and accommodation are provided by the club. From the minute the alarm clock goes at 6 a.m. until they drop off to sleep, exhausted at around 10 p.m., the players are owned by the club.

As well as meals, the club provides entertainment on a small scale during camp in the form of movies. Many clubs show those that are designed to create a sense of teamwork in the players. From over 100 players at the start, the club has a little over a month to reduce this number to a 45-man squad who are ready and willing to die for each other. Football is no place for the individual.

For the first couple of weeks the players may not even see a football. Physical fitness will be the main course of the day. Various forms of exercise, some unique to American football,

Chicago Bears training camp in the Illinois countryside.

are adopted to stretch and strengthen almost every part of the body. One of the main tests is the 40-yard dash. It is assumed that most players will rarely run a distance in excess of 40 yards, but sprints of less than 40 are commonplace. So players will be wired to electrical timers to run their own race. If they do not come up to standards they will be told to run it again. A limit of 4.5 seconds at this distance is considered to be good.

In camp the players will have the use of a fully-equipped gymnasium, weight-training room, swimming pool, treatment rooms, saunas and running track. Each player will undergo exhausting medical tests including a visit to the team's dentist. Every part of the body will be checked to make sure that it is in perfect working order. If there is the slightest doubt a player can be rejected on the spot.

As training camp unfolds the coaching staff will have already decided who's to go and who's to stay. A series of pre-season games will be arranged where clubs are permitted more than their usual number of players. But after each game the squad has to be reduced until, at the end of August, the final 45 are left. Although not part of the regular season, these games are taken very seriously by the coaching staff and players alike. For many players it will be the only time they will get the chance to play professional football.

These games make up the first real test of ability, although many teams are notorious for poor pre-season results—results which have no bearing on the regular season. The Los Angeles Raiders are one such team, yet no one could deny their success once the season has started.

Players receive a differently-structured salary when in camp. In 1986 rookies received $450 per week and the veterans $500. Veterans will also get an additional $200 for every pre-season game they participate in.

Once the final cut is made the players who remain will then receive their negotiated salary—and for some it can amount into millions. Buffalo quarterback Jim Kelly was the NFL's highest-paid player in 1986, receiving over $1.2 million as a basic wage per year plus a lucrative bonus deal.

But, sadly, for the majority, success is very short-lived. Only the very best are retained by the league's 28 clubs. For many it is time to disappear. Yet, most will return the following year still pursuing the impossible dream.

The Teams

The AFC

Buffalo Bills

1 Bills Drive, Orchard Park, New York 14127

Stadium: Rich Stadium

Conference: AFC (Eastern Division)

Colours: scarlet, white and royal blue

1959 Ralph C. Wilson, a shareholder in the Detroit Lions, is awarded a franchise to establish an AFL team in Buffalo. He names them the 'Buffalo Bills' after the archetypal western frontiersman, scout and showman William 'Buffalo Bill' Cody.

1960 Over 100 000 Buffalo citizens turn out to meet the Bills as they return from training camp before their first pre-season game. However, by the end of the season, with a 5–8–1 record, attendances have fallen to an average of 16 000 per game

1962 Running back Cookie Gilchrist becomes the AFL's first 1000-yard runner.

1964 AFL champions, defeating the San Diego Chargers.

1965 After demanding more money following the previous year's championship season, Gilchrist is traded to the Denver Broncos.
AFL champions, again defeating the San Diego Chargers.

1966 Eastern Division champions.

1969 After intense negotiations, Heisman Trophy winner O. J. 'The Juice' Simpson is signed to a long-term contract.

1971 After the Bills win only one game that season, Lou Saban (who had previously coached the team, 1962–65) rejoins as head coach and 'vice president in charge of football'.

1972 Saban proceeds to rebuild the Bills. After two disappointing seasons O. J. Simpson begins to live up to his potential and is named AFC player of the year.

1973 The Bills move into Orchard Park stadium (later renamed Rich Stadium) from their old stamping-ground at the War Memorial Stadium.
The team becomes the first in AFL history to run for more than 3000 yards.

1976 Simpson insists on being traded to the

Los Angeles Rams but later signs a three-year contract worth more than $2 million to stay with the Bills.

After three losses in the first five games of the season, Saban resigns 'in the best interests of the team'.

1977 Simpson is benched with a knee injury for half the season.

1978 Simpson is traded to the San Francisco 49ers.

1980 Eastern Division champions.

1983 Coach Chuck Knox replaced by Kay Stephenson.

1985 Kay Stephenson replaced by Hank Bullough.

1986 Bullough fired, replaced by Marv Levy.

Cincinnati Bengals

200 Riverfront Stadium, Cincinnati, Ohio 45202

Stadium: Riverfront Stadium

Conference: AFC (Central Division)

Colours: black, orange and white

1967 The AFL franchise for Cincinnati is awarded to a group headed by Paul Brown, former head coach of the Clevelend Browns. As previous Cincinnati AFL teams had taken the name of 'Bengals' in 1927, 1930 and 1931, Brown chooses it for his team too.

1969 At the end of the Bengals' second season, with a 4–9–1 record, Brown is named AFL coach of the year.

1970 Central Division champions—a remarkable recovery from being in last place after the first seven games.

1973 Central Division champions.

1976 Paul Brown retires after 41 years as coach; Bill Johnson succeeds him. Brown remains owner, vice-president and general manager.

1978 Johnson resigns after five consecutive losses (but two previous seasons close to the top of the division); he is followed by Homer Rice.

1979 By repeating the 1978 season record of 4–12, Rice is fired and eventually replaced by Forrest Gregg—like Paul Brown, a former Cleveland Browns coach.

1981 The team adopts new uniform with tiger stripes on helmets, jerseys and trousers. Central Division champions.

1982 AFC champions, defeating the San Diego Chargers in appalling weather—a wind chill factor of minus 59°F. Defeated in Super Bowl XVI by the San Francisco 49ers.

1985 Finished second in AFC Central Division.

Cleveland Browns

Tower B, Cleveland Stadium, Cleveland, Ohio 44114

Stadium: Cleveland Stadium

Conference: AFC (Central Division)

Colours: seal brown, orange and white

1946 Entrepreneur Arthur 'Mickey' McBride wins a franchise for a Cleveland team from the newly-formed All-America Football Conference.

Paul Brown is appointed head coach and general manager. In a contest to choose the team's name, 36 entrants plump for 'Panthers'. However, coach Brown rejects the name as it was used by a signally unsuccessful NFL Cleveland team in the 1920s. The majority of the other entrants had chosen 'the Browns'—after the new team's just-appointed coach—and after initially refusing to accept this honour, Brown relents and the Browns become the only team ever to be named after its coach. The first player Brown signs is Otto Graham, who will become one of the greatest T-formation quarterbacks in football history.

AAFC champions, defeating the New York Yankees.

1947 AAFC champions, again defeating the New York Yankees.

1948 AAFC champions, defeating the Buffalo Bills after an unbeaten season.

1949 AAFC champions, defeating the San Francisco 49ers

The AAFC folds, helped to its death by the Browns who, being such dominant champions, caused fans to avoid games which they assumed had foregone conclusions.

1950 The Cleveland Browns are transferred into the NFL.

NFL champions, defeating the Los Angeles Rams.

1951 Eastern Conference champions.

1952 Eastern Conference champions

1953 McBride sells the team for $600 000 to a syndicate headed by Cleveland industrialist David Jones. They take out a large life assurance policy on coach Paul Brown, regarding him as their most important asset.

Eastern Conference champions.

1954 NFL champions, defeating the Detroit Lions, 56–10. In the game, after which he plans to retire, Otto Graham scores three times, as well as throwing three touchdown passes.

1955 After four games, Brown is aware of a yawning gap without Graham, and he persuades him to return.

Eastern Conference champions.

NFL champions, defeating the Los Angeles Rams. Graham scores twice and makes two touchdown passes, before

Bernie Kosar led Cleveland to the play-offs last season. (Fotosports International).

finally retiring at the end of the game, following a standing ovation by all 85 000 fans at the Los Angeles Memorial Coliseum.

1956 The Browns have their first losing season: 5–7–0.

1957 Even though the Browns are only sixth in the queue for the collegiate draft, Paul Brown is fortunate enough to choose Jim Brown, who will prove to be one of the most valuable running backs in NFL history.

Eastern Division champions.

1958 Paul Brown's relationship with his players begins to deteriorate, particularly that with Jim Brown, quarterback Milt Plum and running back Bobby Mitchell.

1961 Former New York advertising executive Arthur Modell buys the Browns for $3 925 000. With his experience in television, he aims to make the team tops in entertainment value—an innovative attitude at the time.

1962 Quarterback Plum is traded, as is Bobby Mitchell, the latter for Syracuse University back Ernie Davis; however, tragically, Davis discovers he is dying of leukemia.

Jim Brown threatens to retire unless Paul Brown is replaced as coach.

1963 Modell fires Paul Brown, who has been coach and general manager of the Browns for 17 years with a record of 158 victories, 48 defeats and 8 ties. However, his abrasive manner and habit of calling plays from the sidelines via messenger guards has finally beaten him, and he is replaced by his trusted assistant Blanton Collier, whose manner is the exact opposite of Brown's.

1964 NFL champions, defeating the Baltimore Colts.

1965 Eastern Conference champions. Jim Brown retires.

1967 Century Division champions.

1968 Eastern Conference champions.

1970 The team is transferred to the AFC Central Division.

1971 Central Division champions.

1974 For the first time, since 1956, the Browns have a losing season (4–10–0).

1975 Forrest Gregg is named head coach.

1977 Despite an improvement in the team's fortunes the previous year, a losing season (6–8–0), partially due to injuries, results in Gregg's resignation.

61

1979 With Sam Rutigliano as head coach, the Browns become known as the 'Kardiac Kids' when 12 out of 16 of their games are cliffhangers as well as victories.

1980 Central Division champions.

1984 Marty Schottenheimer, a former Browns' assistant coach, replaces Sam Rutigliano.

1986 Central Division champions.
Lose out to Denver Broncos in AFC championship game.

Denver Broncos

5700 Logan Street, Denver, Colorado 80216

Stadium: Mile High Stadium

Conference: AFC (Western Division)

Colours: orange, blue and white

1959 The Broncos, with Bob Howsam and his father Lee as majority shareholders, are formed and become charter members of the AFC.

1960 Frank Filchock is appointed as first head coach.
The team has to play in the Bears' baseball stadium, which has limited seating capacity. However, they are watched by 18 372 as they beat the Oakland Raiders in their first home game.
After a losing first season (4–9–1), attendance dwindles to 5861 at the last home game of the year.

1961 The Howsams sell out to a new group headed by Cal Kunz and Gerry Phipps. After an even worse season's record (3–11–0) Filchock is fired.

1962 Jack Faulkner is appointed head coach and general manager.
Faulkner changes the team's uniform from brown and gold to orange, blue and white, and eliminates the vertically-striped socks—hated by team and public alike. A pair of the latter are symbolically burnt at a public ceremony. With wins over the San Diego Chargers and Houston Oilers and a 7–7–0 record, attendances at home games are more than doubled.

1963 Fielding a team including 14 rookies, the Broncos end the season with a 2–11–1 record.

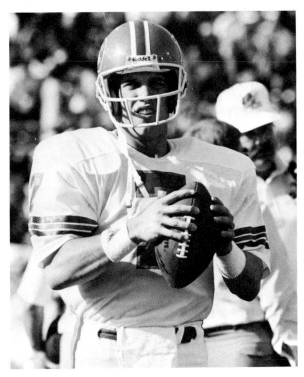

Denver Bronco's quarterback, John Elway.
(Fotosports International).

1964 Without a win after four games, when the Broncos lose a fifth to the Boston Patriots, Faulkner is fired and his place is taken by Mac Speedie.

1965 Part-owner Carl Kunz and his supporters sell the team to the Cox Broadcasting Corporation, who plan to transfer it to Atlanta. Gerry and Alan Phipps, who own 42 per cent of the club, decide that it should remain in Denver and buy out the other shareholders for $1.5 million. The threatened removal of the team does wonders for ticket sales as public support for the Broncos snowballs, and before the beginning of the season, season ticket sales reach an all-time high of 22 000.

1966 Relations between coach Speedie and fullback Cookie Gilchrist, who arrived from the Buffalo Bills the previous year, reach rock-bottom and Gilchrist is traded, with detrimental effects on the team. One week into the season, Speedie is fired.
Late in the year, Lou Saban is named coach and general manager.

1967 In a pre-season game against the Detroit Lions the Broncos become the first AFL team to defeat an NFL side.

1968 With a new $1.8 million upper level, increasing capacity to 50 000, Bears'

Stadium is given as a gift to the city of Denver by a non-profit fund-raising group. Its name is officially changed to the 'Denver Mile High Stadium'.

1969 A disappointing 5–8–1 season is highlighted by the Broncos' first-ever shutout of another team—the San Diego Chargers.

1971 After nine lacklustre games Saban resigns as head coach, following this a month later with his resignation as general manager.

1972 John Ralston of Stanford University is appointed head coach.

Because all season tickets (over 46 500 of them) are already held, there is, for the first time in the Broncos' history, no public sale of season tickets.

1976 With the Mile High Stadium expanded to a 63 500 capacity, season ticket sales are halted at 62 215—the club's seventh sell-out season.

The team's 9–5–0 record is its best ever.

1977 Ralston resigns as head coach (having given up his position as general manager the year before). He is replaced by Robert 'Red' Miller.

Western Division champions.

1978 AFC champions, defeating the Oakland Raiders.

Runners-up at Super Bowl XII, beaten by the Dallas Cowboys.

1981 The Broncos are bought by Edgar F. Kaiser Jr.

Dan Reeves is appointed head coach.

1983 In the most lucrative trade in NFL history, the Broncos sign quarterback John Elway to a five-year contract for $6 million—with the result that Elway becomes known as the 'six-million-dollar man'.

1984 Western Division champions.

1986 AFC champions before losing out 39–20 to NY Giants in Super Bowl XXI.

During their first two seasons of play the Broncos played in brown and gold uniforms. But they won only seven of their first 28 games and decided to look for a change of fortune. Out went those drab colours and in came the colours they wear today – orange and blue.

Houston Oilers

Box 1516, Houston, Texas 770001

Stadium: Astrodome

Conference: AFC (Central Division)

Colours: scarlet, Columbia blue and white

1959 The team is founded by K. S. 'Bud' Adams Jr, a Houston oilman, who names them the 'Oilers' for 'sentimental and social reasons': 'You think I'd ever call them the "Aluminiums" or "Uraniums"?' Adams jokes.

1960 All-America halfback and Heisman Trophy winner Billy Cannon is signed (after a dispute with the Los Angeles Rams, for whom Cannon had also agreed to play), and veteran quarterback George Blanda is lured out of retirement.

Lou Rymkus is appointed head coach. Adams leases Jeppesen High School stadium and spends $200 000 to renovate it and increase seating capacity to 36 000.

Eastern Division champions.

1961 The Oilers win the first AFL Championship, defeating the Los Angeles Chargers on New Year's Day.

After the Oilers win only one of their first five games, Rymkus is replaced by his assistant Wally Lemm. After the changes in coaches, the Oilers are victorious 10 times in a row and become the first professional team to score more than 500 points in one season.

AFL champions, defeating the San Diego Chargers.

1962 Lemm leaves to become coach of the St Louis Cardinals, and is replaced by Frank 'Pop' Ivy—the Oilers' third coach in three years.

Runners-up for the AFL championship, defeated by the Dallas Texans in a historic six-quarter, double-overtime game which ends 20–17.

1963 The Oilers suffer their first losing season: 6–8–0.

1964 Ivy is replaced by Sammy Baugh, who at the end of another losing season (4–10–0) is, in turn, replaced by Hugh 'Bones' Taylor. Baugh stays on to help his successor, and the Oilers' coach, Lou Rymkus, also returns as offensive line coach.

1965 Although the new Houston Astrodome

Houston Oilers Warren Moon – one of a very few band of black quarterbacks in the NFL.

is now complete, the team management announces that the Oilers will not play there because of 'an unrealistic lease agreement', and sign a lease to play at the Rice University stadium instead.

1966 'Bones' Taylor is also unable to come up with the goods—he had a 4–10–0 season the previous year—and Wally Lemm returns as coach.

1967 Eastern Division champions: with this success, the Oilers become the first team ever to go from the bottom of the league to the division championship in one season.

1968 The teams moves into the Astrodome after all.

1970 The Oilers, in one of the most emotional games in the AFL's history, defeat the Dallas Cowboys for the first time in a pre-season game.

1971 On Lemm's retirement, Ed Hughes is named head coach. However, during the dismal 4–9–1 season, during which both the offensive line and offensive backfield

coaches are sacked, Hughes' contract is terminated 'by mutual consent'. He is replaced by Bill Peterson of Rice University.

1973 When the team under Peterson wins only one game in 19 outings, he is fired and replaced by the veteran Sid Gilman as head coach and general manager.

1974 The Oilers finish with seven wins and seven losses—their best record since 1969. However, the management announce a record loss of $459 281.

1975 O. A. 'Bum' Phillips is named head coach, but although Gilman wants to remain general manager, he is forced to give that up to Phillips as well.
The Oilers end the season with a 10–4–0 record, their first winning season since 1967. Houston home attendance reaches an all-time high.

1979 Runners-up for the AFC Championship, defeated by the Pittsburgh Steelers.

1980 Runners-up for the AFC Championship, again defeated by the Pittsburgh Steelers. After the Oilers are defeated in the play-offs by the eventual Super Bowl winners—this time, the Oakland Raiders—for the third time in a row, 'Bum' Phillips is relinquished as coach.

1981 Ed Biles becomes head coach.

1983 After the team won only one game the previous year, Biles is relieved of duty after six games and is replaced by Chuck Studley, who only manages a 2–14–0 season.

1984 Studley is replaced by Hugh Campbell: the Oilers' record for the year is 3–13.

1985 With a second losing season under his belt (5–11), Campbell is released and replaced by Jerry Glanville.

Indianapolis Colts

PO Box 5400, Indianapolis, Indiana 46254

Stadium: Hoosier Dome

Conference: AFC (Eastern Division)

Colours: royal blue, white and silver

1952 After the franchise in Baltimore folds (after being active 1946–50), the NFL faces a lawsuit by Baltimore shareholders unless it is reinstated. NFL Commissioner Bert Bell agrees that the Dallas Texans can transfer to Baltimore if 15 000 season tickets can be sold within six weeks. The target is met in 4½ weeks.

1953 With ticket sales resulting in $300 000 in the bank, Carroll D. Rosenbloom takes over as majority shareholder.

Keith Molesworth is named first head coach of the reconstituted team, which is now called the 'Colts' after the defunct Baltimore team.

1954 Molesworth becomes chief talent scout and is replaced by Wilbur C. 'Weeb' Ewbank. He promises to produce a championship team within five years.

1956 At the end of an erratic season, Ewbank's job is saved by a 53-yard scoring pass against the Washington Redskins by understudy quarterback Johnny Unitas, who had been signed that year.

1958 After winning five consecutive games, the Colts come up against the Green Bay Packers. This is a 56–0 shutout, but it costs the team Unitas, who suffers broken ribs and a punctured lung.

After the team loses one and wins one, Unitas returns, wearing a special harness to protect his ribs. The team goes on to win the Western Conference championship.

NFL champions, defeating the New York Giants. Trailing 17–14 with 8 seconds left on the clock, linebacker Steve Myrha kicks a 20-yard field goal to even the score and enter the two teams into sudden-death overtime for the first time in league history. A pass from Unitas to fullback Alan Ameche enables the latter to score a touchdown and bring victory to the Colts, 23–17. A crowd of 30 000 fans meet the team at the airport on their return from New York.

1959 NFL champions, again defeating the New York Giants.

1960 Unitas suffers a cracked vertebra and, although he can pass well (his 47-game touchdown passing streak is only stopped by the Los Angeles Rams in mid-December), he is forbidden to run. With this and other team injuries, the Colts finish 6–6–0.

1963 Weeb Ewbank is replaced by Don Shula, who is only 33.

1964 Rosenbloom buys all the stock in the Colts that is held in other hands and becomes sole owner of the club.

Western Conference champions.

1965 With a team record of 9–1–1, both Unitas and number-two quarterback Gary Cuozzo are injured. Running back Tom Matte is transferred to the quarterback position and performs flawlessly, but the Colts are defeated in sudden-death overtime in the Western Conference playoffs by the Green Bay Packers.

1967 The Colts are transferred into the Coastal Division.

1968 NFL champions, defeating the Cleveland Browns to end the season with a ten-game winning streak. Some critics compare the Colts to the best NFL teams of all time.

1969 Super Bowl III runners-up, losing to the New York Jets (who are now coached by Weeb Ewbank, formerly of the Colts).

The Colts are moved into the new American Conference of the NFL.

1970 Despite protests by owner Rosenbloom, Shula moves to Miami to coach the Dolphins. This is the beginning of a long-standing feud between the two men.

1971 AFC champions, defeating the Oakland Raiders.

Super Bowl V champions, defeating the Dallas Cowboys 16–13 after a field goal kicked by rookie wide receiver Jim O'Brien in the final 5 seconds.

1972 Runners-up for the AFC championship, defeated by Shula's Miami Dolphins 21–0, the Colts' first shutout since 1965.

Winnetka, Illinois, executive Robert Irsay gains control of the Colts: he first buys the Los Angeles Rams and then trades them to the Rosenblooms for the Colts.

1973 Unitas is transferred to the San Diego Chargers—the end of an era.

With a 4–10–1 record, the Colts tie for last place in the division, winning the fewest games since 1954.

1975 Ted Marchibroda is named head coach: his appointment marks the fifth since Shula left in 1969.

Eastern Division champions.

1976 After the Colts lose four of its six pre-season games, Irsay lashes out against both the team and coach Marchibroda. The latter resigns, but after the players issue a statement saying that Irsay and general manager Joe Thomas 'have completely destroyed this team', Marchibroda agrees to return with complete control over football matters. Eastern Division champions.

1977 Eastern Division champions.

1980 After two 5–11–0 seasons, Marchibroda is replaced by Mike McCormack.

1981 Team manages to win only two of its 16 games, McCormack is fired and Frank Kush, a Canadian Football League coach, takes over.

1983 After a miserable 0–8–1 season in 1982, the Colts have first pick of the collegiate draft. However, first choice John Elway states that he would rather play baseball than join the Colts (he eventually goes to the Denver Broncos for $6 million).

1984 The team is transferred to Indianapolis, where there are 143 000 season ticket requests in two weeks.

1985 The new Indianapolis Colts, now under coach Rod Dowhower, finish their second season in their new home with a 5–11–0 record.

1986 Dowhower axed, makes way for new head coach Ron Meyer.

Kansas City Chiefs

1 Arrowhead Drive, Kansas City, Missouri 64129

Stadium: Arrowhead Stadium

Conference: AFC (Western Division)

Colours: red, gold and white

1959 Texas millionaire Lamar Hunt, unable to get an NFL franchise for his home city of Dallas, establishes and organizes the American Football League and its six original teams, one of which is the Dallas Texans. (NB: this is a completely different team from the Dallas Texans which formed the basis of the Indianapolis Colts.) After the league is formed and the Texans are in place, the NFL establishes the Dallas Cowboys.
Hunt appoints Hank Stram as coach, a disciplinarian who is notable for having said: 'Show me a good loser, and I'll show you a loser—period'.

1962 AFL champions, defeating the Houston Oilers.

1963 The mayor of Kansas City promises Hunt three times as many season ticket sales and the enlargement of the Municipal Stadium there if he will move the Texans to Kansas City. This Hunt does, also persuaded by the fact that the nearest professional football franchise is 250 miles away (whereas the Texans had been competing against the Dallas Cowboys and the Houston Oilers.) He renames the team the 'Chiefs'.
The Chiefs arrive to ill omens as rookie Stone Johnson suffers a fatal injury in a pre-season game.

1964 The Chiefs play erratically during a season when ten regulars are injured, including tight end Fred Arbanas, who is mugged on a Kansas City street and blinded in one eye. With a 7–7–0 record, attendances fall (an average of only 18 125 people watch seven home games) and there are discussions among the AFL owners about whether the team should be moved again.

1966 Following the Chiefs' first winning season in 1965, and intrigued by the signing of Heisman Tophy winner, running back Mike Garrett for $400 000, attendance picks up dramatically, with 43 885 turning out to see the Chiefs lose to the Buffalo Bills at the season's opening game at home.
Western Division champions.

1967 AFL champions, defeating the Buffalo Bills. The Chiefs are mobbed at the airport in Kansas City on their return.
Runners-up of the first Super Bowl, losing to the Green Bay Packers. More than 6300 fans travel to Los Angeles to see the game, but despite this, only 61 946 people fill Memorial Coliseum, leaving 30 000 empty seats.

1970 AFC champions, defeating the Oakland Raiders.
Super Bowl IV champions, defeating the Minnesota Vikings.
Relations between star running back Garrett and coach Stram become strained, and Garrett is traded to the San Diego Chargers. In the final game of the season, he is instrumental in the Chargers' defeat of the Chiefs.

1971 Western Division champions.

New Los Angeles Rams quarterback Jim Everett. (Fotosports International).

Above: New Jersey's Meadowlands – home of both the Giants and the Jets. (Fotosports International).

Left: Jim McMahon suffered a torn shoulder in 1986. (Fotosports International).

Right: Mick Luckhurst, Atlanta's British Kicker. (Fotosports International).

Below: The half-time show at the 1985 Sun Bowl. (Amy L. Carr).

Above: San Diego kick off the 1986 season at Jack Murphy Stadium, the venue for Superbowl XXII. (Fotosports International).

Right: San Diego's veteran quarterback Dan Fouts. (Sporting Pictures).

Above left: Robert F. Kennedy Stadium, Washington. (Fotosports International).

Far left: Rueben Mayes – New Orleans' rookie star of 1986. (Fotosports International).

Left: John Elway led the Denver Broncos to Superbowl XXI. (Fotosports International).

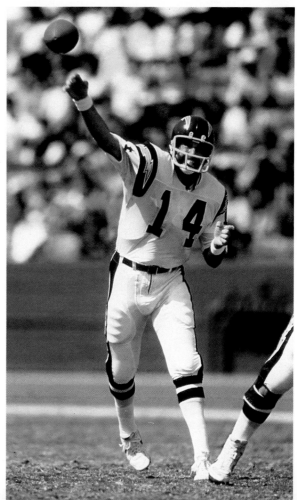

Joe Cribbs joined San Francisco in 1986 from Buffalo. (Fotosports International).

Above: Outrageous Washington fans – 'The Hoggettes'. (Fotosports International).

Left: Dan Marino came to London in 1986 as president of the Budweiser League. (Fotosports International).

Below: St Louis Cardinals veteran fullback Stump Mitchell. (Fotosports International).

Above left: Patriots star receiver Irving Fryar. (Thomas J. Croke).

Above right: Lionel 'Little Train' James. (Fotosports International).

Left: Chris Chandler, Washington's highly-rated quarterback.

Above: Candlestick Park, home of the San Francisco 49ers. (Sporting Pictures).

Right: New England Patriots quarterback Tony Eason. (Thomas J. Croke).

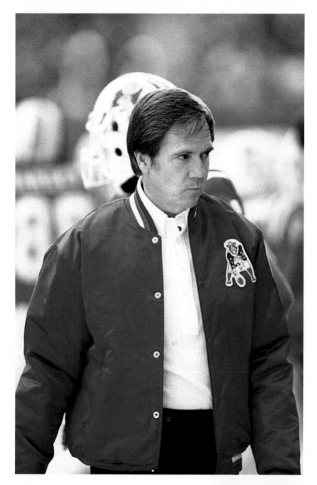

Above left: Patriots head coach Raymond Berry. (Thomas J. Croke).

Above right: New England quarterback Tony Eason. (Thomas J. Croke).

Right: Football is a fun game, as this Los Angeles Rams fan proves. (Fotosports International).

Left: Washington punter Steve Cox. (Fotosports International).

Above: Candlestick Park, home of the San Francisco 49ers.

Left: Marcus Allen, Los Angeles Raiders. (Fotosports International).

Below: Los Angeles Raiders defensive player of the year, Howie Long

Right: Jim McMahon leads the Chicago Bears in last summer's American Bowl at Wembley Stadium. (Fotosports International).

Left: Action from a Cleveland Browns–Los Angeles Raiders game in 1986. (Fotosports International).

Right: Walter Payton and William Perry in a sprint race at training camp.

Left: Raiders fans show their loyalty to their team. (Fotosports International).

Right: Seattle Seahawks Curt Warner. (Fotosports International).

Don McNeal, Miami Dolphins cornerback. (Fotosports International).

1972 The team moves into the futuristic Arrowhead Stadium.

1974 The Chiefs have their first losing season since 1963: 5–9–0.

Stram, the team's first and only coach, is dismissed after 15 years.

1975 Paul Wiggin of the San Francisco 49ers is appointed head coach.

1976 After losing six of their first seven games, Wiggin is fired and succeeded by Tom Bettis. The team dedicates its next game, against the Green Bay Packers, to Wiggin, and win. However, a six-game losing streak results in Bettis's contract not being renewed.

1981 The Chiefs, now with Marv Levy as coach, have their first winning season since 1973: 9–7–0.

1983 John Mackovic, formerly of the Dallas Cowboys, is appointed head coach.

1986 Mackovic leads Chiefs to playoffs, but still loses his job.

Los Angeles Raiders

332 Center Street, El Segundo, California 90245

Stadium: Los Angeles Memorial Coliseum

Conference: AFC (Western Division)

Colours: silver and black

1960 Following the withdrawal of the Minneapolis-St Paul franchise from the newly-formed American Football League, Barron Hilton, owner of the Los Angeles Chargers, threatens to pull out too if another franchise is not given to a city on the West Coast. Oakland is that city, and the franchise becomes the property of a syndicate headed by Y. C. 'Chet' Soda. The squad is formed with players from the other seven new teams.

The team is named the 'Raiders' and Eddie Erdelatz is appointed head coach. When the University of California refuses permission for the team to use their stadium, the Raiders move into Kezar Stadium in San Francisco, which they share with NFL rivals, the 49ers.

1961 The Raiders move to Candlestick Park in San Francisco. Ed McGah, Robert Osborne and Wayne Valley buy out the other shareholders, and McGah is made president of the club.

After the Raiders lose their first two games in shutouts—55–0 against the Houston Oilers and 44–0 against the Chargers (who had by now moved to San Diego)—Erdelatz is fired after admitting: 'I don't know what to do about it.'

Marty Feldman is named head coach, but his tenure sees the Raiders scoring the fewest and allowing the most points in the league, winning only two games in front of mostly empty seats. In disgust, Robert Osborne sells his interest in the club.

1962 When co-owner Valley threatens Oakland city officials that the club will be moved unless a new stadium is built, the team is given Frank Youell Field, a high-school stadium, which, when expanded to hold 20 000, still loses money even when every seat is filled.

Feldman is replaced with Bill 'Red' Conkright after two games, but the Raiders fail to win until the very last game of the season—ending a 13-game losing streak.

1963 After refusing several times, Al Davis of the San Diego Chargers agrees to replace

Rod Martin is feared in the NFL for his no-nonsense style of play.

the luckless Conkright and become head coach and general manager. He proceeds to reorganize both the management and the team sides of the franchise completely.

The Raiders have their first winning season since their formation—10–4–0—winning their last game, against the Houston Oilers, 52–49: the highest scoring game in AFL history.

1966 Davis leaves the Raiders to become AFL commissioner, and is succeeded by John Rauch. However, when the AFL and NFL merge, Davis resigns and takes over as managing general partner of the Raiders.

The team moves into the new Oakland-Alameda County Coliseum.

1967 AFL champions, defeating the Houston Oilers.

1968 Runners-up at Super Bowl II, defeated by the Green Bay Packers.

One of the highlights of the 1968 season was what game to be known as the 'Heidi game'. The Raiders were trailing the New York Jets 32–29 when the TV network showing the game switched over to the film *Heidi* when there were still 65 seconds to play. Despite the fact that the switchboard at NBC was immediately swamped with angry protests, viewers were not allowed to see the two last-minute touchdowns by the Raiders, which won them the game, 43–32.

Western Division champions.

1969 Rauch leaves to become head coach of the Buffalo Bills and is replaced by Raiders' assistant John Madden who at 32 is the youngest head coach in professional football.

Western Division champions.

1970 The Raiders are the first AFC team to become Western Division champions four times in a row, largely thanks to the veteran 43-year-old quarterback/kicker George Blanda, who that season produced four victories and a tie in the final seconds of five consecutive games.

1972 Western Division champions.

1973 Western Division champions.

1974 Western Division champions.

1975 Western Division champions.

1976 George Blanda retires after a 15-year career in professional football.

Western Division champions: the

Raiders' ninth divisional title in ten years. AFC champions, defeating the Pittsburgh Steelers.

1977 Super Bowl XI champions, defeating the Minnesota Vikings.

1978 The Raiders miss the AFC playoffs for the first time since 1971 (they had taken part the year before in the wild card game).

1979 After 10 years of producing divisional victories and winning the Super Bowl, John Madden retires as head coach. Former Raiders' quarterback Tom Flores replaces him.

1980 The Raiders, with an 11–5–0 record, win a wild card spot in the AFC playoffs.

1981 AFC champions, defeating the San Diego Chargers.

Super Bowl XV champions, defeating the Philadelphia Eagles.

The Raiders' management, along with the Los Angeles Coliseum Commission, want the team to move into the Memorial Coliseum, the Los Angeles Rams having transferred to Anaheim Stadium, but are blocked by the NFL. The Raiders and the Commission bring a lawsuit against the NFL monopoly, but this ends in a mistrial.

The Raiders have their first losing season (7–9–0) since 1964.

1982 In a retrial, the Raiders win the right to move to the Los Angeles Memorial Coliseum, which has the largest seating capacity of any football stadium in the US. In December, in a game between the Raiders and their rivals, the Los Angeles Rams, more than $1 million worth of tickets are sold—a first in the NFL. The Raiders win.

1984 AFC champions, defeating the Seattle Seahawks on New Year's Day.

Super Bowl XVIII champions, defeating the Washington Redskins.

The Raiders are awarded the key to the city of Los Angeles in recognition of their achievements.

1985 Western Division champions.

The first season in which players wore their names on the back of their jerseys was in 1970.

Miami Dolphins

4770 Biscayne Boulevard, Suite 1440, Miami, Florida 33137

Stadium: Orange Bowl

Conference: AFC (Eastern Division)

Colours: aqua, coral and white.

1965 Minneapolis attorney Joseph Robbie, while representing a friend in his bid for an AFL franchise for Philadelphia (he did not succeed), is persuaded by AFL Commissioner Joe Foss to apply for one for Miami. Robbie joins forces with entertainer Danny Thomas, and together they raise the $7.5 million for the franchise. Miami Mayor, Robert King High, agrees to invite the AFL to Miami after some behind-the-scenes advice from Vice-President Hubert Humphrey, a friend of Robbie's.

In a statewide 'name the team' contest, Mrs Robert Swanson of West Miami wins two lifetime passes for her entry (out of 20 000): 'Dolphins'. According to Mrs

Dan Marino in action for Miami.

Swanson: 'The dolphin is intelligent and indigenous to this area.' Co-owner Robbie expands on this at the naming ceremony on 8 October. 'The dolphin is one of the fastest and smartest creatures of the sea. Dolphins can attack and kill a whale or a shark. Sailors say bad luck will come to anyone who harms a dolphin.'

1966 George Wilson, formerly of the Detroit Lions and the Washington Redskins, is named head coach.

Conditions for the team are, at first, rather less than perfect. They practise on a gravel-covered field; their dormitory is next door to Sea World and they are kept awake by the barking of the seals. Their first pre-season game against the San Diego Chargers follows a miserable 10-hour flight to California in a propeller-driven aeroplane: they lose, 30–10.

Although the Dolphins are defeated in their first regular game, against the Oakland Raiders, the 26 776 Florida fans thrill to the sight of running back Joe Auer (who is also notable for owning a pet lion) returning the opening kickoff 95 yards for a touchdown.

When quarterbacks Rick Norton and Dick Wood are injured, coach Wilson sends in his son George Jr, who leads the Dolphins to their first AFL victory, against the Denver Broncos.

1967 W. H. Keland of Racine, Wisconsin buys out three of the minority shareholders. Then Keland and Robbie buy out Danny Thomas.

1969 Robbie buys Keland's interest in the team to become the majority shareholder.

As the Dolphins plummet to last place, due to injuries to a large extent, George Wilson is fired.

1970 Don Shula, former coach of the Baltimore Colts, is named head coach and vice-president of the club. Shula says that 'The only way I know is hard work', and goes on to prove it with the team as they embark on a gruelling training camp schedule involving two-mile runs every morning at 7 o'clock, two daily 90-minute practices and an evening walk-through.

All the practice pays off as the Dolphins win four pre-season games running and have a four-game winning streak at the beginning of the regular season. They go on to win a wild card spot in the play-

The longest game in NFL history took place on Christmas Day 1971 between Miami and Kansas City. The game lasted 82 minutes and 42 seconds with the Dolphins winning by 27–24.

offs, finally losing to the Oakland Raiders.

1971 Eastern Division champions.

In the divisional playoffs the Dolphins defeat the Kansas City Chiefs 27–24 in the longest game in NFL history: 82 minutes, 40 seconds.

1972 AFC champions, defeating the Baltimore Colts.

Runners-up at Super Bowl VI, beaten by the Dallas Cowboys.

The Dolphins are the first team in NFL history to go unbeaten and untied all season, including post-season games.

With the Dolphins' 52–0 shutout over the New England Patriots, Shula becomes the first coach to win 100 games in 10 seasons (with both the Baltimore Colts and the Dolphins).

AFC champions, defeating the Pittsburgh Steelers.

1973 Super Bowl VII champions, defeating the Washington Redskins.

The Dolphins' perfect record is broken with two defeats in the 1973 season, but this still leaves them with the best two-year record in NFL history: 26–2–0.

AFC champions, defeating the Oakland Raiders, the first time any team has won the championship three times in a row.

1974 Super Bowl VIII champions, defeating the Minnesota Vikings.

In a shock announcement, star players Larry Csonka, Jim Kiick (both running backs) and Paul Warfield (wide receiver) reveal they have signed a deal worth $3.3 million to play for the Toronto Northmen in the World Football League, and will be leaving the Dolphins in 1975.

Eastern Division champions.

In the playoffs the Dolphins' domination of professional football ends when the Oakland Raiders win with a touchdown pass thrown in desperation in the last seconds of the game.

1976 Shula experiences his first losing season in 14 years as an NFL head coach when

the Dolphins end the year with a 6–8–0 record.

1979 Eastern Division champions.

1980 A shoulder injury ends the career of quarterback Bob Griese, who has been with the team since their record season.

1981 Eastern Division champions.

1982 AFC champions, defeating the San Diego Chargers.

1983 Runners-up at Super Bowl XVII, beaten by the Washington Redskins.

In a first in Dolphin history, a quarterback, Dan Marino, is drafted, after 26 other NFL teams pass him up. He goes on to make 20 touchdown passes and becomes the first rookie quarterback ever voted to start in the Pro Bowl.

1984 Eastern Division and AFC champions. Marino becomes the first NFL quarterback to pass for over 5000 yards.

1985 Runners-up at Super Bowl XIX, defeated by the San Francisco 49ers.

Marino holds out from joining the team in a contract dispute; this is resolved later in the season.

Eastern Division champions.

New England Patriots

Sullivan Stadium, Route 1, Foxboro, Massachusetts 02035

Stadium: Sullivan Stadium

Conference: AFC (Eastern Division)

Colours: red, white and blue

1959 The AFL's eighth franchise is awarded to Boston and William H. 'Billy' Sullivan Jr—the first time a professional football team has been established in the city since the demise of the Boston Yanks in 1949.

1960 Lou Saban of Western Illinois University is named head coach. He is described by the team's general manager, Ed McKeever, as 'a Paul Brown [of Cleveland Browns' fame] with heart'.

A Boston newspaper runs a contest to pick the team's name. 'Patriots' is the winner, submitted by 74 people in the light of Boston's position in the history of the American Revolution.

The team signs to play at Boston University's football field for at least two years. In April the Patriots become the first club to issue public stock. By the end of the year, the team has lost about $350 000.

1961 With the club managing to sell fewer than 3500 season tickets, they enter the year on rocky financial ground. The situation is made worse as the team loses two of its first five games, and the fans stay away. Saban is fired, and Mike Holovak is named head coach. The Patriots, now stressing defense, continue with a 7–1–1 record, and attendance increase to an average of more than 19 000 per game. Financial losses continue but not at the same perilous rate.

1963 The team moves to Fenway Park, home of the Boston Red Sox baseball team. Eastern Division champions.

1964 At the end of a 10–3–1 season, the club announces that they have made profits for the first time.

1969 After two consecutive losing seasons, Holovak is replaced by Clive Rush, who

Craig James had another good season for the New England Patriots last year.

proceeds to lose the first seven games of the season.

All home games are now played at Boston College Alumni Stadium.

1970 Joe Kapp is transferred from the Minnesota Vikings for a large sum, but by the end of the year the out-of-condition quarterback has made only three touchdown passes and 17 interceptions.

By mid-season, coach Rush is fired and replaced by John Mazur, but the Patriots still end the year with a dismal 2–12–0 record.

After failing to find financing for a projected $80 million stadium in central Boston, the club selects Foxboro, Massachusetts (about 35 miles south-west of Boston) as the team's future home. In the meantime the Patriots play at home at Harvard Stadium.

1971 Because of the move out of Boston the team's name is changed to the 'New England Patriots'.

The new Schaefer Stadium at Foxboro (so named because the Schaefer brewing company bought $1 million worth of Patriots' stock) is inaugurated by a preseason win over the New York Giants.

1972 Mazur and general manager Upton Bell feud over plans to build up the team.

Quarterback Jim Plunkett, rookie star of the previous year, is subjected to massive physical punishment by a leaky offensive line, and the defense is notable for its inexperience as several veteran players are transferred.

The Mazur–Bell feud is resolved when the head coach resigns before the end of the season and Bell is fired soon after.

1973 Chuck Fairbanks of the University of Oklahoma is hired as head coach and general manager.

1975 With Plunkett frequently out of action through injury, Fairbanks begins to depend more and more on his number two quarterback, Steve Grogan. When Plunkett returns to health, there is controversy over which quarterback is the best.

Club president Sullivan buys additional voting stock to become majority shareholder with 83 per cent of the franchise.

1976 Plunkett is traded to the San Francisco 49ers and Grogan reigns supreme.

With an 11–3–0 record, the Patriots have

their best season ever, winning a wild card spot in the playoffs, only to be defeated by the Oakland Raiders, the eventual Super Bowl champions, in the last 39 seconds of the game.

1978 Eastern Division champions.

Shortly after Fairbanks announces that he is resigning to return to collegiate coaching at the University of Colorado, the Patriots lose their final game of the regular season to the Miami Dolphins.

The team loses the divisional playoff game against the Houston Oilers.

1979 Ron Erhardt, former Patriots' assistant, is named head coach.

1981 Following a 10–6–0 season in 1980, the Patriots collapse, ending with the worst record (2–14–0) in the NFL. Erhardt is fired at the end of the season.

1982 Ron Meyer of Southern Methodist University is named the new head coach.

1983 The Patriots make it to the playoffs for the first time since 1978 but lose to the Miami Dolphins.

Schaefer Stadium is officially renamed 'Sullivan Stadium' in honour of the team's owner.

1984 Raymond Berry replaces Ron Meyer as coach in mid-season, four days after the Patriots lose 44–24 to the Miami Dolphins and the day after Meyer fires popular defensive co-ordinator Rod Rust. Rust is given his job back.

1985 Eastern Division and AFC champions.

1986 Runners-up at Super Bowl XX, defeated by the Chicago Bears.

New York Jets

598 Madison Avenue, New York, New York 10022

Stadium: Giants Stadium

Conference: AFC (Eastern Division)

Colours: Kelly green and white

1959 New York City and Harry Wismer are awarded an AFL franchise.

The team is named the 'Titans', with blue and gold as team colours.

Sammy Baugh, former Redskins' quarterback, is hired as head coach at the (then) astronomical annual salary of $28 000.

1960 Wismer leases the Polo Grounds for the Titans' home games. He also signs a five-year deal to have the Jets' games televised: their fee for the first year is $1 785 000.

In its first game of the regular season the team draws an audience of just 9607, of which 3880 get in on free tickets.

1962 After two seasons with records of 7–7–0 Clyde 'Bulldog' Turner replaces Baugh, after Wismer agrees to pay off the remainder of Baugh's contract.

Wismer cannot meet the club's costs from its revenue and the AFL agree to assume the team's running costs until the end of the season.

1963 A five-man syndicate (comprising David 'Sonny' Werblin, Townsend B. Martin, Leon Hess, Donald Lillis and Phil Iselin) buy the Titans from Wismer for $1 million.

After the team's first losing season the year before, Turner is let go and Weeb Ewbank is appointed the new head coach by the new owners. At the same time they change the team's name to the 'Jets'. Attendances improve with the newly-revitalized club.

1964 The team moves to Shea Stadium, where 45 665 watch them defeat the Denver Broncos and, later, 60 300 are dismayed to see them beaten by the Buffalo Bills. The club trades draft rights so that they can pick University of Alabama quarterback Joe Namath—perhaps the most significant deal in the history of the NFL.

1965 Namath signs a Jets' contract worth $427 000. His start with the team is delayed by a knee operation but he is well enough by mid-September to play against the Kansas City Chiefs. In his first outing for a full game (in the Jets' loss to the Buffalo Bills) he throws for 287 yards. By the end of the season, Namath is twice named rookie of the year: he has gained 2220 yards and has thrown 18 touchdown passes.

1966 Namath is responsible for the Jets' trouncing of the New England Patriots 38–28, ending the latter's hopes for the Eastern Division championship. Less than two weeks later he is back in hospital again, for further knee surgery.

1967 The Jets have their first winning season: 8–5–1. Namath finishes the season having thrown for 4007 yards—a record that stood for many years. His performance results in every home game being a sellout.

1968 Sonny Werblin is bought out by his partners, and later in the year, Don Lillis dies.

One of the highlights of the Jets' best-ever season is the 'Heidi game', when NBC TV show the beginning of a children's film rather than the final few minutes of the contest between the Jets and the Oakland Raiders: the Raiders score twice in the final 42 seconds to win. The television network's switchboard is inundated with protest calls from irate football fans.

AFL champions, defeating the Oakland Raiders.

1969 Namath 'guarantees' in an interview with sports reporters that the Jets will win Super Bowl III—a claim that helps to make the quarterback a legend.

Super Bowl III champions, defeating the Baltimore Colts. The Jets are the first AFL team to win the championship, and Ewbank is the first coach to have won it in both leagues.

In June Namath announces his retirement because of a dispute over his ownership of the New York nightclub Bachelors III. However, by mid-July Namath has sold the night-spot and joins the team at training camp.

Eastern Division champions.

1970 The Jets reverse their record, from 10–4–0 the year before to 4–10–0 this year, largely due to Namath's absence after a Baltimore Colts game in October when he fractured his right wrist.

1971 Running back John Riggins from the University of Kansas is signed up.

Namath misses 19 games after injuring his knee again.

1972 Namath signs a contract for $250 000 a year, making him the highest-paid player in professional football.

1973 In his last season before his retirement, Ewbank is joined by Charley Winner as an assistant for one year; Winner will succeed as coach in 1974.

Namath's shoulder is dislocated during a tackle by Baltimore Colts linebacker Stan White, and the quarterback returns to the sidelines for two months.

1975 Namath turns down a multi-million-dollar offer from the New World Football League and signs a two-year contract with the Jets.

After the team loses seven out of nine games (including six consecutive losses), Winner is fired.

1976 Lou Holtz of North Carolina State University is named head coach.

The Jets match the previous year's losing record, 3–11–0. Despite his relatively new five-year contract, Holtz resigns to return to collegiate football before the end of the season.

Phil Iselin dies: now only Leon Hess and Townsend B. Ward remain of the original five-man syndicate of owners.

1977 Walt Michaels, the Jets' defensive coach, is promoted to head coach.

Jim Kensil is named club president and chief operating officer.

Namath leaves the Jets and signs as a free agent with the Los Angeles Rams: it is the end of an era. He announces his retirement from professional football eight months later.

Again, the team ends the year with a 3–11–0 record.

1978 The Jets adopt a new logo and a new uniform.

1981 Leon Hess acquires more of the club until he is now owner of 75 per cent of the team.

New York Jets' Joe Klecko also appeared in a Burt Reynolds film in 1986. (Fotosports International).

The Jets have their first winning season (10–5–1) since 1969 and land a wild card spot in the playoffs, where they are defeated by the Buffalo Bills.

1983 Joe Walton, Jets' offensive co-ordinator and quarterback coach, takes over as head coach.

1984 The team leaves Shea Stadium for Giants Stadium in New Jersey, which they share with the NFC team.

Pittsburgh Steelers

Three Rivers Stadium, 300 Stadium Circle, Pittsburgh, Pennsylvania 15212

Stadium: Three Rivers Stadium

Conference: AFC (Central Division)

Colours: black and gold

1933 Former boxer and semi-pro football player Art Rooney Sen. buys an NFL franchise for Pittsburgh for $2500, naming the team the 'Pirates' after the home town professional baseball team.
When Rooney comes up against state laws forbidding sporting events on Sunday, he solves the problem by giving free box seats at Forbes Field to the super-intendent of police.
The team's first head coach is Forrest 'Jap' Douds.

1934 After a disappointing 3–6–2 season the previous year, Rooney replaces Douds with Luby DiMelio as head coach.

1935 DiMelio obviously doesn't have the winning touch either—the 1934 season ended with the Pirates at the bottom of the league for the second year running— so Rooney tries his third coach in three years, Joe Bach of Duquesne University.

1936 The Pirates have their best season yet. However, with only one game to win to clinch the divisional title, they are forced to travel by train all the way to California to play an exhibition game for a friend of Rooney's, then travel all the way to the East Coast to meet the Boston Redskins. Exhausted, the Pirates lose in a 30–0 shutout.

1937 Bach returns to college coaching and

Rooney hires as player-coach Johnny Blood (né McNally) who had been a member of the team in 1934 but did not play because of injury. At 32, Blood (who took his name from the Rudolph Valentino film *Blood and Sand*) is irresponsible and unreliable. However, his extraordinary behaviour is offset by some stunning football: in his first game against the Philadelphia Eagles, he returns the opening kickoff to score a touchdown. This inspires the rest of the team.

1938 Rooney hires Byron 'Whizzer' White for $15 800—the most money paid for a player at the time. White agrees to play only after postponing his acceptance of a Rhodes' scholarship.
By mid-season, the Pirates are in contention for the divisional title, but unbeknown to Blood, Rooney sells quarterback Frank Filchock and the team's offense crumbles.

1939 'Whizzer' White leaves for Oxford University; in his absence, Rooney sells the rights to him to the Detroit Lions.
After a 32–0 shutout against the Chicago Bears, Blood packs his bags and walks out.
Walt Kiesling, Blood's assistant as well as a former Pirates' guard, takes over as head coach: he enforces curfews and makes bed checks just to make sure. Despite this, the team ends the year 1–9–1.

1940 Rooney decides to change the team's image and their name: a contest results in the winning name 'the Steelers'—a reference to Pittsburgh's important steel industry.
The altered name makes no difference: the new Steelers end the season with a 2–7–2 record. Rooney is so disappointed that he sells the franchise to Alexis Thompson, a Philadelphia resident.

1941 Rooney buys an interest in the Philadelpia Eagles, but when he and Thompson discover they are both homesick for their respective hometowns, they swap franchises.
Bert Bell, who had been involved in Rooney's Philadelphia deal, takes over as the Steelers' head coach, but leaves after they lose two games. He is replaced by Buff Donelli, who tries to coach both the Steelers and the Duquesne University

team at the same time. Eventually AFL Commissioner Elmer Layden rules that Donelli's dual coaching interests are inappropriate and Walt Kiesling again takes over.

1942 The Steelers have their first winning season (7–4–0), thanks to rookie halfback 'Bullet' Bill Dudley, who despite physical shortcomings wins through on sheer will power.

1943 The Second World War takes away many of the Steelers' players, so the team is merged with the Philadelphia Eagles to form the 'Phil-Pitt Steagles'.

1944 After having a creditable 5–4–1 season in tandem with the Eagles, the Steelers leave them to join the less effective Chicago Cardinals to form the 'Card-Pitts'. They are so bad that they become known as the 'Carpets: the team everybody walks on'.

After the third loss, three players are fined for 'indifferent play'. One is fullback Johnny Grigas, one of the few decent players; he becomes so disgusted with the team that he walks out minutes before the last game of the season—a 49–7 defeat by the Chicago Bears.

1945 The Steelers are back in Pittsburgh with Jim Leonard as head coach, but the team wins only two games all season, even though Dudley rejoins after military service.

1946 Leonard is replaced by Dr John B. 'Jock' Sutherland, a former winning college coach and a strict disciplinarian.

Dudley and Sutherland dislike each other on sight, but this does not affect the former's performance on the field. However, when Sutherland forces the halfback to play four games with injured ribs, Dudley tells Rooney that he will leave football unless the owner trades him at the end of the season. Rooney reluctantly lets him go to the Detroit Lions.

1947 With their first winning season since 1942, the team ties for the Eastern Division championship with the Philadelphia Eagles. Just before the playoff game, the players go on a one-day strike, demanding to be paid extra for an extra week's practice. This outrages Sutherland, and the upset tears the club apart: Eagles win 21–0.

1948 Sutherland dies of a stroke and is replaced by his assistant John Michelosen. He, too, believes in strict discipline, but lacks Sutherland's ability. The Steelers begin to lose, ending the season 4–8–0.

1949 The team has a winning season (barely), 6–5–1, despite the fact that Michelosen retains single-wing formation, at a time when all other NFL teams have gone over to the T-formation.

1952 Rooney woos back Joe Bach as coach. Bach installs the T-formation and makes Finks a quarterback, and after taking time to adjust to the new regime, the team begins to win.

1954 Bach resigns due to illness and Walt Kiesling takes over for the third time.

The Steelers do well, but after a battering contest with (and win over) the Philadelphia Eagles, the two teams are so knocked about that they both win only four of their next 14 games.

1955 The Steelers fall to last place for the first time since 1945.

1957 Kiesling is replaced by Buddy Parker, former head coach of the Detroit Lions.

1958 Parker signs up quarterback Bobby Layne, who had played for him with the Detroit Lions. Layne is instrumental in producing a 7–4–1 winning season—the team's best since 1947.

1962 After two seasons plagued by injuries, Layne makes a startling comeback and leads the Steelers to their best-ever record: 9–5–0, finishing second in the Eastern Conference, with a wild card spot in the playoffs, which they lose to the Miami Dolphins.

1963 Layne retires, and tackle Gene 'Big Daddy' Lipscomb (acquired from the Baltimore Colts in 1961) dies of an apparent drug overdose.

After a good start, the Steelers lose to the St Louis Cardinals after a 13-point lead. After coach Parker shrieks at them, 'You disgraced me, you disgraced yourselves', the team wins all but one of its next eight games, although usually only by the smallest of margins.

1965 After a 1964 season in which the Steelers fell to sixth place with a record of 5–9–0, coach Parker walks out just before the opening game, saying, 'I can't win with this bunch of stiffs'.

Under interim coach Mike Nixon, the Steelers have their worst season since 1945, winning only two of 14 games.

1966 Bill Austin is signed as head coach. He had been a line coach under Vince Lombardi at Green Bay, and with verbal abuse and battering practice sessions, he follows Lombardi's style. However, like Michelosen before him, he lacks his mentor's ability, and grumbling increases among the team members.

1968 A poor 2–11–1 season was notable for the 'O. J. game' against the Philadelphia Eagles. The Steelers, Eagles and the Buffalo Bills were all 'fighting' to have the poorest record so that they could have first pick of the college draft and thus obtain the miraculous Heisman Trophy winning running back O. J. Simpson. The Steelers won against the Eagles and so lost Simpson (he eventually went to the Bills).

Bill Austin is fired at the end of the season.

1969 Chuck Noll, a former Baltimore Colts assistant, is hired as head coach.

1970 The Steelers are one of three NFL teams to be transferred to the American Football Conference following the merger of the NFL and AFL.

Because of the team's previous dismal record the year before (1–13–0), they have first pick of the college draft and choose quarterback Terry Bradshaw, who single-handedly seems to raise the spirits of the team.

The Steelers move to their new home, Three Rivers Stadium.

1972 Rookie fullback Franco Harris joins the team and, in partnership with Bradshaw, lifts the team to its first winning season since 1963 and their best-ever record so far: 11–3–0.

Central Division champions—the first division title in the Steelers' 39-year history.

In the first of the playoffs, against the Oakland Raiders, Bradshaw and (particularly) Harris prove their worth. On their own 40-yard line, after a fourth-and-ten, the Steelers were behind 7–6 with 22 seconds left on the clock. Following three unsuccessful passes, Bradshaw tried one more time, aiming at John 'Frenchy' Fuqua; it missed him, bounced off the

Frank Pollard (Pittsburgh) resists a tackle from Keith Butler (Seattle). (Fotosports International).

Raiders' Jack Tatum and was caught by Harris in full stride, who took the 60-yard pass across the goal line to make the winning touchdown. This play came to be called the 'immaculate reception'. The Steelers went on to be defeated by the Miami Dolphins in the AFC championship game.

1973 Despite many players sidelined because of injuries—including Bradshaw, Harris and Fuqua—the Steelers end the year with a 10–4–0 record and a wild card spot in the play-offs.

1974 AFC champions, defeating the Oakland Raiders.

1975 Super Bowl IX champions, defeating the Minnesota Vikings.

In the regular season, after a 1–1 start the Steelers go on to win 11 in a row, showing their now awesome offensive and defensive power. In fact, the defense is now called the 'steel curtain'. A player of note is running back Rocky Bleier.

Central Division champions.

1976 AFC champions, again defeating the Oakland Raiders.

Super Bowl X champions, defeating the Dallas Cowboys. Despite hugging last place for the first eight weeks of the regular season, the Steelers then win ten straight (including five shutouts) to gain their fourth Central Division title since 1972.

1977 After breaking his wrist early in October, Bradshaw comes back in a plaster cast to lead the team to its fifth Central Division championship.

1978 Central Division champions.

1979 AFC champions, defeating the Houston Oilers.
Super Bowl XIII champions, defeating the Dallas Cowboys—the first team in the NFL to win the Super Bowl three times.
Central Division champions.

1980 AFC champions again defeating the Houston Oilers.
Super Bowl XIV champions, defeating the Los Angeles Rams—the only team to have won it four times, and twice consecutively.
Because of injuries, including to the all-important Bradshaw, the Steelers' record falls to 9–7–0, and they miss the playoffs for the first time since 1971.

1982 Central Division champions.

1983 Bradshaw and Harris retire, the former as the Steelers' all-time leading passer, and the latter as the team's all-time leading rusher.
Central Division champions.

1984 Central Division champions.

1985 The Steelers have their first losing season (7–9–0) since 1971.

San Diego Chargers

San Diego Jack Murphy Stadium, PO Box 20666, San Diego, California 92120

Stadium: San Diego Jack Murphy Stadium

Conference: AFC (Western Division)

Colours: blue, gold and white

1959 A Los Angeles team is one of the original six franchises of the newly-formed American Football League. Barron Hilton (of the hotel chain) becomes owner of the team, which is to play at the Los Angeles Memorial Stadium.

Gerald Courtney of Hollywood wins a holiday to Acapulco for entering the winner of the 'name the team' contest: he bases his entry—'The Chargers'—on the battle cry of the University of Southern California football team: 'Cha-a-a-rge!'

1960 Sid Gillman, former coach of the Los Angeles Rams, is signed as head coach and, later, general manager. The player chosen to model the team's new uniform (blue and gold with lightning bolts on the helmet) is quarterback Jack Kemp, who as Senator Kemp of New York is being groomed for the 1988 US presidential election.
At the start, audiences are sparse: the first game of the regular season (a 27–7 win over the New York Titans) is played in front of only 27 778 people—filling only about 30 per cent of the massive Coliseum's seats.
Western Division champions: the championship game against the Denver Broncos is watched by a crowd of only 9928.

1961 Hilton reveals that he has lost almost $1 million in the Chargers' first season.
The city of San Diego, aiming to persuade Hilton to move his team there, increase ticket sales and enthusiasm for the Chargers among its citizens. The ploy works, and Hilton agrees. With permission from the AFL, the team moves into its new home, the enlarged (to 34 000 seats) Balboa Stadium.
With August temperatures soaring to 35°C, the Chargers defeat the Houston Oilers in their pre-season debut in San Diego.
Western Division champions.

1962 With Kemp (suffering from an injured throwing hand) traded to the Buffalo Bills for $100 and 23 players on the injury list for two or more games—and despite the signing of rookies Lance Alworth and John Hadl, wide receiver and quarterback

The 1973 Super Bowl was the first for which the TV blackout was lifted and the game was screened locally. 90 182 tickets were sold, but because of the local coverage 8476 ticket holders didn't turn up.

respectively—the Chargers decline to a 4–10–0 season record.

1963 Barron Hilton and his father Conrad sell one-third of their interest in the team to a consortium of San Diego and Los Angeles business executives.

After training camp in the desert, the Chargers emerge at the end of the season with a winning 11–3–0 record. Western Division champions.

1964 NFL champions, defeating the Boston Patriots in the first week of January. Western Division champions.

1965 Star back Keith Lincoln and linebacker Frank Buncom hold out for more money, but eventually sign with the club. Defensive end Earl Faison and 22½-stone defensive tackle Ernie Ladd both announce that they will be working out their options: Ladd is fined, suspended and then finally reinstated.

1966 A syndicate of 21 businessmen, led by Eugene Klein and Sam Schulman of Beverly Hills, buy the Chargers for $10 million. Klein becomes president of the club (as well as co-general partner with

Lionel 'Little Train' James – one of the smallest players in the League. (Fotosports International).

Schulman) in place of Barron Hilton, but the latter, with his father, hang on to a substantial part of the club. They are joined as minority shareholders by George Pernicano, a restaurateur, and James Copley, publisher of a San Diego newspaper.

Despite signing a new five-year contract, coach Gillman is unable to lift the team from a 7–6–1 record: the first time they have not won the Western Division title since their establishment.

1967 The team moves into the new San Diego Jack Murphy Statium (Jack Murphy was the sports editor of the *San Diego Union* newspaper). In the pre-season inaugural game the Chargers meet their first NFL opponents, being defeated by the Detroit Lions.

1969 The Chargers have their biggest crowd yet (54 042) attracted by the chance to see Joe Namath and the New York Jets in action; despite Broadway Joe's presence, the Chargers win.

Gillman announces his retirement as coach, due to ill health; he will continue as general manager. The Chargers' offensive backfield coach Charlie Waller succeeds him.

1970 The team has its first losing season (5–6–3) since 1962.

At the end of the year Gillman returns as head coach and Waller goes back to offensive backfield duties.

1971 Club president, Eugene Klein, announces Gillman's retirement 'by mutual consent'. Harland Svare, a former Los Angeles Rams coach who had already taken over as general manager, is now also appointed head coach.

1973 After two further losing seasons, Svare announces the signing of the Baltimore Colt's star quarterback Johnny Unitas, who is now 40 years old. However, after only three games, an old back injury is aggravated during a contest with the Pittsburgh Steelers and Unitas is rendered virtually motionless. He spends most of the rest of the year on the bench, and retires from professional football in July of the following year. When Unitas is injured, rookie quarterback Dan Fouts takes over.

Svare resigns as head coach, staying on as general manager.

1974 Tommy Prothro, also a former LA Rams coach, is hired as head coach.

Training camp is interrupted by veteran players picketing as part of an NFL Players' Association dispute.

1975 The Chargers have their worst season ever: 2–12–0.

1976 Svare is fired as general manager and replaced by Johnny Sanders.

In the first NFL game outside the US, the Chargers are defeated by the St Louis Cardinals in Tokyo in August.

1978 After a disappointing 1–3 start, Prothro resigns and is succeeded by Don Coryell, formerly of the St Louis Cardinals, as head coach.

The Chargers have their first winning season (9–7–0) since 1969, helped by Dan Fouts' 24 touchdown passes.

1979 With their best record for 16 years (12–4–0), the Chargers become Western Division champions for the first time since 1965.

1980 Western Division champions.

1981 A hold-out during a contract dispute leads to the trading of star wide receiver John Jefferson to the Green Bay Packers. Western Division champions, achieved with the aid of Dan Fouts' spectacular 4802-yard passing record.

1984 Wide receiver Charlie Joiner sets an NFL record with his 650th pass reception. The mayor of San Diego proclaims 11 December 'Charlie Joiner Day'.

1986 Don Coryell resigns. London-born Al Saunders takes over hot-seat.

Seattle Seahawks

5305 Lake Washington Boulevard, Kirkland, Washington 98033

Stadium: Kingdome

Conference: AFC (Western Division)

Colours: blue, green and silver

1974 The NFL awards a franchise to Seattle Professional Football Inc. (a group of business executives and community leaders) for $16 million. Lloyd W. Nordstrom and his family become majority shareholders.

1975 A contest is held to decide on the team's name. More than 20 000 entries are received, and 'Seahawks' is the winner, chosen by 151 entrants.

On 28 July, the first day of season-ticket sales, 24 168 requests arrive; 27 days later an overwhelming 59 000 have been bought.

1976 Jack Patera, formerly of the Minnesota Vikings, is appointed the first head coach.

Lloyd Nordstrom dies of a heart attack while holidaying in Mexico.

The team plays at the new $67 million Kingdome, the walls of which anchor the world's largest self-supporting concrete roof.

The Seahawks finish their first season with a 2–12–0 record. Jim Zorn establishes an NFL record for passing 2571 yards—the most by any rookie quarterback.

1977 The team improves its record to 5–9–0: the best of any previous second-year expansion team.

1978 After only three years the Seahawks have

Seattle's Curt Warner recovered from a 1985 injury to lead the Seahawks in 1986. (Fotosports International).

their first winning season: 9–7–0. Two of these victories are against the Oakland Raiders, the first time any team has beaten the Raiders twice during the regular season since 1965.

1980 Following another winning season, the Seahawks' defense collapses, allowing 408 points—the most in the AFC. The team finishes with a 4–12–0 record, including eight straight losses at the Kingdome.

1983 Patera having been replaced by Chuck Knox, who had successfully rebuilt both the Los Angeles Rams and the Buffalo Bills, the Seahawks go all the way to the playoffs making Knox the first coach to take three different teams into the play-offs in NFL history.

1984 The team wins a wild card spot in the divisional play-offs, where it defeats the Super Bowl champions, the Los Angeles Raiders. The Seahawks are themselves beaten by the Miami Dolphins the following week.

After his two successful years as the team coach, Knox is wooed by Henry Ford, a personal friend and owner of the Detroit Lions, who promises him part of that team if he will move to the Motor City. To keep him in Seattle, the Seahawk owners pay him an enormous sum.

The NFC

Atlanta Falcons

1–85 Suwannee Road, Suwannee, Georgia 30174

Stadium: Atlanta-Fulton County Stadium

Conference: NFC (Western Division)

Colours: red, black, silver and white

1965 Rivalry between the NFL and AFL to establish an expansion team in Atlanta results in Atlanta being the first city able to choose which league to join. The citizens opt for the NFL.

The franchise is bought by Rankin M. Smith, the vice-president of an insurance company, for about $8.5 million. He gives the team the corporate name of Five Smiths Inc., after his five children. The team's nickname is chosen via a local radio contest; the winner asserts that the falcon is a 'proud bird full of courage and fight'.

Season ticket sales reach 45 000 in the first year.

1968 The team's uniforms are changed by the elimination of the black falcon emblem from jersey sleeves, to be replaced by stripes.

Head coach Norb Hecker is replaced by Norm Van Brocklin, previously with the Minnesota Vikings. Under the latter's direction, the Falcons break an 11-game losing streak with a win over the New York Giants on 13 October. At the end of the season, Van Brocklin fires five assistant coaches.

1969 Under Van Brocklin, the Falcons have their best-ever season: 6–8–0.

1970 Van Brocklin takes over as general manager in addition to his coaching responsibilities.

1971 The Falcons' uniform is altered again, from black to red jerseys.

1973 In their opening game, the Falcons set 35 team records during their massive defeat (62–7) of the New Orleans Saints.

Atlanta Falcons' Gerald Riggs. (Fotosports International).

1974 Due to the team's lack of wins, Van Brocklin is fired mid-season and replaced as head coach by Marion Campbell.

The Falcons gain the dubious record of 40 202 'no-shows' (people who do not attend the game, despite having tickets) for their game against the Los Angeles Rams on 1 December—they lost, 30–7. They beat this record two weeks later with 48 830 no-shows in a rain-swept victory over the Green Bay Packers.

1976 Campbell is sacked and general manager Pat Peppler takes over. However, after a humiliating defeat at the hands of the Los Angeles Rams (59–0) he, too, is sacked, to be succeeded the following year by Eddie LeBaron as general manager and Leeman Bennett as head coach.

1978 Once again, the uniform is changed, but it has remained the same ever since. The Falcons have their first winning season since 1973: 9–7–0. This results in a wild card place in the divisional playoffs, where they lose to the Dallas Cowboys.

1980 Western Division champions.

1982 The Falcons participate in the playoffs, but lose their first game to the Minnesota Vikings, 30–24.

1984 Englishman Mick Luckhurst, a kicker, becomes the team's all-time leading scorer on 9 September.

1987 Marion Campbell replaces Dan Hemming as head coach.

Chicago Bears

Halas Hall, 250 North Washington, Lake Forest, Illinois 60045

Stadium: Soldier Field

Conference: NFC (Central Division)

Colours: orange, navy blue and white

1960 Team founded in Decatur, Illinois by starch manufacturer A. E. Staley as a company team, and run by employee George Halas on company time. Halas's favourite ploy is the T-formation.

Co-champions of the then American Professional Football Association (APFA).

1921 Because of the business recession, Staley withdraws sponsorship and Halas becomes co-owner with former school-mate Dutch Sternamen. They move the team to Chicago, where they play at Cub Park, the stadium of the city's baseball team, the Chicago Cubs. Team known as the 'Chicago Staleys' for one year, after their former sponsor pays $5000 for the privilege.

APFA champions.

1922 Team renamed 'Chicago Bears' to show relationship with the baseball team in whose stadium they play. At Halas's suggestion, the APFA changes its name to the National Football League.

1925 Halas signs Red Grange on 22 November, the day after the latter left the University of Illinois, to play for the Bears for the rest of the season; in return, Grange receives a large share of the gate. By the end of January 1926 Grange and his agent C. C. Pyle each earn $100 000.

1926 When Halas refuses to pay Grange a five-figure salary and give him one-third ownership of the Bears, Pyle starts the American Football League and Grange leaves to join an AFL team, the New York Yankees. (He returns to the Bears in 1929, retiring as a member of the team in 1934).

Chicago's Willie Gault won an Olympic medal in 1984. (Fotosports International).

JOE MONTANA

On the day that Joe Montana came of age, he and the San Francisco 49ers swamped the Cincinnati Bengals to win Super Bowl XVI.

The 24 January 1982 marked the day that the 49ers quarterback gained the nickname of 'Cool' Joe, a name made even more remarkable by his antics on the bus before the big game.

The bus carrying the team to the stadium, some 25 miles east of Detroit, was stuck in a huge traffic jam. They could see the Silverdome, but they couldn't reach it. Frustration began to set in as players, already nervous at the prospect of the imminent proceedings, were beginning physically to show signs of discomfort.

Montana casually reached into his kit bag for his tape of Kenny Loggins singing, 'This is It!', stuck it into the cassette player and turned the volume up loud.

Loose and cool inside the bus, Montana kept his cool later inside the Silverdome and throughout the whole game as the west coast team waltzed to a 26–21 victory.

In that game he scored on a one-yard sneak as the 49ers used time-consuming plays to seal a dramatic triumph. Three years later, and still at the helm, it was Montana's day again as he outgunned the brilliant young pretender to his crown—Dan Marino.

Today Joseph C. Montana, out of New Eagle, Pennsylvania, is one of the highest paid footballers in NFL history. His annual salary with the 49ers exceeds $1 million, which coupled with the endorsements give him a gross yearly earning power of around a staggering $3 million.

In 1985, the field general was rumoured to have recieved a whopping $25 000 for turning up at a celebrity golfing tournament—and he was only there for 20 minutes!

In footballing terms, Joe Montana is big business, but the fame and the glory he has helped to heap upon his team must make him one of the wisest investments coach Bill Walsh has ever made.

But if it wasn't for Notre Dame, Walsh might never have got the chance. Montana was a standout at both football and basketball at high school in Monongahela, Penn. He was all set for a basketball career at North Carolina before the fighting Irish stepped in.

During a sparkling career with the Irish, Montana, whose original name, of Italian descent, is Montagna (the 'g' was dropped generations ago), led the South Bend school to numerous victories including the staging of a dramatic comeback show in the Cotton Bowl of 1979. Montana brought the Irish back from a 34–12 fourth quarter deficit to a 35–34 win with no time showing on the clock over Bill Yeoman's Houston Cougars.

With the young Montana at the helm, Notre Dame stormed to a national championship in 1977, a year after missing an entire season to study. He once figured that he was only the seventh choice quarterback at the school.

The rise from Notre Dame No 7 to NFL No 1 has been meteoric to say the least.

Because of those feats in Super Bowls XVI and XIX, Joe Montana has etched his name in the record book as only the third player to win the coveted MVP title twice, an honour he shares with Bart Starr and Terry Bradshaw.

What makes Montana a cut above the rest is his ability to improvise, even under the most extreme pressure. This ability, or gift, as some have called it, has brought glowing praise from other NFL quarterbacks. 'What makes Joe so tough', exclaimed former Washington quarterback Joe Theismann, 'is when things start breaking down he's got great peripheral vision. He has the ability to move and see everything that's happening around him.'

His coolness has also brought praise from

fellow team mates. 'I don't know what it is about him', says Dwight Clark, 'but he never lets on that he's nervous. I'm sure he is inside but you never see him blow his cool.'

The two Super Bowls were the games that brought him instant stardom. However, one or maybe two games do not make a career, and Super Bowls XVI and XIX were merely excerpts from the long-running serial entitled, 'The Joe Montana Story.'

That story, fact not fiction, is almost certain to add quite a few more exciting chapters yet, as Joe Montana, golden boy of the San Francisco 49ers goldrush, enters his ninth year in the NFL, still scrambling around at the top of the heap.

1930 Sternaman and Halas argue, and Halas steps down as coach and retires as a player, while remaining co-owner.

1932 NFL champions, defeating Portsmouth (Ohio) Spartans. The game is played indoors in the 80-yard-long Chicago Stadium because of Chicago's notorious icy winter temperatures.

Because of the team's financial losses, Sternaman sells his share of the team to Halas for $38 000; Halas is now full owner.

1933 NFL champions, defeating the New York Giants.

1934 Beattie Feathers becomes first back to gain 1000 yards.

Runners-up in the NFL championship: the New York Giants win when some of their players put on tennis shoes to have better traction on the icy ground.

1937 Western Division champions.

1940 NFL champions, defeating the Washington Redskins by a record score of 73–0.

1941 NFL champions, defeating the New York Giants. The Bears are now known as the 'Monsters of the Midway'.

1942 Western Division champions, despite losing many players to the armed services, including Halas to the US Navy.

1943 NFL champions, defeating the Washington Redskins.

1946 NFL champions, defeating the New York Giants; many pre-Second World War stars have returned to the team.

1956 George Halas retires as head coach.

Runners-up in the NFL championship, losing to the New York Giants, who again have an edge due to their tennis shoes.

1958 George Halas returns as head coach.

1963 NFL champions, defeating the New York Giants.

1968 George Halas, aged 73, retires as head coach, after 40 years of coaching and a record of 320 wins, 147 defeats and 30 draws.

1969 Bears finish last in the league, having won only once in 14 games—their poorest record since they were founded almost 50 years before.

1971 The team moves to Soldier Field.

1982 Mike Ditka becomes head coach.

1983 George 'Papa Bear' Halas dies, aged 88.

1984 Central Division champions.

1986 Super Bowl XX champions.

Dallas Cowboys

1 Cowboy Parkway, Irving, Texas 75063

Stadium: Texas Stadium

Conference: NFC (Eastern Division)

Colours: royal blue, metallic blue, white

1960 The team is founded with 36 players from other NFL teams and Tom Landry as coach. They play at the Cotton Bowl.

1964 Landry signs a ten-year contract—at that time, the longest contract of any coach in any professional sport.

1967 Runners-up for NFL championship, losing 34–27 to Green Bay Packers on New Year's Day. The game was one of the most exciting in NFL history, with both sides battling it out to the limits of their endurance. Quarterback Don Meredith was particularly outstanding.

Runners-up for NFL championship, losing again to Green Bay Packers. The game is played on the coldest 31 December in Green Bay history—minus 25°C.

1970 Eastern Division champions.

1971 NFC champions, defeating the San Francisco 49ers.

The team moves to Texas Stadium.

1972 NFC champions, defeating the San Francisco 49ers.

Super Bowl VI champions, defeating the Miami Dolphins.

1973 The Cowboys celebrate their 100th NFL win—over the New Orleans Saints, 40–3.

1976 NFC champions, defeating the Los Angeles Rams. Roger Staubach throws four touchdown passes to clinch the victory.

1978 NFC champions, defeating the Minnesota Vikings.

Super Bowl XII champions, defeating the Denver Broncos.

1979 NFC champions, defeating the Los Angeles Rams.

The team releases a film of the season's highlights entitled *America's Team*, and the nickname has stuck.

1981 NFC East champions.

1984 Missed playoffs for first time for ten years.

Dallas Cowboys' cheerleaders wowed the capacity crowd at Wembley.

Detroit Lions

Pontiac Silverdome, 1200
Featherstone Road, Pontiac,
Michigan 48057

Stadium: Pontiac Silverdome

Conference: NFC (Central Division)

Colours: Honolulu blue and silver

1934 Radio station owner George Richards buys the Portsmouth (Ohio) Spartans (who had entered the NFL in 1930) for $21 500, and moves them to Detroit. The winner of a contest on Richards' station renames them the Detroit Lions, to make the team 'the king of beasts' over the Detroit Tigers baseball team.

1935 NFL champions, defeating the New York Giants.

1938 The Lions move from the University of Detroit stadium to Briggs Stadium. Head coach Dutch Clark accuses owner Richards of 'meddling' in the possible transfer of a player from the Pittsburgh Steelers; the player is not transferred, and Clark leaves.

1939 The NFL fines Richards $5000 for having given money to a potential player while he was still at college.
Richards sells the Lions to Chicago department store magnate Fred Mandel for $225 000.

1948 After owning the club for nine years—during which they ended five seasons near or at the bottom of the league (and one year, 1942, in which they won no games at all)—the disenchanted Mandel sells out to a syndicate of Detroit sportsmen and society people.
End Bob Mann is hired as the team's first black player.

1949 The Lions finish fourth in the NFL, the first time since 1945 they have not been bottom of the league.

1950 The players revolt against head coach Alvin 'Bo' McMillin and he is dismissed with a $60 000 golden handshake to cover the remaining two years of his contract. The management vow never to sign contracts longer than one year with any further coaches.

1952 National Conference champions, defeating the Los Angeles Rams in a playoff.
NFL champions, defeating the Cleveland

James Jones – the new running back sensation in Detroit.

1967 With the NFL's reorganization, the Lions are placed in the Central Division of the Western Conference.

The Lions became the first NFL team to be beaten by an AFL team, in a preseason inter-league game against the Denver Broncos.

1971 Wide receiver Chuck Hughes dies of a heart attack on the field during a game against the Chicago Bears.

1975 The Lions move to the Pontiac Metropolitan Stadium (later renamed the 'Silverdome'), the largest air-supported dome structure in the world.

1983 Central Division champions.

1985 Daryll Rogers takes over as head coach.

Green Bay Packers

1265 Lombardi Avenue,
Green Bay, Wisconsin 54307

Stadia: Lambeau Field, Milwaukee County Stadium

Conference: NFC (Central Division)

Colours: dark green, gold and white

1919 Earl 'Curly' Lambeau persuades his employers, the Indian Packing Company, to provide $500 for equipment for a football team. The team takes its name from this association.

1921 The team joins the American Football Association.

The franchise for the team is awarded to John Clair of the Acme Packing Company, with Lambeau as star halfback, passer, publicity man, general manager and coach.

1922 Clair is ordered to return the franchise to the APFA because he had been paying players who were still at college. Curly Lambeau is awarded the franchise for $50.

Lambeau's tenure is in doubt: an insurance company refuses to pay out for a 'rain policy' when precipitation amounting to 0.09 of an inch stops a game, 0.01 of an inch less than that specified in the policy. When another game is washed out and there is no insurance, Lambeau almost gives up, but help is at hand in the form of Andrew Turnbull, publisher of the Green Bay *Press-Gazette*.

Browns and ending the Lions' best season since 1934.

1953 NFL champions, again defeating the Cleveland Browns.

1954 Western Conference champions.

1957 Head coach Buddy Parker negotiates a two-year contract (having suffered under one-year contracts since 1950) and immediately announces, 'I can no longer control this team', and resigns. His leaving may have been spurred by seeing his players socializing with the club's owners at a cocktail party—a practice he deplored.

1962 The Lions win the most games (11) in one season in the club's history, finishing second in the league.

1963 Star player, defensive tackle Alex Karras, and five other players, as well as the Lions' management, are fined by the NFL for betting on football games. Karras is suspended for a minimum of one year.

1964 William Clay Ford of the motor car dynasty buys out all the other shareholders for $6.5 million to take control of the club.

Cal Hubbard, who played on New York Giants' and Green Bay Packers' defense in the 1920s and 1930s, was the first really large football player. He was 6ft 5in tall and weighed 250lb.

1923 Turnbull forms a group—the 'Hungry Five'—who cancel the Packers' debts and campaign for civic support. The community of Green Bay rises to the occasion, shares are sold and the Green Bay Football Corporation is born.

1930 The Packers' string of 22 wins and no defeats finally ends when they lose to the St Louis Cardinals.
NFL champions.

1931 NFL champions.

1933 When a fan falls out of the temporary stands at the Packers' stadium and sues, and then the team's insurance company fails, the Packers go into receivership. Once again, the 'Hungry Five' come to the rescue: a 'Save the Packers' fund is started, and Green Bay residents, from school children and policemen to businessmen, raise $15 000. The club is incorporated with all profits to go to retired servicemen's organizations.

1936 NFL champions, defeating the Boston Redskins.

1938 Western Division champions.

1939 NFL champions, defeating the New York Giants.

1941 Western Division champions.

1944 The Packers field a team of untried newcomers, older players and servicemen on leave, to become NFL champions, defeating the New York Giants.

1947 Lambeau is criticized by the executive committee of the club for buying a training camp with land and cottages for coaching staff and their wives. Club management is reorganized into sub-committees.

1948 With the team winning fewer than half their games, Lambeau begins to fine each player half-a-week's salary for each loss.

1950 After 31 years with the club, Lambeau resigns amid a dispute with the citizen-owned club corporation. To make matters worse, the training camp burns down and attendances (and income) have hit bottom. New shares are sold to raise $125 000.

1957 The team moves into the new $1 million City Stadium.

1958 The executive committee hires Ray 'Scooter' McLean as head coach. Players take advantage of his 'nice guy' manner, which leads to the worst season in Packers' history: 1 win, 10 defeats.

1959 Vince Lombardi, hired as head coach and general manager, on the first day of his eventual 10-year career with the club states: 'Let's get one thing straight; I'm in complete command here.' He spends three months watching films of the previous season's Packers games. By the end of the year, the team has had its best season since 1945: 7–5–0.

1960 Western Conference champions, after a win over the Los Angeles Rams highlighted by a 91-yard touchdown pass by quarterback Bart Starr.

1961 NFL champions, defeating the New York Giants. Running back/kicker Paul Hornung scores 19 points in that game.

1962 NFL champions, again defeating the New York Giants at Yankee Stadium in temperatures plummeting to minus 7°C with a 40 mph wind.

1963 NFL suspends Hornung, the team's top scorer, indefinitely for betting on the Packers and other teams.

1964 Hornung is back on the squad after his suspension but apparently has lost the ability to kick successfully under pressure.

1965 NFL champions, defeating the San Francisco 49ers by a field goal (kicked by Don Chandler) in the 14th minute of sudden death.

1966 City Stadium is renamed Lambeau Stadium in honour of the team's founder. NFL champions, defeating the Cleveland Browns.

1967 NFL champions, defeating the Dallas Cowboys on 2 January.
Champions of the first Super Bowl, defeating the Kansas City Chiefs.
NFL champions, defeating the Dallas Cowboys in Arctic conditions (−25°C) at Green Bay on 31 December, in what came to be known as the 'Ice Game'.

1968 Champions of Super Bowl II, defeating the Oakland Raiders.
In a shock announcement, Vince

Lombardi retires as coach; he stays on as general manager.

1969 Lombardi leaves the Packers for the Washington Redskins. (He dies of cancer the following year.)

1970 The Packers tie for the last place in their division.

1971 New coach Dan Devine's leg is broken when he is run over on the sidelines by a New York Giant player during the first game of the season.

1972 Central Division champions. Bumper stickers appear carrying the slogan 'The Pack Is Back'.

1975 Former star player Bart Starr appointed head coach.

1984 Starr replaced by former teammate Forrest Gregg.

Los Angeles Rams

2327 West Lincoln Avenue, Anaheim, California 92801

Stadium: Anaheim Stadium

Conference: NFC (Western Division)

Colours: royal blue, gold and white

1937 Team founded in Ohio as the Cleveland Rams. Owner Homer Marshman chooses their name because 'wild rams butt heads harder than any other animal' and also because he admires the Fordham University Rams.

1941 Team sold to Fred Levy Jr and Daniel F. Reeves, who at 29 becomes the youngest owner in professional football.

1943 Reeves becomes sole owner of the team. He obtains permission from the NFL to suspend operations for a year, because of the Second World War.

1945 NFL champions, defeating the Washington Redskins. Despite the Rams being league champions, the team attracts only 45 000 fans during the whole season and Reeves loses $50 000. He buys Los Angeles Memorial Coliseum in preparation for his bid for an LA franchise.

1946 Initially the other owners in the NFL refuse Reeves permission to move his franchise to Los Angeles, but when he threatens to sell the Rams and get out of football altogether, they finally agree. The Rams hire Kenny Washington and Woody Strode, the first black players in the NFL since 1933.

1947 Having fired general manager Chile Walsh, Reeves takes over that position. Increasing financial losses force him to take on partners; these receive 'one of the best bargains in sports history', one obtaining 30 per cent of the stock for one dollar and a share of the debts (15 years later, Reeves has to pay $4.8 million to buy them out). The losses were partly due to the fact that the Los Angeles Dons, the All-America Football Conference team, attracted far larger crowds.

1949 Western Division champions.
With the acquisition of a second quarterback, a controversy raged over which man was number one—an argument which continued (with a number of different personnel involved) for many years.

1950 The AAFC folds, and the Rams are the only team left in Los Angeles.
National Conference champions.

1951 NFL champions, defeating the Cleveland Browns. The Rams' backfield is now known as the 'Bull Elephants'.

1954 Rumours of dissent between coach Hampton Pool on the one hand and the coaching staff on the other seem proved as the Rams decline into fourth place and all the assistant coaches resign.

1955 Pool resigns. Reeves and the other owners then set out on a widely publicized hunt for a new coach, finally (and anti-climactically) appointing Sid Gillmann of the University of Cincinnati. Western Conference champions.
After arguments among the owners, Reeves is relieved of his directorship of the club.

1957 Pete Rozelle is appointed general manager.

1959 After the Rams finish the season at the bottom of the Western Conference, Gillmann and his entire staff resign.

1960 Rozelle leaves to become NFL commissioner; Reeves appoints former player Elroy 'Crazy Legs' Hirsch to replace him. Another former star, Bob Waterfield, is hired as head coach, and he brings along former coach Hampton Pool as an assistant.

Eric Dickerson starred for the Los Angeles Rams at Wembley Stadium in August 1987. (Fotosports International).

1962 In an auction which involves celebrity Bob Hope and others, Reeves reacquires control of the franchise for $7.1 million. A new corporation, the Los Angeles Rams Football Company, is formed with Reeves owning 51 per cent of shares and the rest distributed between 11 minority shareholders.

1963 The recurring quarterback problem causes the team to lose its first five games, and it is only when Roman Gabriel is appointed number one quarterback that the Rams go on to win five of their last nine games. David 'Deacon' Jones, Merlin Olsen, Lamar Lundy and Roosevelt 'Rosey' Grier make an impact in the defensive front line, and become known as the 'Fearsome Foursome'.

1966 George Allen is appointed head coach.

1967 Coastal Division champions.

1968 Personal differences lead Reeves to fire coach Allen, resulting in an outcry from the team, many members of which appear at a televised press conference on his behalf.

1969 Allen reluctantly returns.

1970 At the end of the year it is announced that Allen's contract is not to be renewed.

He has tied with Sid Gillmann for lasting the longest of any of the Rams' coaches—five years.

1971 Reeves dies of Hodgkins' disease.

1972 The Reeves estate sells the franchise to industrialist Robert Irsay for $19 million. He trades it to Carroll Rosenbloom for the Baltimore Colts and $3.4 million.

1973 Western Division champions.

1974 Western Division champions. James Harris becomes the first black quarterback to lead a professional team to a championship.

1975 Western Division champions.

1976 Western Division champions.

1977 Western Division champions.

1978 When coach Chuck Knox resigns to go to the Buffalo Bills, George Allen returns. However, after two losses before the official season, he is 'released' and is succeeded by Ray Malavasi.
Western Division champions.

1979 Rosenbloom drowns while swimming off Florida coast; his wife Georgia (now Georgia Frontiere) becomes majority owner of the club.
Western Division champions.

1980 NFC champions, defeating Tampa Bay Buccaneers on 6 January.

1983 Western Division champions.

1984 Western Division champions.

1985 New head coach John Robinson leads the Rams to the play-offs, where they lose to Chicago.

Minnesota Vikings

9520 Viking Drive, Eden Prairie, Minnesota 55344

Stadium: Hubert H. Humphrey Metrodome

Conference: NFC (Central Division)

Colours: purple, white and gold

1960 Max Winter wins a franchise from the NFL to set up a team in Minnesota.

1961 General manager Bert Rose invents the team name 'Vikings' and the first team is formed, comprising mainly players past their prime, with Norm Van Brocklin, former quarterback with the Los Angeles Rams and the Philadelphia Eagles, as head coach. However, the draft results in the hiring of one Fran(cis) Tarkenton, an outstanding quarterback from the University of Georgia, who threw four touchdown passes as, well as scoring himself in the Viking's first NFL game—a 37–13 upset over the Chicago Bears.

1964 Despite the Vikings becoming accepted as a full-blooded NFL team, Rose is replaced as general manager.

In a game with the San Francisco 49ers, defensive end Jim Marshall gains a place in the record books by picking up a fumble and carrying it 66 yards *the wrong way*, for a 49ers' safety. The Vikings still won, 27–22.

1965 When the Vikings fail to win the Western Conference title as expected, coach Van Brocklin announces he is resigning. He changes his mind the next day.

1968 Central Division champions.

1969 Western Conference champions.

1970 NFC champions, defeating the Cleveland Browns in a freezing minus 13°C.

Runners-up at Super Bowl IV, losing to the Kansas City Chiefs.

Central Division champions. The Vikings' strength lies in their mighty defense: they allow only 14 touchdowns in 14 games during the regular season.

1971 Central Division champions.

Defensive tackle Alan Page named the most valuable player in the NFL—the first time a defensive lineman has received the award.

1972 Fran Tarkenton returns to the Vikings and has an outstanding year, although the team itself finishes with a disappointing 7–7.

1973 NFC champions, defeating the Washington Redskins.

1974 Runners-up at Super Bowl VIII, losing to the Miami Dolphins.

NFC champions, defeating the Los Angeles Rams.

1975 Runners-up at Super Bowl IX, losing to the Pittsburgh Steelers.

Central Division champions.

1976 In a game against the New York Giants, Tarkenton becomes the first man to reach 3000 completions.

NFC champions, defeating the Los Angeles Rams.

1977 Runners-up at Super Bowl XI, losing to the Oakland Raiders.

Central Division champions.

1978 Central Division champions.

1979 Long-serving star Fran Tarkenton retires. The team has its first losing season since 1967.

1980 Central Division champions.

1982 The team moves from Metropolitan Stadium to Humphrey Metrodome.

New Orleans Saints

1500 Poydras Street, New Orleans, Louisiana 70112

Stadium: Louisiana Superdome

Conference: NFC (Western Division)

Colours: old gold, black and white

1966 The NFL grant a franchise to New Orleans. Millionaire racing-car buff John W. Mecom Jr becomes majority shareholder. One of his partners is jazz trumpeter Al Hirt.

1967 Team named the 'Saints' after the Dixieland classic (and one of Hirt's favourite numbers) 'When the Saints Go Marching In'.

The Saints play their first game at Tulane University stadium against the Los Angeles Rams in front of 80 789 fans (20 000 of whom had bought season tickets the day the box office opened). Despite rookie John Gilliam returning the opening kickoff 94 yards for a touchdown the team loses.

1970 In the first game helmed by new coach J. D. Roberts, the Saints upset the Detroit Lions. The two-point win is achieved on a 63-yard field goal by Tom Dempsey, a free-agent kicker born with no toes on his right foot and with no right hand.

1972 Former astronaut Richard F. Gordon Jr is appointed executive vice-president of the club. Despite the assistance of the man who had piloted *Apollo XII* to the moon and back, the Saints equal their worst-ever season: 2–11–1.

1975 The team moves into the Louisiana Superdome, the world's largest indoor stadium.

1976 Hank Stram is appointed head coach—the fifth since the team was formed ten years before. (He lasts only two years.)

1977 The Saints become the first team ever to lose to the Tampa Bay Buccaneers (33–14).
1980 The Saints finish a disastrous season, winning only once and losing 15 times. Coach Dick Nolan (after the standard two years) is fired the day after the 12th loss.
1981 O. A. 'Bum' Phillips is named head coach.
1983 The Saints equal their best season (1979): 8 wins and 8 defeats.
1984 Owner John Mecom Jr puts the Saints on the market for $75 million. They are bought for $70 million by Tom Benson.
1985 'Bum' Phillips retires. He is replaced as head coach by his son Wade Phillips.
1986 Jim Mora named new head coach.

The Giants played in what Sports Illustrated *called the best game of football ever played against Baltimore in the NFL championship game of 1959. But New Yorkers never saw or read of the game. Eleven million TV viewers in the USA did, but New York suffered a TV blackout and to make matters worse all the local newspapers were on strike!*

New York Giants

Giants Stadium, East Rutherford, New Jersey 07073

Stadium: Giants Stadium

Conference: NFC (Eastern Division)

Colours: blue, red and white

1925 Timothy J. Mara purchases an NFL franchise for $2500 (he had intended to buy an interest in champion boxer Gene Tunney). He names his team the 'Giants' after the baseball team whose stadium (the Polo Grounds) they will share. One of the players of that first team is Jim Thorpe, the 1912 Olympic champion.
With the assistance of 5000 free tickets, 25 000 attend to watch the Giants' first game on their home ground; they lose to the Frankford (Pennsylvania) Yellowjackets. Despite winning the next seven in a row, the team fails to pull in the crowds until the Chicago Bears, with star player Red Grange, come to town: 70 000 turn out to watch and Mara suddenly finds that owning a pro football team is financially rewarding.
1926 Mara and his Giants find themselves fighting for audiences with the rival New York Yankees, an AFL team also named after a local baseball club. Mara hits back by issuing free tickets and providing entertainment and games between school teams before each Giants game, but by the end of the season, he has lost $40 000. However, the Yankees lose 2½ times that and the AFL folds.
1927 The NFL ensures that the Yankees play only when their games will not conflict with those of the Giants.
NFL champions.
1930 Tim Mara's two sons, Wellington and Jack, take over ownership of the club.
At the end of a season which saw them second only to the Green Bay Packers, the Giants play a charity game against Knute Rockne's Notre Dame All-Stars, winning 21–0 and raising $115 153 (an astronomical sum for the time) for the New York Unemployed Fund.
1933 Eastern Division champions.
1934 NFL champions, defeating the Chicago Bears. This contest became known as the 'Sneakers' Game', after the Giants' equipment manager made a quick trip to Manhattan College and returned with basketball shoes (i.e. 'sneakers') for some of the Giants' players to give them more grip on the icy turf.
1935 Eastern Division champions.
1938 NFL champions, defeating the Green Bay Packers.
1939 Eastern Division champions.
1941 Eastern Division champions.
1944 Eastern Division champions.
1946 Eastern Division champions.
Just before the NFL championship game against the Chicago Bears (which the Giants lost), quarterback Frank Filchock and Merle Hapes are both questioned about an attempt by a New York bookmaker to fix the game. Filchock is immediately suspended for not reporting the contact, but Hapes is allowed to play. Both are subsequently suspended indefinitely.
1949 New York now has three pro football

teams: the Giants and the Bulldogs, both NFL and both sharing the Polo Grounds; and the Yankees, a new All-America Football Conference team founded in 1946.

1952 Frank Gifford (later an ABC-TV football commentator) joins the team as a defensive back.

The Giants' fortunes dip dramatically, with Steve Owen, coach since 1931, still employing A and T formations.

1954 Jim Lee Howell is appointed head coach. In turn, he hires the young Vince Lombardi as his offensive coach.

1956 The Giants sign a contract to play at Yankee Stadium.

NFL champions, defeating the Chicago Bears.

1958 Runners-up for NFL championship, losing to the Baltimore Colts. The sudden-death finish, seen on television by millions of people, is credited with dramatically raising public interest in the sport.

1959 Founder Tim Mara dies.

Vince Lombardi leaves to become head coach of the Green Bay Packers.

Eastern Conference champions.

1961 Eastern Conference champions.

1962 Eastern Conference champions.

1963 Eastern Conference champions, with quarterback Y.A. Tittle having his best year, including 36 touchdown passes.

1965 Club co-owner Jack Mara dies; his responsibilities are taken over by his brother Wellington.

1967 The Giants obtain quarterback Fran Tarkenton from the Minnesota Vikings, but the trade uses up most of the team's draft choices and leads to a lack of new players the following year.

1973 The Giants play their last game at Yankee Stadium, finishing off the season at the Yale Bowl in New Haven, Connecticut, preparatory to moving to the new Giants Stadium.

1975 As the new stadium is not yet completed, the Giants are forced to share Shea Stadium with the New York Jets, their games having to be scheduled for Saturday afternoons so that they do not conflict with the Jets.

1976 The Giants finally move into Giants Stadium in East Rutherford, New Jersey. They lose to the Dallas Cowboys in their

Lawrence Taylor – the NFL's 1986 player of the year.

first game there, the fifth in a nine-game losing streak; after the seventh, head coach Bill Arnsparger is sacked.

1980 After a brilliant start with a victory over the St Louis Cardinals, the team fall to eight defeats in a row, prompted by a deluge of injuries which left 35 players out of action.

1981 The Giants defeat the Philadelphia Eagles in the wild card game for the divisional championship. (They are later defeated by the San Francisco 49ers for the championship itself.)

1984 In playoffs, but lose to eventual Super Bowl champions San Francisco 49ers.

1985 Saw playoffs again. Quarterback Phil Simms finishes third among top ten quarterbacks.

1986 The Jackpot! The Giants win their first NFL championship in 30 years defeating Denver 39–20 in Super Bowl XXI. Quarterback Phil Simms is named the game's most valuable player.

Philadelphia Eagles

Veterans Stadium, Broad
Street and Pattison Avenue,
Philadelphia, Pennsylvania 19148

Stadium: Veterans Stadium

Conference: NFC (Eastern Division)

Colours: Kelly green, white and silver

1933 Bert Bell and Lud Wray buy the franchise for the Frankford Yellowjackets and move it from the Philadelphia suburbs to the city proper, when a state law banning sports on Sunday is about to be repealed. Bell renames the team after the eagle which is the symbol of President Franklin Roosevelt's National Recovery Administration (established to deal with the effects of the Great Depression). The Eagles lose 56–0 in their first game, against the New York Giants, but then go on to win four in a row.

1935 Bell proposes instituting a 'draft', with the weakest clubs getting first pick of each year's graduating college players. The Eagles win only two games despite the efforts of halfback Alabama Pitts, who learnt to play while serving time at Sing Sing prison.

1936 After the Eagles have lost $80 000, Bell buys out his partners for $4000 and takes over as coach from Wray. The first draft is held, and Bell has first pick as coach of the lowliest team.
The team moves from the Baker Bowl to the Municipal Stadium.

1939 Bell signs Davey O'Brien, a 5 ft 7 in quarterback, for $12 000 plus a percentage of the gate. He also has him insured by Lloyds of London, with the policy having to pay out $1500 for every game O'Brien misses through injury; the money never had to be paid.

1940 The Eagles move from the Municipal Stadium to Shibe Park in North Philadelphia.
O'Brien retires to join the FBI.

1941 The Eagles have a new owner in Alexis Thompson of New York.
New coach Earle 'Greasy' Neale makes the most of his star quarterback Tommy Thompson who, despite being blind in one eye, is a deadly long passer.

1942 The Eagles are one of the few NFL teams not to lose their quarterback to war service, since Thompson is rejected by the army because of his 'disability'.

1943 Because of squad losses due to the military call-up, and subsequent financial troubles, the Eagles and the Pittsburgh Steelers join forces. The result: the 'Phil-Pitt Steagles'.

1944 After a surprisingly successful year, the 'Steagles' separate.
Steve Van Buren of Louisiana State University, a halfback, is taken on during the college draft, and proves to be the making of the Eagles.

1947 Runners-up in the NFL championship, losing to the Chicago Cardinals. The Eagles are banned from wearing cleated shoes after being discovered sharpening their cleats to gain better traction on the slippery ground. Van Buren, in flat-soled shoes, slips and slides and gains only 26 yards in 18 carries.
'Greasy' Neale's 'Eagle' defense is overwhelmingly successful: a 5–2–4 alignment which is extremely physical and intimidating.

1948 NFL champions, defeating the Chicago Cardinals 7–0 in heavy snow. This might not have happened since the scorer of the game's only touchdown, Van Buren, had woken to discover the snow and, presuming that the game would be called off, went back to sleep; it was only after a frantic phone call from coach Neale that Van Buren raced to a trolley and reached the stadium in time to score.

1949 Alexis Thompson sells the franchise to a syndicate of 100 businessmen headed by James P. Clark for $250 000.
NFL champions, defeating the Los Angeles Rams in a game which saw the field turned into a muddy bog by heavy rain.

1950 The Eagles' fortunes begin to decline.
Coach 'Greasy' Neale and owner Clark start a feud which has its climax in the locker room at the Giants' Polo Grounds, where the two have to be physically separated; Neale is fired at the end of the season.

1951 Alvin 'Bo' McMillin is hired as head coach but has to resign due to ill health after just two games. Wayne Millner succeeds him.

1952 'Bo' McMillin dies of stomach cancer, and

Van Buren suffers the serious knee injury that forces him to retire.

Coach Millner is fired, and Jim Trimble replaces him.

1956 After a losing season, Trimble is usurped by Hugh Devore as head coach, but the latter is left with the weakest team in the Eastern Division as the Eagles' veteran line retires.

1958 Devore, too, is relieved of duty, and this time Buck Shaw is taken on as head coach. One of the first acts is to sign on the 32-year-old Norm Van Brocklin from the Los Angeles Rams—a decision that has much to do with the upturn in the Eagles' fortunes.

The Eagles move to the University of Pennsylvania's Franklin Field; attendances double.

1959 Bert Bell, former Eagles' owner and now NFL commissioner, suffers a fatal heart attack while watching the Eagles beat the Pittsburgh Steelers.

1960 NFL champions, defeating the Green Bay Packers. After the game, both coach Shaw and Norm Van Brocklin retire.

1961 Van Brocklin is outraged when Shaw's former assistant Nick Skorich is appointed head coach instead of him. He refuses to stay on as player-coach and leaves to become head coach of the Minnesota Vikings.

Sonny Jurgenson, the remaining and relatively untried quarterback, surprises everyone and proves to be one of the best players the Eagles have ever had, setting two league records and tying a third in his first season in the big time.

1962 Chairman of the board and former president James P. Clark dies.

1963 Quarterback Jurgenson and his back-up King Hill dramatically leave training camp to try to force management to increase their money. They do and the two players return.

Jerry Wolman, a building tycoon, buys the franchise for $5.5 million.

1964 Wolman hires as head coach and general manager Joe Kuharich, who promptly trades most of the Eagles' previous stars—for example Jurgenson and Tommy McDonald.

1966 Kuharich trades off more popular players, but the team ends up with its first winning season in five years.

1968 After the Eagles lose their first 11 games, fans begin to hope that they will remain winless and thus be able to nab college All-American O. J. Simpson in the draft; unfortunately (?), the team wins two of its last three games and the Buffalo Bills qualify for Simpson. Fans, disillusioned with Kuharich, starts a 'Joe Must Go' campaign, complete with buttons as well as a skywriter over Franklin Field. Meanwhile, Wolman is fighting bankruptcy.

1969 Wolman is forced to sell the franchise to haulage magnate Leonard Tose of Norristown, Pennsylvania for $16.1 million. Tose fires Kuharich, and replaces him as general manager with former player Pete Retzlaff; Retzlaff himself hires another former player Jerry Williams as head coach.

Keith Byars overcame a foot injury to play a few games for Philadelphia. (Fotosports International).

1971 The Eagles move to Veterans Stadium. After two losing seasons and the beginning of another which saw three defeats in as many games, Tose fires Williams who, with the players' support, denounces the owner as 'a man of little character'. Williams' replacement, Ed Khayat, a fan of General George Patton, orders all the players to cut their hair and shave off their moustaches—an order that several team members, led by linebacker Tom Rossovich who was the star player the previous season, resist before acceding.

1972 Khayat's strict discipline and punishing contract drills result in three players being seriously injured during training camp.

Safety Lee Bradley and Rossovich jointly refuse to sign their contracts in a power struggle with general manager Retzlaff; Rossovich is traded and Bradley finally signs.

The moment following the Eagles' staggering 62–10 defeat by the New York Giants, Tose accepts Retzlaff's resignation and then fires the entire coaching staff.

1973 Mike McCormack is appointed head coach. One of his first acts is to sign on veteran quarterback Roman Gabriel from the Los Angeles Rams.

1975 After the favourites, the Eagles, fail to win over the Giants and Bears, coach McCormack states that he has 'two dogs' on his squad—a statement which angers his whole team. McCormack's contract is not renewed at the end of the season.

1976 Dick Vermeil becomes head coach—the fifth in nine years.

1978 The Eagles have their best season since 1960, finally reaching the playoffs (they lose to the Atlanta Falcons).

1979 The Eagles again reach the playoffs but are defeated by the Tampa Bay Buccaneers.

1980 NFC East champions.

1981 NFC champions, defeating the Dallas Cowboys.

Runners-up at Super Bowl XV, losing to the Oakland Raiders.

1985 Coach Marion Campbell fired.

1986 Former Chicago defensive coordinator Buddy Ryan named club's new head coach.

St Louis Cardinals

Busch Stadium, Box 888,
St Louis, Missouri 63188

Stadium: Busch Stadium

Conference: NFC (Eastern Division)

Colours: cardinal red, black and white

1899 Painter-decorator Chris O'Brien forms a neighbourhood team in Chicago's South Side.

1901 The team moves to a new field on a corner of Racine Avenue. O'Brien buys secondhand, faded maroon jerseys from the University of Chicago, the colour of which O'Brien dubs 'cardinal'. The team is now named the Racine Cardinals.

1906 Lack of competition forces O'Brien to disband the team.

1913 O'Brien reforms the team and hires a coach; by 1917, they are champions of the Chicago Football League.

1918 After disbandment during the First World War and a subsequent flu pandemic, O'Brien forms the team for the third and last time.

1920 The Racine Cardinals become a charter member of the American Professional Football Association, the forerunner of the NFL.

John 'Paddy' Driscoll joins the team for $3000 a year; an outstanding all-round athlete, he is probably the best dropkicker of all time. He scores the only touchdown in a game with the Chicago Tigers—the winner of which (the Cardinals) would remain the only team to represent Chicago, the other one going out of business.

1921 Driscoll becomes player-coach.

For unknown reasons, O'Brien agrees that the Decatur Staleys (later to become the Chicago Bears) can move to Chicago, where they will compete for fans.

1922 The team changes its name to the 'Chicago Cardinals', and move to White Sox Park (where the eponymous baseball team plays).

1923 Quarterback Arnold Horween takes over as player-coach. A Harvard graduate and member of a wealthy family, Horween often takes to the field under the alias of McMahon and only occasionally takes money for playing.

The first NFL game to be played outside the USA took place in Tokyo, Japan on 16 August 1976. The St Louis Cardinals defeated the San Diego Chargers 20–10.

1925 NFL champions.

1926 Under financial pressure, O'Brien is forced to sell Paddy Driscoll to the Chicago Bears for $3500. In addition, the new American Football League's Chicago team, the Bulls, take a lease on the Cardinal's field; the latter are forced to move to the smaller Normal Field, which can hold fewer spectators, but without Driscoll, fewer people come anyway.

1929 After three losing seasons, O'Brien sells the team to a Chicago doctor, David Jones, for $25 000.
Jones moves the team to Comiskey Park and brings Ernie Nevers out of retirement to be player-coach. Nevers responds by scoring 40 points in six touchdowns and two field goals against the Chicago Bears.

1930 The Cardinals play a charity game against the Bears (with proceeds going to unemployment relief) in the indoor Chicago Stadium which is only 80 yards long. Earth is brought in to make a playing surface 6 in deep.

1932 Ernie Nevers retires.
After three years of seeing the Cardinals on a downward slide, a chance remark during dinner on a yacht owned by Chicago magnate Charles W. Bidwell Sen. leads to Dr Jones offering to sell the team to Bidwell, who is vice-president of the Chicago Bears. The asking price: $50 000—twice what Jones had paid for it in 1929. Bidwell rids himself of his Bears' holdings.

1941 For the first time since 1937, the Cardinals do not finish last, even though they win only three games.

1942 The Second World War takes a heavy toll of the squad, with most of the best players going into the armed forces.

1944 Because of the lack of players, the Cardinals join forces with the Pittsburgh Steelers to form the 'Card-Pitts'. They fail to win any games.

1945 The Card-Pitts dissolve back into their previous forms.

1946 With the advent of the new All-America Football Conference and the birth of its Chicago team, the Rockets, Bidwell resolves to back his own team strongly, acquiring an outstanding set of rookies and hiring Jimmy Conzelman (coach between 1940 and 1942) for a second term.

1947 Bidwell hires Charley Trippi, the Georgia All-American halfback, for a then record $100 000 spread over four years. Trippi forms part of what Bidwell calls 'my million-dollar backfield'.
Charles Bidwell dies. His widow Violet authorizes Ray Bennigsen to carry on.
Wearing tennis shoes to counteract the frosty ground, the Cardinals become NFL champions, defeating the Philadelphia Eagles.

1948 After the Cardinals lose to the Philadelphia Eagles for the NFL championship on a snow-covered field, Conzelman resigns.

1949 Violet Bidwell marries Walter Wolfner, a St Louis executive; together they become involved in team management.

1950 Earl 'Curly' Lambeau, former coach of the Green Bay Packers, is hired as coach by Bennigsen, who resigns shortly after.

1951 Violet Bidwell Wolfner becomes chairman of the board; her sons Charles Jr ('Stormy') and Bill are named president and vice-president respectively. However, it is Walter Wolfner, now managing director, who has control. He quarrels with Lambeau for most of the season, until the latter resigns.

1955 With Ray Richards as coach, the Cardinals have their best season since 1950: 4–7–1. Highlight of the year is a devastating win over arch rivals, the Bears, 53–14.

1960 The Cardinals are moved to St Louis by the NFL to prevent the American Football League establishing a team there. They must share Busch Stadium with the Cardinals baseball team, and have nowhere to practise, having to settle for a city park.

1961 Violet Bidwell Wolfner dies, bequeathing 90 per cent ownership of the Cardinals (10 per cent had been sold to brewery tycoon Joseph Griesedieck) to her two sons. Walter Wolfner contests the will, but it is declared valid. 'Stormy' and Bill Bidwell retain their previous titles.

St Louis Cardinals receiver Earnest Gray hangs on to a long pass. (Fotosports International).

1963 With a record of 9–5, the Cardinals have their best season since 1948, finishing third in the Eastern Conference.

1964 The Bidwells are approached by an Atlanta, Georgia, syndicate with a view to moving the team to that city where a new stadium is almost ready (the new St Louis stadium was far behind schedule). When better terms are offered by the St Louis stadium authority and there is evidence of increased public support for the team, the Bidwells reject the Atlanta proposal.

1966 The Cardinals move into the new Busch Memorial Stadium.

1972 Bill Bidwell buys out his brother Charles' ('Stormy') share of the team.

1973 Bill Bidwell names Don Coryell as the Cardinal's 26th head coach.

1974 Eastern Division champions.
In the NFC divisional playoffs (the first time the team had been involved in any post-season competition since 1948) the Cardinals lose to the Minnesota Vikings.

1975 Eastern Division champions.

1978 When coach Coryell resigns after the Cardinals fail to make the playoffs for two years running, veteran university coach Bud Wilkinson is appointed.

1979 Despite a losing season for the Cardinals, Ottis Anderson has the greatest season of any rookie running back in NFL history: he rushes for 1605 yards and has nine 100-yard games—both league records.
Wilkinson is fired as head coach.

1980 Jim Hanifan is hired as coach.

1982 Eastern Division champions.

1985 With a dismal 5–11 record, key players on the injury list and plummeting morale, Bill Bidwell fires Jim Hanifan and his entire staff.

San Francisco 49ers

711 Nevada Street, Redwood City, California 94061

Stadium: Candlestick Park

Conference: NFC (Western Division)

Colours: 49er gold and scarlet.

1946 Anthony J. 'Tony' Morabito, partner in Lumber Terminals of San Francisco, forms a team that is a charter member of the new All-America Football Conference (having been refused an NFL franchise). E. J. Turre and Allen E. Sorrell, both partners of Morabito, are both credited with giving the team its name, a reference to the prospectors who flocked to California following the discovery of gold in 1849. Its first emblem showed a gold prospector in tartan trousers and lumberjack shirt, with his hat blown off, hair mussed, feet set apart while firing two six-shooters. Lawrence 'Buck' Shaw is named as head coach.

1947 Morabito—a 'nut with a hearing aid in San Francisco', according to a Washington Redskins broadcaster—buys out his partners for $100 000 and splits ownership of the team 75/25 per cent with his brother Vic.

1949 The 49ers enter the NFL.

1951 Quarterback Y. A. Tittle is acquired from the defunct Baltimore Colts franchise.

1952 Tony Morabito suffers a heart attack. Rookie Hugh McElhenny, a halfback, has a spectacular first season.

1953 After their best season since they joined the NFL, losing only three games, Morabito gives fullback Joe Perry a bonus cheque for $5090—$5 for each of the 1018 yards he had rushed.

1954 The 49ers now have one of the best backfields in pro football history, with fullback John Henry Johnson from the Pittsburgh Steelers joining Tittle, McElhenny and Perry. The latter, by the end of the season, has rushed 1049 yards—the first runner to gain over 1000 yards, two years in a row.

1955 Buck Shaw, the team's first and only coach, is fired after nine years with the 49ers. His replacement is Norman 'Red' Strader, who is unpopular for his strict discipline.

1956 Strader is replaced by Frankie Albert, a former 49ers' quarterback.

1957 Tittle and rookie end R. C. Owens (standing 6 ft 5 in tall) invent the 'Alley-Oop' pass: Tittle throws the ball in a high arc, and Owens outjumps any opponents to catch it.
Trailing the Chicago Bears 17–7 at half-time, coach Albert tells the team that owner Tony Morabito, aged only 47, has suffered a fatal heart attack; the team rallies to make an emotional comeback and win 21–17.

1958 Vic Morabito takes over the team's operation.

1960 Coach Howard 'Red' Hickey (who had succeeded Frankie Albert in 1959) institutes the 'shotgun' formation: the quarterback, standing 3 to 5 yards back, takes a long snap from the centre, then passes or hands off. Using this, the 49ers win four of their last five games.

1961 After an appalling loss to the Chicago Bears, Hickey abandons the shotgun formation and returns to the T formation; he says, however, that he would have continued with the shotgun if his players had not lost confidence in it.

1962 The 49ers have their first losing season since 1956; six wins and eight losses.

1963 Hickey resigns and is replaced by Jack Christiansen. The 49ers have their worst season in their history: two wins and twelve losses.

Jerry Rice – San Francisco's top rated wide receiver. (Fotosports International).

1964 Vic Morabito dies of a heart attack, aged just 44. Josephine and Jane Morabito widows of the two brothers, retain ownership and place the team's operations in the hands of Lou Spadia, general manager since 1952.

1968 Spadia takes over as president of the club and names Jack White as general manager. Dick Nolan succeeds Christiansen as head coach.

1970 Western Division champions, the first time in their 25-year history that the 49ers have won a title.

1971 The team moves from Kezar Stadium, which they have been renting from the time of their formation, to Candlestick Park.
Western Division champions.

1972 Western Division champions.
The 49ers lose to the Dallas Cowboys (coach Dick Nolan's former team) for the third time in a row in the NFC championship game.

1976 After the team has been in a slump for three years, Nolan is replaced by Monte Clark. The 49ers go on to have their first winning season since 1972.

1977 The 49ers are bought by Edward J. DeBartolo Jr, at 31 the youngest owner in the NFL.

1978 With a new coach (Pete McCulley) and many changes in the squad, the 49ers have the worst season in their history: 2–14. Midway through their disasters, McCulley is replaced by Fred O'Connor, who lasts only until the end of the season.

1979 Bill Walsh from Stanford University is appointed head coach.

1981 Western Division champions.

1982 NFC champions, defeating the Dallas Cowboys
Super Bowl XVI champions, defeating the Cincinnati Bengals.

1983 Western Division champions.

1984 NFC champions.

1985 Super Bowl XIX champions, defeating the Miami Dolphins.

Tampa Bay Buccaneers

1 Buccaneer Place, Tampa, Florida 33607

Stadium: Tampa Stadium

Conference: NFC (Central Division)

Colours: Florida orange, white and red

1974 Tampa Bay is awarded an NFL franchise, first to Philadelphia construction boss Tom McCloskey, who withdraws after two weeks, and then to Hugh F. Culverhouse, an attorney and property developer from Jacksonville, Florida, who pays $16 million. In awarding the franchise, NFL commissioner Pete Rozelle says that the league has been impressed by the audiences for pre-season games in Tampa—the first of which, the Washington Redskins versus the Atlanta Falcons, had taken place in 1968.

1975 An advisory board headed by Culverhouse sifts through over 400 names for the team submitted by the public; the owner eventually settled on 'Buccaneers' (which was soon shortened to 'Bucs'), with a swashbuckling figure for a logo.

1976 In their first season, the Bucs become the first team to have a 0–14 record (including five shutouts) in NFL history, and also the first team to go winless since the Dallas Cowboys in 1960.

1977 After losing 12 games running in the new season, the Bucs finally have their first win on 11 December against the New Orleans Saints, ending a total winless streak of 26 consecutive games. More than 8000 fans came out to welcome home the team.

1979 After such a dismal start, the Bucs gradually become much stronger and more frequently victorious until, in a tie-breaker, they win Central Division.

1981 Central Division champions.

1983 Central Division champions (2 January).

1985 Worst record in NFL.

1986 No 1 draft choice Bo Jackson spurns team to play professional baseball. Once again, worst record in NFL.

1987 Ray Perkins replaces Leeman Bennett as head coach.

Washington Redskins

Redskin Park, PO Box 17247, Dulles International Airport, Washington DC 20041

Stadium: Robert F. Kennedy Stadium

Colours: burgundy and gold

1932 The team is founded in Boston by a syndicate headed by George Preston Marshall of Washington DC, and named the Boston Braves after the baseball team whose field they use.
By the end of a mediocre 4–4–2 season and with a loss of $46 000, all the syndicate partners drop out except Marshall, who becomes sole owner.

1933 The team is moved to Fenway Park (home of the Red Sox baseball team), renamed the Boston Redskins and supplied with a full-blooded Indian coach—Will 'Lone Star' Dietz. For the team picture taken on the first day of practice the players all wear Indian headdresses, feathers and warpaint.
The team has so little money that, when the ball goes into the stands, owner Marshall approaches the stands and asks for it back.
Marshall suggests major rule changes (subsequently adopted by the NFL) which lead to a set schedule, two divisions with a championship playoff, moving the goal posts to the goal line and a slimmer ball to aid passing.

1936 Newly-hired coach Ray Flaherty insists that Marshall stay off the field and in the stands.
Eastern Division champions.

1937 Team transferred to Washington, DC, to play at Griffith Stadium. Marshall organizes elaborate half-time shows with marching bands.
Marshall signs Sammy Baugh, an All-America tailback, who in his 16 years with the team will set passing and punting records which still stand today.
Eastern Division champions, after a decisive win over the New York Giants (the second such game in two years). More than 10 000 Redskins fans travel to New York to see the game, then march up Broadway behind their band and overwhelm the Polo Grounds.
NFL champions, defeating the Chicago Bears.

1940 Before becoming Eastern Division champions, the Redskins defeat the Chicago Bears. The latter complains about some of the umpires' decisions, and Marshall retaliates by calling the Bears 'quitters' and 'crybabies'.
The Redskins lose the NFL championship game to the Bears, 73–0—the most one-sided score in a championship game and the first to be broadcast coast-to-coast.

1941 During a home game in the nation's capital on 7 December, a number of high-ranking military men and government officials are called out of the stands, but it is not until the game is over that the crowd discovers that the Japanese have bombed Pearl Harbor and the US is at war.

1942 NFL champions, beating the Chicago Bears.

1943 Eastern Division champions, defeating the New York Giants in a playoff.

1945 Eastern Division champions.

1949 With the Redskins producing mediocre football, there is much criticism in the sports press of Marshall's failure to hire any black players.

1950 The team becomes, with the Los Angeles Rams, the first to have all their games televised.

1952 After head coach Dick Todd resigns, saying he has received no respect, Marshall signs Earl 'Curly' Lambeau as Todd's successor.

1953 NFL champions, defeating the Philadelphia Eagles.
Lambeau retires after his 231st NFL victory.

1954 Dave Sparks, guard, dies of a heart attack after his team loses to the Cleveland Browns.

1956 Vic Janowicz, superb former All-American halfback, suffers irrevocable brain damage in a car accident during training camp.

1957 Roy Barni, defensive back, is shot dead in a bar room brawl during training camp.

1961 The Redskins move to the new DC Stadium (later renamed Robert F. Kennedy Stadium), but the team still ends the season with a 1–12 record.

1962 Marshall finally drafts his first black player, Ernie Davis, then transfers him for another black player, Bobby Mitchell. By the time the squad is complete, there are four black men on the team.

1964 Marshall signs quarterback Sonny Jurgensen.

1965 In the biggest upset in their history, the Redskins fight back from a 21-point deficit to defeat the Dallas Cowboys 34–31, with Jurgensen passing for more than 400 yards and three touchdowns.
Cornerback Johnny Sample is suspended for insubordination.

1966 Otto Graham is appointed head coach and general manager.

1969 Legendary coach Vince Lombardi leaves Green Bay Packers to become part-owner, executive vice-president and head coach of the Redskins.

1970 Lombardi dies of cancer at the beginning of the season.

1971 George Allen, former coach of the Los Angeles Rams, becomes head coach. He begins trading to obtain as many good veteran players as he can (including quarterback Billy Kilmer from the New Orleans Saints and linebacker Jack Pardee from the Rams), with the result that, by the end of the season, the team is known as the 'over-the-hill gang'. This bunch of 'old men' give the Redskins their best record in 29 years (9–4–1).

1972 Eastern Division champions.
NFL champions, defeating the Dallas Cowboys.

1973 Runners-up at Super Bowl VII, losing to the Miami Dolphins.

Jay Schroeder took over from Joe Theismann in 1985.
(Fotosports International).

1975 After celebrating his 40th birthday by leading the NFC in passing the previous year, Jurgensen retires after 11 years with the Redskins.

1976 Allen signs away his first draft choice to get quarterback Joe Theismann from the Miami Dolphins.

1978 George Allen leaves to return to the Rams and is replaced by former Redskins player and Chicago Bears coach Jack Pardee.

Guided by Theismann, the team has six victories in a row—the best start in the Redskins' history.

1979 Jack Pardee is named NFL coach of the year.

1981 After a losing season the previous year, Pardee is released and succeeded by Joe Gibbs.

1982 NFL champions.

1983 Super Bowl XVII champions, defeating the Miami Dolphins and earning their first world title in 41 years.

1984 NFC champions, defeating the San Francisco 49ers.

1985 Runners-up in Super Bowl XIX, losing to the Los Angeles Raiders by the largest margin in the history of the Super Bowl, 39–9.

1986 Lose NFC championship to NY Giants.

1986 Season Statistics

National Football Conference

Scoring

Touchdowns	td	rush	rec	ret	pts
Rogers, Washington	18	18	0	0	108
Rice, San Francisco	16	1	15	0	96
Morris, New York Giants	15	14	1	0	90
Walker, Dallas	14	12	2	0	84
Dickerson, Los Angeles Rams	11	11	0	0	66
Payton, Chicago	11	8	3	0	66
Jones, Detroit	9	8	1	0	54
Quick, Philadelphia	9	0	9	0	54
Riggs, Atlanta	9	9	0	0	54
Mayes, New Orleans	8	8	0	0	48

Kicking	ep-a	fg-a	lg	pts
Butler, Chicago	36–37	28–41	52	120
Wersching, San Francisco	41–42	25–35	50	116
Nelson, Minnesota	44–47	22–28	53	110
Andersen, New Orleans	30–30	26–30	53	108
Allegre, New York Giants	33–33	24–32	46	105
Septien, Dallas	43–43	15–21	50	88
McFadden, Philadelphia	26–27	20–31	50	86
Lansford, Los Angeles Rams	34–35	17–24	50	85
Murray, Detroit	31–32	18–25	52	85
Del Greco, Green Bay	29–29	17–27	50	80

Passing

	att	cmp	pct	yds	td	int
Kramer, Minnesota	372	208	55.9	3000	24	10
Montana, San Francisco	307	191	62.2	2236	8	9
Hipple, Detroit	305	192	63.0	1919	9	11
Simms, New York Giants	468	259	55.3	3487	21	22
Lomax, St Louis	421	240	57.0	2583	13	12
Schroeder, Washington	541	276	51.0	4109	22	22
Archer, Atlanta	294	150	51.0	2007	10	9
Jaworski, Philadelphia	245	128	52.2	1405	8	6
Pelluer, Dallas	378	215	56.9	2727	8	17
Wright, Green Bay	492	263	53.5	3247	17	23
Wilson, New Orleans	342	189	55.3	2353	10	17
Young, Tampa Bay	363	195	53.7	2282	8	13

Rating based on pct. comp, avg yds, pct. td, pct. int.

Pass receivers

Receptions	no	yds	avg	td
Rice, San Francisco	86	1570	18.3	15
Craig, San Francisco	81	624	7.7	0
J. Smith, St Louis	80	1014	12.7	6
Walker, Dallas	76	837	11.0	2
Clark, Washington	74	1265	17.1	7
Monk, Washington	73	1068	14.6	4
Bavaro, New York Giants	66	1001	15.2	4
Lofton, Green Bay	64	840	13.1	4
C. Brown, Atlanta	63	918	14.6	4
Clark, San Francisco	61	794	13.0	2
Quick, Philadelphia	60	939	15.7	9
Jordan, Minnesota	58	859	14.8	6
Ferrell, St Louis	56	434	7.8	3
Jones, Detroit	54	334	6.2	1
Chadwick, Detroit	53	995	18.8	5
D. Nelson, Minnesota	53	593	11.2	3

Yards	yds	no	avg	td
Rice, San Francisco	1570	86	18.3	15
Clark, Washington	1265	74	17.1	7
Monk, Washington	1068	73	14.6	4

	yds	no	avg	td
J. Smith, St Louis	1014	80	12.7	6
Bavaro, New York Giants	1001	66	15.2	4
Chadwick, Detroit	995	53	18.8	5
Quick, Philadelphia	939	60	15.7	9
C. Brown, Atlanta	918	63	14.6	4
Jordan, Minnesota	859	58	14.8	6
Lofton, Green Bay	840	64	13.1	4
Walker, Dallas	837	76	11.0	2
Gault, Chicago	818	42	19.5	5
Clark, San Francisco	794	11	13.0	2
Hill, Dallas	770	49	15.7	3
Sherrard, Dallas	774	41	18.1	5
Stanley, Green Bay	723	35	20.7	2

Interceptions

	no	yds	lg	td
Lott, San Francisco	10	134	57	1
Waymer, New Orleans	9	48	17	0
Lee, Green Bay	9	33	11	0
Gray, Los Angeles Rams	8	101	28	0
Holt, Minnesota	8	54	27	0
Richardson, Chicago	7	69	32	0
Irvin, Los Angeles Rams	6	150	50	1
Duerson, Chicago	6	139	38	0
Downs, Dallas	6	54	31	0
A. Waters, Philadelphia	6	39	21	0
McKyver, San Francisco	6	33	21	1
Young, Philadelphia .	6	9	9	0

Rushing

	att	yds	avg	lg	td
Dickerson, Los Angeles Rams	404	1821	4.5	42	11
Morris, New York Giants	341	1516	4.4	54	14
Mayes, New Orleans	286	1353	4.7	50	8
Payton, Chicago	321	1333	4.2	41	8
Riggs, Atlanta	343	1327	3.9	31	9
Rogers, Washington	303	1203	4.0	42	18
Jones, Detroit	252	903	3.6	39	8
Craig, San Francisco	204	803	4.1	25	7
Mitchell, St Louis	174	800	4.6	44	5
D. Nelson, Minnesota	191	793	4.2	42	4
Dorsett, Dallas	184	748	4.1	33	5
Walker, Dallas	151	737	4.9	84	12
Wilder, Tampa Bay	190	704	3.7	45	2
James, Detroit	159	688	4.3	60	3
Cribbs, San Francisco	152	590	3.9	19	5
Byars, Philedelphia	177	577	3.3	32	1
Ferrell, St Louis	124	548	4.4	25	0
Cunningham, Philadelphia	66	540	8.2	20	5
Davis, Green Bay	114	519	4.6	50	0
Redden, Los Angeles Rams	110	567	4.2	41	4

Punting

	no	lg	avg	blk	x-net
Landetta, New York Giants	79	61	44.8	0	37.1
Donnelly, Atlanta	78	71	43.9	1	35.0
Cox, Washington	75	58	43.6	0	36.4
Hansen, New Orleans	81	66	42.7	1	36.6
Teltschik, Philadelphia	108	62	41.6	1	33.6
Runager, San Francisco	83	62	41.6	2	34.3
Coleman, Minnesota	67	69	41.4	0	34.9
Buford, Chicago	69	59	41.3	1	36.9
Saxon, Dallas	86	58	40.7	1	34.4
Garcia, Tampa Bay	77	60	40.1	0	32.7
Bracken, Green Bay	55	63	40.1	2	32.8
Black, Detroit	46	57	39.5	1	31.3
Hatcher, Los Angeles Rams	97	57	38.6	1	32.9
Cater, St Louis	61	52	37.2	1	33.2

x-net (team efficiency)—total punt yards minus return yards, minus 20 yards for each punt over goal-line divided by total attempts including punts blocked.

Punt returns

	no	yds	avg	lg	td
Sikahema, St Louis	43	522	12.1	71	2
Griffin, San Francisco	38	377	9.9	76	1
Mandley, Detroit	43	420	9.8	81	1
Jenkins, Washington	28	270	9.6	39	0
Stanley, Green Bay	33	316	9.6	83	1
Martin, New Orleans	24	227	9.5	39	0
Barnes, Chicago	57	482	8.5	35	0
Sutton, Los Angeles Rams	28	234	8.4	32	0
McConkey, New York Giants	32	253	7.9	22	0
Bess, Minnesota	23	162	7.0	16	0

Kick-off returns

	no	yds	avg	lg	td
Gentry, Chicago	20	576	28.8	91	1
Gray, New Orleans	31	866	27.9	101	1
Sikahema, St Louis	37	847	22.9	44	0
Bess, Minnesota	31	705	22.7	43	0
Brown, Los Angeles	36	794	22.1	55	0
Stamps, St Louis	24	514	21.4	35	0
Hunter, Detroit	49	1007	20.6	54	0
Jenkins, Washington	27	554	20.5	37	0
Stanley, Green Bay	28	559	20.0	55	0
Elder, Detroit	22	435	19.8	36	0

Sacks

Taylor, New York Giants	20.5
Manley, Washington	18.5
White, Dallas	18.0
Jeffcoat, Dallas	14.0
Haley, San Francisco	12.0
Marshall, New York Giants	12.0
Dent, Chicago	11.5
Stover, San Francisco	11.0
A. Baker, St Louis	10.5
Millard, Minnesota	10.5

American Football Conference

Scoring

Touchdowns	td	rush	rec	ret	pts
Winder, Denver	14	9	5	0	84
Warner, Seattle	13	13	0	0	78
Hampton, Miami	12	9	3	0	72
Walker, New York Jets	12	0	12	0	72
Duper, Miami	11	0	11	0	66
Paige, Kansas City	11	0	11	0	66
Clayton, Miami	10	0	10	0	60
Collinsworth, Cincinnati	10	0	10	0	66
Mack, Cleveland	10	10	0	0	60
Morgan, New England	10	0	10	0	60

Kicking	ep-a	fg-a	lg	pts
Franklin, New England	44—45	32—41	49	140
N. Johnson, Seattle	42—42	22—35	54	108
Karlis, Denver	44—45	20—28	51	104
Breech, Cincinatti	50—51	17—32	51	101
Lowery, Kansas City	43—43	19—26	47	100
Bahr, Los Angeles Raiders	36—36	21—28	52	99
Anderson, Pittsburgh	32—32	21—28	45	95
Reveiz, Miami	52—55	14—22	52	94
Zendejas, Houston	28—29	22—27	51	94
Leahy, New York Jets	44—44	16—19	50	92

Passing

	att	cmp	pct	yds	td	int
Marino, Miami	623	378	60.7	4746	44	23
Krieg, Seattle	375	225	60.0	2921	21	11
Eason, New England	448	276	61.6	3328	19	10
Esiason, Cincinnati	469	273	58.2	3959	24	17

	att	comp	pct	yds	td	int
O'Brien, New York Jets	482	300	62.2	3690	25	20
Kosar, Cleveland	531	310	58.4	3854	17	10
Kelly, Buffalo	480	285	59.4	3593	22	17
Plunkett, LA Raiders	252	133	52.8	1986	14	9
Elway, Denver	504	280	55.6	3485	19	13
Fouts, San Diego	430	252	58.6	3031	16	22
Kenney, Kansas City	308	161	52.3	1922	13	11
Wilson, LA Raiders	240	129	53.8	1721	12	15
Malone, Pittsburgh	425	216	50.8	2444	15	18
Moon, Houston	488	256	52.5	3489	13	26
Trudeau, Indianapolis	417	204	48.9	2225	8	18

Rating based on pct. comp, avg yds, pct. td, pct. int.

Pass receivers

Receptions

	no	yds	avg	td
Christensen, LA Raiders	95	1153	12.1	8
Toon, New York Jets	85	1176	13.8	8
Morgan, New England	84	1491	17.8	10
Anderson, San Diego	80	871	10.9	8
Collins, New England	77	684	8.9	5
Bouza, Indianapolis	71	830	11.7	5
Largent, Seattle	70	1070	15.3	9
Shuler, New York Jets	69	675	9.8	4
Duper, Miami	67	1313	19.6	11
Brooks, Indianapolis	65	1131	17.4	8
D. Hill, Houston	65	1122	17.1	5
Winslow, San Diego	64	728	11.4	5
Willhite, Denver	64	529	8.3	3
Collinsworth, Cincinnati	62	1024	16.5	10
Givins, Houston	61	1062	17.4	3
Hampton, Miami	61	446	7.3	3

Yards

	yds	no	avg	td
Morgan, New England	1491	84	17.8	10
Duper, Miami	1313	67	19.6	11
Toon, New York Jets	1176	85	13.8	8
Christenson, LA Raiders	1153	95	12.1	8
Clayton, Miami	1150	60	19.2	10
Brooks, Indianapolis	1131	65	17.4	8
D. Hill, Houston	1112	65	17.1	5
Largent, Seattle	1070	70	15.3	9
Givins, Houston	1062	61	17.4	3
Collingsworth, Cincinnati	1024	62	16.5	10
Walker, New York Jets	1016	49	20.7	12
Brown, Cincinnati	964	58	16.6	4
Chandler, San Diego	874	50	15.6	4
Anderson, San Diego	871	80	10.9	8
Williams, LA Raiders	843	43	19.6	8
Brennan, Cleveland	838	55	15.2	6

Interceptions

	no	yds	lg	td
Cherry, Kansas City	9	150	49	0
Lippett, New England	8	76	43	0
McElroy, LA Raiders	7	105	28	0
Breeden, Cincinnati	7	72	36	1
Harden, Denver	6	179	52	2
Holmes, New York Jets	6	29	28	0
Burruss, Kansas City	5	193	72	3
Brown, Seattle	5	58	24	1
Byrd, San Diego	5	45	18	0
Lyles, New York Jets	5	36	22	0
Lynn, New York Jets	5	36	26	0
Dixon, Cleveland	5	35	19	0

Rushing

	att	yds	avg	lg	td
Warner, Seattle	319	1481	4.6	60	13
Brooks, Cincinnati	205	1087	5.3	56	5
Jackson, Pittsburgh	216	910	4.2	31	5
Abercrombie, Cleveland	214	877	4.1	38	6
McNiel, New York Jets	214	856	4.0	40	5
Hampton, Miami	186	830	4.5	54	9
Winder, Denver	240	789	-3.3	31	9
Allen, LA Raiders	208	759	3.6	28	5
Mack, Cleveland	174	655	3.8	20	10
Rozier, Houston	199	662	3.3	19	4
Riddick, Buffalo	150	632	4.2	41	4
McMillan, Indianapolis	189	609	3.2	28	3
Hector, New York Jets	164	605	3.7	41	8
Williams, Seattle	129	538	4.2	36	0
McCallum, LA Raiders	142	536	3.8	18	1
Dickey, Cleveland	135	523	3.9	47	5
Kinnebrew, Cincinnati	131	519	4.0	39	8
Pruitt, Kansas City	139	448	3.2	16	2
Anderson, San Diego	127	442	3.5	17	1
James, New England	154	427	2.8	16	4

Punting

	no	lg	avg	blk	x-net
Stark, Indianapolis	76	63	45.2	0	37.2
Roby, Miami	56	73	44.2	0	37.4
Camarillo, New England	89	64	42.1	3	33.1
Mojsijnk, San Diego	72	62	42.0	2	32.9
Gossett, Cleveland	83	61	41.2	0	35.6
L. Johnson, Houston	88	66	41.2	0	35.7
Colbert, Kansas City	99	56	40.7	0	33.7
Kidd, Buffalo	75	57	40.4	0	34.5
Guy, LA Raiders	90	64	40.2	0	33.8
Newsome, Pittsburgh	86	64	40.1	3	32.2
Jennings, New York Jets	85	55	39.4	0	36.1
Gamache, Seattle	79	55	36.5	0	33.0
Hayes, Cincinnati	56	52	35.1	2	29.7

x-net (team efficiency)—total punt yards minus return yards, minus 20 yards for each punt over goal-line divided by total attempts including punts blocked.

Punt returns

	no	yds	avg	lg	td
Edmonds, Seattle	34	419	12.3	75	1
Willhite, Denver	42	468	11.1	70	1
Fryar, New England	35	366	10.5	59	1
Anderson, San Diego	25	227	9.1	30	0
Walker, LA Raiders	49	440	9.0	70	1
Woods, Pittsburgh	33	294	8.9	41	0
McNeil, Cleveland	40	348	8.7	84	1
J. Smith, Kansas City	29	245	8.4	48	0
Sohn, New York Jets	35	289	8.3	27	0
Drewrey, Houston	34	262	7.7	25	0

Kick-off returns

	no	yds	avg	lg	td
Sanchez, Pittsburgh	25	591	23.6	64	0
McGee, Cincinnati	43	1007	23.4	94	0
Humpherey, New York Jets	28	655	23.4	96	1
Bell, Denver	23	531	23.1	42	1
Lang, Denver	21	480	22.9	42	0
Edmonds, Seattle	34	764	22.5	46	0
Starring, New England	36	802	22.3	52	0
Ellis, Miami	25	541	21.6	41	0
Bentley, Indianapolis	32	687	21.5	37	0
Adams, LA Raiders	27	573	21.2	51	0

Sacks

Jones, LA Raiders	15.5
Lee Williams, San Diego	15.0
B. Smith, Buffalo	15.0
Jones, Denver	13.5
O'Neal, San Diego	12.5
Green, Seattle	12.0
Willis, Pittsburgh	12.0
Pickel, LA Raiders	11.5
Townsend, LA Raiders	11.5
Smith, San Diego	11.0
Veris, New England	11.0

SAMMY BAUGH

Every once in a while a single character has come along in football who has made contributions to the game that have been so great that, after he had departed from the scene the sport would forever be a better, but a different game.

Sammy Baugh was such a history maker, the passer deluxe of the Washington Redskins for 16 seasons and a charter member of the Pro Football Hall of Fame in Canton, Ohio, when that institution was first set up in 1963.

But it was in 1937 when a highly publicized cowboy from Sweetwater, Texas first appeared in Washington DC. Redskins owner George Preston Marshall 'had just moved his team from Boston and he knew that he badly needed a promotional shot in the arm to make pro football go in the nation's capital.

When the cowboy retired so many years later in 1952—no other full-time player had endured such a long tenure—football was not only established in Washington but it was beginning its rise to the peaks of popularity that it enjoys today.

When Slingin' Sammy Baugh first started playing pro football, the game was largely a rock-em, sock-em infantry battle on the ground. The forward pass was something very rarely used and when it was it was with extreme caution. You rarely used it inside your own 30-yard line. Green Bay did.

By the time Baugh retired, the forward pass was an anywhere-on-the-field weapon enjoying almost equal use with the bread and butter ground game. Pro football was still a rugged game between rugged men but it was beginning to evolve as a certain test of finesse where the object was to outguess the opposition rather than just overpower him.

In school Sammy Baugh was good at many sports—basketball, football and baseball. In fact, it was on a baseball scholarship that he

first attended Texas Christian University and he was still considering a career in that sport when George Preston Marshall was offering him a $5000 a year salary in his plush Washington office. It turned out to be the best investment that Marshall or pro football, for that matter, had ever made.

It is quite interesting to discover that Baugh started his career as a single wing tailback and didn't actually make the switch to the T-formation until 1944—half-way through his career. In fact he made the All-NFL team only twice as a quarterback, but four times as a halfback, in 1937, 1940, 1943, and 1947.

His record-setting NFL passing titles were evenly split, three as a tailback and three as a quarterback in 1945, 1947 and 1949.

Statistically, Sammy Baugh was way ahead of his time. His records stood for many years and the feats of the man were not just in the passing game. He also won four NFL punting titles and led the NFL in interceptions in 1943 with 11 and during the game with Detroit in 1943 picked off four.

But perhaps the most telling factor as far as Baugh's value to the Redskins was concerned is that the Redskins won five divisional and two NFL titles during his career. In the years that followed his departure, they didn't even come close.

Sammy Baugh was one of those pioneering, cheerful individuals, with a never say die good-natured attitude to the game.

In 1940, the Redskins suffered badly at the hands of the Chicago Bears in the championship game. They were massacred 73–0. Early in the game, a Redskin end had dropped a potential scoring pass in the end zone at a time when the Bears were only leading 7–0. Asked afterwards if the outcome might have been different had that pass been caught, Baugh replied in his usual Texan drawl, 'Yeah, it

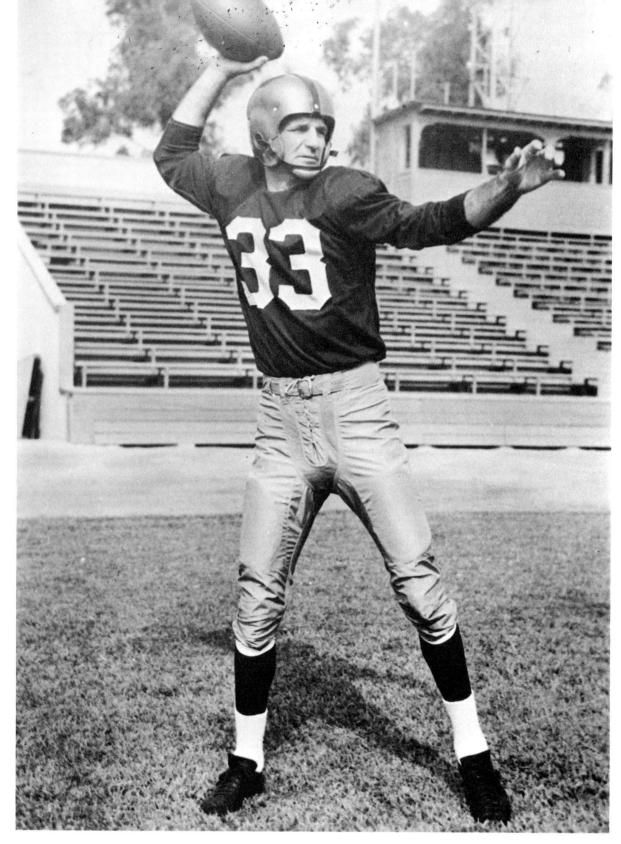

would have made the score 73–7!'

Obviously, the changes in football at that time were brought about by more than just one man, but as fellow Hall of Fame member Sid Luckman, himself one of Baugh's greatest rivals, insists, 'Sammy Baugh was the best. Nobody is ever going to equal him. Not anybody.'

3 College Football

Introduction

Football in the USA is big business, and nowhere is it bigger than in the colleges throughout this vast country. Under the aegis of the National Collegiate Athletic Association (NCAA), over 650 universities compete at four levels of excellence in probably one of the toughest schedules in the world.

Just as professional as its senior counterparts, in management terms at least, the college football circuit is the breeding ground for the stars of tomorrow.

Under NCAA rules players do not receive salaries, although rumours abound every year of inducements being made that break the rules. Colleges found guilty by the tough disciplinarian NCAA of violating their rules are usually banned from the lucrative Bowl games at the end of the season.

Whilst the players are not paid, their mentors, the coaches, are among the highest-paid sports coaches in the USA. Alabama's Paul Bryant was reported to have earned in excess of $450 000 in 1981. Not only do the coaches earn substantial basic salaries, but they can command huge fees for seminars and summer training camps and from the media.

Almost all of today's NFL and USFL coaches started life in college ranks. Los Angeles Rams' head coach John Robinson was for many years the top man at the University of Southern California, and Darryl Rogers, one of the newest coaches in the NFL at Detroit Lions, served his time at Arizona State.

Everything about college football is on a big scale. The Division One universities use stadiums that are big enough to attract massive crowds, and massive crowds do turn up. In 1981 the University of Michigan averaged a crowd of 104 292 for its regular season games. The top twenty teams will have an average

Shane Conlan will be in action in the NFL this year.

crowd attendance for a season of over 60 000 people who cram into huge dome-like stadiums to cheer on their favourites.

In 1979, Michigan again set a new record for crowd attendance at a single game when over 106 000 fans packed into the Ann Arbor Stadium to watch the Wolverines play their arch rivals in the Big Ten, Ohio State.

More than three times as many fans watch the college football games as attend the professional action of the NFL.

Football has certainly come a long way from its early pioneering days back in the latter part of the last century. In 1892 Stanford and the University of California met in the first recorded west coast game, and three years later the first conference or league was formed. Originally called the Western Athletic Conference, it is known today as the 'Big Ten'.

Over the past century many more confer-

106

ences have been formed, not only to play football but to enable groups of universities to participate in all sports.

Many of these conferences are based on geographical areas, with teams vying every year for their conference championship and a chance to represent their league in a money-spinning Bowl game.

The teams in each conference will play a certain number of games against local conference rivals. Other games will be played against colleges from other conferences and some will arrange schedules that include fixtures with universities who are labelled as 'Independents'. Notre Dame, Pittsburgh, Miami and Penn State number in these ranks, and choose to run their own athletic policies and play games against some of the top colleges in the USA. Some of these games have longstanding traditions predating the formation of conferences. The USC versus Notre Dame fixture is an annual affair that can be traced back to the 1920s.

Like any sport, college-style football has a habit of developing dynasties, and these have constantly varied over the years.

The team from the University of Michigan in the early 1900s, with Willie 'The Wisp' Heston at the helm, was undefeated for 56 games between 1901 and 1905. Because of their ability to score almost at will, they became known as the 'point-a-minute' team, and their record in the year 1901 (11–0), with a total score of 550 points for and none against, showed how powerful they were.

A few hundred miles to the west, and some twenty years later, Illinois, under Red Grange, set about rewriting the record books with four touchdowns in 12 minutes during one game.

The 1920s saw Notre Dame rise to prominence, with the legendary Knute Rockne as coach. Rockne is still regarded by many as the greatest coach ever.

The 'Thundering Herd' of USC became almost invincible during the 1930s on the west coast, whilst on the eastern seaboard New York's Fordham University went a whole

Penn State quarterback John Shaffer.

season in 1936 without conceding a single touchdown.

The war years naturally saw the emergence of the military academies, and the Army with Glenn Davis and Doc Blanchard achieved an NCAA record high of 56 points per game.

The post-war years once again saw the emergence of Notre Dame, before Oklahoma and Texas decided it was time that the southwest achieved some fame.

The late 1950s saw the arrival of new coaches with new ideas. One of the leading lights of this era was John McKay of USC. McKay favoured a new I-version for his offensive formations, and after going through only 8 wins and 11 losses, a powerful I-formation gave the Trojans three national titles and perfect seasons of 11–0–0 and 12–0–0.

The formations used by colleges are much more varied than those used in the professional leagues. College football tends to try the unusual and some say it is far more exciting than its big league brothers.

Naturally, the large colleges across the nation play their football within one of the major division IA conferences, or as a division IA Independent. There are a few exceptions such as Baylor, a small baptist university from Waco, Texas, which plays in the Southwest Conference.

'Football is not a contact sport. It's a collision sport. A good example of a contact sport is ballroom dancing.' Duffy Daugherty, *former head coach of Michigan State and a member of the College Hall of Fame.*

The Major Conferences

Division IA

Atlantic Coast
Clemson
Duke
Georgia Tech.
Maryland
North Carolina
North Carolina State
Wake Forest
Virginia

Big Eight
Colorado
Iowa State
Kansas
Kansas State
Missouri
Nebraska
Oklahoma
Oklahoma State

Big Ten
Illinois
Northwestern
Indiana
Iowa
Michigan
Michigan State
Minnesota
Ohio State
Purdue
Wisconsin

Pacific 10
Arizona
Arizona State
California
Oregon
Oregon State
Southern California
Stanford
University of California at Los
  Angeles
Washington
Washington State

Southeastern
Florida
Louisiana State
Alabama
Auburn
Georgia
Kentucky
Mississipi
Mississippi State
Tennessee
Vanderbilt

Southwest
Arkansas
Baylor
Houston
Rice
Southern Methodist
Texas
Texas A&M
Texas Christian
Texas Tech.

Western Athletic
Air Force
Brigham Young
Colorado State

Hawaii
New Mexico
San Diego State
Texas-El Paso
Utah
Wyoming

Mid-American
Toledo
Western Michigan
Miami, Ohio
Ball State
Bowling Green
Central Michigan
Eastern Michigan
Kent State
Northern Illinois
Ohio University

Division IA

Independents
Boston College
West Virginia
Florida State
South Carolina
Syracuse
Virginia Tech.
Temple
Penn State
Miami, Florida
Southwest Louisiana
Memphis State
Notre Dame
Southern Mississippi
Pittsburgh
Rutgers
Tulane
Louisville
East Carolina

Missouri Valley
Illinois State
Tulsa
Southern Illinois
Drake
Indiana State
West Texas State
Wichita State

Ohio Valley
Eastern Kentucky
Youngstown State
Akron
Austin Peay
Middle Tennessee
Morehead State
Murray State
Tennessee Tech.

Pacific Coast
Nevada-Las Vegas
San Jose State
Cal State Fullerton
New Mexico State
Fresno State
Long Beach State
Pacific
Utah State

Southern
Western Carolina

Maryland's fullback Alvin Blount avoids the despairing tackles of the Duke defense.

Davidson
Appalachian State
Citadel
East Tennessee State
Furman
Marshall
Tennessee-Chattanooga

Division IAA

Big Sky
Boise State
Idaho
Idaho State
Montana
Montana State
Nevada-Reno
Northern Arizona
Weber State

Gulf Star
Southwest Texas State
Stephen F. Austin
Sam Houston State
Northwest Louisiana
Southeast Louisiana
Nicholls State

Ivy League
Brown
Columbia
Cornell
Dartmouth
Harvard
Penn
Princeton
Yale

Southland
Arkansas State

Lamar
Louisiana Tech.
McNeese State
North Texas State
Northeast Louisiana
Texas-Arlington

Southwestern
Alcorn State
Jackson State
Southern University
Texas Southern
Grambling
Alabama State
Mississippi Valley State
Prairie View A&M

Yankee
New Hampshire
Maine
Boston University
Connecticut
Massachusetts
Rhode Island

Division IAA

Independents
Tennessee State
Delaware
Cincinnati
William and Mary
Lehigh
Bucknell
Colgate
Richmond
Western Kentucky
Lafayette
Florida A&M

108

The major conferences are the Big Ten, comprising colleges from the northern midwest; the Big Eight, whose teams come predominantly from the farming belt of the midwest (Nebraska and Kansas to name but two); the Pacific Ten Conference, the major universities from the far west; the Southeastern Conference, whose members are located, as the name suggests, in the deep south of the country; the Southwest Conference, with some of the best known teams in the land: Texas, Houston, Arkansas, SMU; the Atlantic Coast Conference, geographically not far from the Southeastern, but with most of the colleges from the Carolinas, Virginia and Georgia; and the Western Athletic Conference, whose biggest college is without doubt the Mormon Brigham Young University, the 1984 National Champions. Other major conferences are the Pacific Coast Athletic Association, the Missouri Valley Conference and, of course, the grandfather of them all the Ivy League, with such distinguished members as Harvard, Princeton, Yale, Brown, Dartmouth and Cornell. The Ivy League has, though, in recent years decided to downgrade its athletic ability and is now rated in football as a division IAA league.

Other important division IAA conferences are the Big Sky, Ohio Valley, Southern, Mid-Continent, Mid-Eastern and the Yankee.

Below this grade of football are the smaller divisions II and III conferences, normally situated within one or two states. Some of the titles of these conferences are quite delightful. Lone Star, Rocky Mountain and Little Three are amongst their number with quaintly named colleges like Slippery Rock, Wooster, Bowie State and Kutztown.

At this end of the scale really small-town football is to be found; most of these colleges only have two or three thousand students, whereas some of the giants of the division 1A circuit will have an enrolment in excess of 40 000.

But whatever the size, every August over 50 000 young men the length and breadth of the USA are going through the pain barrier in an attempt to lift their Alma Mater to glory and fame.

The Bowl Games

Every year the major college teams vie for places in the 18 Bowl games that currently take place around the country. In late November and early December the scouts from the various bowl organizations travel the land signing up the best teams in the country to play in the games, which usually start the week before Christmas.

A trip to a Bowl game can mean money for a college, and the chance to appear on national TV. In the 1985 Rose Bowl, the teams were paid a staggering $5.6 million in a very different game from that of 1 January 1902 when the University of Michigan played Stanford in the first 'East-West' Bowl game.

The Tournament of Roses had begun in 1890 as a winter floral celebration and parade in Pasadena, California. The first parade took place along the dirt streets of Pasadena and was organized by the local Valley Hunt Club. Flowers grown by local residents adorned the parading horses and carriages. The festival quickly caught the attention of people throughout the nation, and many travelled to the west coast to see the unique parade. Within five years the parade had become so famous and complex that the Valley Hunt Club relinquished its sponsorship to a committee of community leaders who formed the Pasadena Tournament of Roses Association.

At the end of the 1901 season, Michigan was prevailed upon to play Stanford in an 'East-West' game at Tournament Park. The contest took place on 1 January 1902, and Michigan won by a score of 49–0. The game was played on a 110-yard field and 8000 spectators turned out to watch this very first Bowl game.

In 1903 polo replaced football as the sports attraction, but lured a crowd of only 2000 people. So in 1904 the tournament decided to introduce chariot races. These were very popular and the 1915 event attracted 25 000 spectators. Eventually interest dwindled and in view of this fact, and the high cost of staging the races, the tournament committee decided to return to football as its main attraction for 1916.

During the 1929 Rose Bowl in which California's Roy Riegels became famous for his wrong-way run, the ball burst. On a quick California kick the air went completely out of the ball during its flight and it fell to the ground like a pancake, denying the Bears much needed ground in the battle with Georgia Tech.

President Gerald Ford was center and captain of Michigan University in the mid 1930s. In 1934 he was voted their most valuable player. He played in the annual college all-star game but chose not to enter into the professional ranks, opting for a brilliant political career instead.

Other famous presidents of the gridiron include John F. Kennedy, who played for Harvard as an end; Franklin D. Roosevelt, who captained Harvard's freshman team in 1900; Dwight D. Eisenhower, who played for Army until he broke a leg against the Carlisle Indians on 12 November 1912; and although President Ronald Reagan played only prep-school football, he achieved fame when he played Notre Dame's legendary George Gipp in a 1940 Warner Brothers film. Reagan sped some 50 yards downfield for a touchdown, where he bounced the ball on the ground, and became the very first player to spike a football in the end-zone.

Southern California has long been famous for its temperate climate, but the 1916 Bowl game was hit by a rain storm and the game between Washington State and Brown University was played in atrocious conditions as the Cougars became the first western winners, defeating Brown 14–0.

In 1918 the country was at war and college football was virtually non-existent. However, a game was arranged between two military teams: the Mare Island Marines and Camp Lewis Army. President Woodrow Wilson approved the game and all the profits were handed over to the Red Cross. For the record the Marines won the game 19–7, largely thanks to Hollis Hunington, who had played for Oregon in 1917. Hollis ran for 111 yards and was named player of the game.

The 1919 game was a similar affair to that of the previous year. Great Lakes Navy travelled out west and handed a 17–0 defeat to the Mare Island Marines. One of the stars that day was a certain George Halas, who ran a 45-yard pass for the final touchdown. Halas was later to become one of the founding fathers of the NFL.

The 1920 bowl game between Harvard and Oregon attracted a capacity crowd of 30 000 fans paying a mere 65 cents for their seats, and because of the success of the event, the City of San Diego decided to inaugurate its own bowl. Called the Christmas Classic, the first game took place on Boxing Day 1921 when Center, a small college from Danville, Kentucky, walloped a lack-lustre Arizona team 38–0.

The Christmas Classic only lasted that one year though. Crippling financial problems forced the premature death of the only other bowl game to challenge the Pasadena 'East-West' event.

In 1923 the new Rosebowl stadium was officially opened and the 'East-West' bowl was given its new name.

In the first game played in the new stadium, the University of Southern California, a late replacement for California, which had declined the invitation, beat Penn State 14–3.

The Nittany Lions arrived 45 minutes late for the game due to a traffic jam and the game was concluded in moonlight as sportwriters struck matches to complete their stories.

The 1925 Rosebowl classic was the confrontation the country wanted to see: Notre Dame vs. Stanford; the Four Horsemen vs. Ernie Nevers; Knute Rockne vs. Pop Warner. Although Pop Warner's Cardinals won the battle of the statistics—beating Notre Dame in virtually every offensive category—the Irish, led superbly by Rockne, capitalized on Stanford's mistakes and came out on top on the scoreboard.

Stanford's Ernie Nevers, recovering from two broken ankles, rushed for 114 yards but Elmer Layden's three touchdowns for Notre Dame proved the decisive factor. Another of the fabled horsemen quartet, Harry Stuhl-dreher, actually broke his ankle early in the game, but despite the painful injury continued to play in what proved to be the Indiana college's finest hour.

The 1929 game produced one of the most famous bone-headed moves in history. California center Roy Riegels picked up a Georgia Tech fumble on the Tech's 20-yard line. In those days a fumble could be advanced, so Riegels then proceeded to race down the pitch, but in the wrong direction, towards his own goal! As his teammates blocked fiercely, Cal's Benny Lom saw the mistake and chased Riegels down on his own one-yard line. In the next play, Lom's punt was blocked by Georgia and a two point safety resulted that won the game 8–7. The play, one of the most bizarre in all football history, brought the capacity 53 000 crowd to their feet. Riegels was later to explain that he had thought that the noise he had heard was the fans yelling encouragement!

Riegels' mistake gained him overnight fame. He received a proposal of marriage in which the couple would walk up the aisle and not down, and daft sponsorship ideas were put forward like an upside-down cake and a new necktie with the stripes the wrong way round.

Despite the Depression, the 1930s saw the emergence of new games to rival the Rose. El Paso, Pittsburgh and New York tried to stage games in 1931, but as in San Diego, their games did not go as planned, and financial problems once again forced their abandonment.

It was not until 1935 that the Rosebowl received worthy competition. The newly-completed Orange Bowl Stadium in Miami decided to stage its own east coast game, and in that year on New Year's Day the Orange Bowl game was born. The neighbouring state of Louisiana was also preparing for a new Bowl game. New Orleans, a city already known for its *Mardi Gras* festivities, inaugurated the Sugar Bowl on 1 January 1935. Playing in Tulane Stadium, the local Tulane University beat Temple 20–14.

Bowl fever had once again hit the nation, and two years later football-mad Texas at last got the formula right with their own festival of football. The Cotton Bowl was designed to add attraction to the annual state fair in Dallas and almost overnight became a hit.

Football went to Cuba in 1937 when the first and only Bacardi Bowl was staged in Havana. Organized by the Cuban National Festival it was the first major game to have been played outside the USA.

During the Second World War the major Bowl games continued to thrive, and it was in 1942 that the Orange Bowl came of age. The first seven games in Miami had failed to attract the big college teams, and until 1942 the Bowl was a confrontation between small schools.

'A pro game is motion. A college game is emotion.' Bob Zuppke

'Football is all very well as a game for rough girls, but it's hardly suitable for delicate boys.' Oscar Wilde

---

Arizona State's quarterback Jeff van Raaphorst led his school to its first ever Rose Bowl victory in 1986. (Fotosports International).

That year also saw a change of venue for the Rosebowl. Because of a threatened Japanese air attack on the US mainland, the game was switched to Durham, North Carolina. The game between Oregon State and the local Duke University was a sell-out three days after the tickets went on sale. A total of 56 000 crammed into the Durham Stadium to watch the west coast team beat Duke 20–16 on a 68-yard pass from quarterback Bob Dethman to Gene Gray.

After the war a new era began at the Pasadena-based Rose. Until then a western team was always invited to participate by the tournament committee, then the western university would itself select its opponents. In 1946 the two conferences, the old Pacific Coast (now the Pacific Ten) and the Big Ten selected their own competing teams. In 1947 and 1948 Bowl hysteria hit football. Overnight games came and went as every city in the country wanted to stage their own version. San Antonio in Texas staged the Alamo Bowl in 1947, and in California Fresno held the Raisin Bowl. There were Grape Bowls, Dixie Bowls, Delta Bowls, even the Salad Bowl in Phoenix, Arizona.

Of the 15 or so Bowl games inaugurated during this period, only two remain today. The Gator Bowl in Jacksonville, Florida and the Tangerine Bowl across state in Orlando. Beginning, as the Orange had done, with small town colleges and even with high schools, these two Bowl games now attract some of the best college teams in the division IA ranks. The Bluebonnet Bowl in Houston, Texas started life in 1959 as did the Liberty Bowl. The Liberty is one of the most travelled of all bowls. It started in Philadelphia in 1959 then moved to Atlantic City in 1964, before settling down for good in Memphis, Tennessee the following year. With the inevitable TV coverage, the 1960s saw the establishment of many more Bowl games, until today there are 18 major Bowls for division IA teams.

There are Bowl games as well for division IAA and division II and III colleges. Until recently the division III championship game was known as the 'Amos Alonzo Stagg' Bowl, after one of the founding fathers of football.

Bowl games attract huge attendances. The annual Rosebowl classic is a sell-out every year, with over 100 000 fans packed into the Pasadena stadium, and the same is true of the other three 'big' Bowl games: the Orange, Sugar, and Cotton, which all receive enormous patronage.

The TV coverage of these games is not only financially beneficial, it also gives the players a national audience for their skills.

Because of the time zones it is possible, by switching channels, to watch all four of the major Bowl games on New Year's Day.

The Orange Bowl has a tendency to try and match up the country's top two teams, and in recent years with the appearance of Nebraska, Miami, Oklahoma and Penn State it has achieved National Championship status. The Sugar Bowl is region-proud and puts together the champions of the southeast with one of the other major local teams. The Cotton Bowl like the Sugar matches the champions of the Southwest Conference with another of the top colleges across the USA. The University of Texas, which is one of the teams most often selected, has taken part in the Cotton 18 times, winning on 10 occasions. For some unknown reason the Cotton Bowl produces some of the closest battles in college history. Because of the number of Bowl games now being played (there are 18 in all), many observers feel that the status of the Bowl has been reduced, but

in today's money-go-round of football fantasia, the colleges find the Bowl circuit very attractive.

College Bowl Records

Alabama, The Nation's No 1 Bowl Team

Alabama has appeared in more Bowl games (38), than any other team in collegiate football.

Its 1983 Sun Bowl victory equalled USC's record of 20 victories in Bowl games.

The Crimson Tide's 29 appearances in the four major Bowls (the Rose, Sugar, Cotton and Orange) also places them top of the college teams. Alabama is the only team to have won all four major Bowl games twice. The following is a listing of the nation's top twenty Bowl teams according to the number of games played up to (1986):

Team	No. of games	All Bowls W L T	Big Four W L T
1 Alabama	38	21 14 3	17 11 1
2 Texas	32	15 15 2	12 9 1
3 USC	29	21 8 0	18 6 0
4 Tennessee	27	13 14 0	5 9 0
5 Oklahoma	26	17 8 1	14 5 0
6 Georgia	25	10 13 2	7 9 1
7 Louisiana State	25	11 12 2	7 6 0
8 Nebraska	24	13 11 0	8 9 0
9 Georgia Tech.	23	15 8 0	9 3 0
10 Penn State	23	14 7 2	6 5 1
11 Arkansas	22	9 10 3	4 7 1
12 Mississippi	21	11 10 0	6 6 0
13 Ohio State	20	10 10 0	6 8 0
14 Missouri	19	8 11 0	2 5 0
15 Auburn	18	9 8 1	2 3 0
16 Pittsburgh	16	7 9 0	3 5 0
17 Michigan	16	6 10 0	5 8 0
18 Texas Tech.	16	3 12 1	0 1 0
19 Florida	15	7 8 0	1 2 0
20 North Carolina	15	6 9 0	0 3 0

College Bowl results 1986

California Bowl – San Jose State	37–7	Miami, Ohio
Liberty Bowl – Tennessee	21–14	Minnesota
Hall of Fame Bowl – Boston	27–24	Georgia
Gator Bowl – Clemson	27–21	Stanford
Aloha Bowl – Arizona	30–21	North Carolina
Sun Bowl – Alabama	28–6	Washington
Independence Bowl – Mississippi	20–17	Texas Tech.
Holiday Bowl – Iowa	39–38	San Diego
Bluebonnet Bowl – Baylor	21–9	Colorado
Freedom Bowl – UCLA	31–10	Brigham Young
Peach Bowl – Virginia Tech.	25–24	North Carolina State
All-American Bowl – Florida State	27–13	Indiana
Orange Bowl – Oklahoma	42–8	Arkansas
Sugar Bowl – Nebraska	30–15	LSU
Cotton Bowl – Ohio State	28–12	Texas A & M
Rose Bowl – Arizona State	22–15	Michigan
Florida Citrus Bowl – Auburn	16–7	USC
Fiesta Bowl – Penn State	14–10	Miami

Bowl Games No Longer With Us

Alamo (San Antonio, Texas); 1947
Aviation (Dayton, Ohio); 1961
Bacardi (Havana, Cuba); 1937
Bluegrass (Louisville, Kentucky); 1958
Camelia (Lafayette, Louisiana); 1948
Charity (New York); 1930–31
Charity (El Paso, Texas); 1933
Charity (Pittsburgh, Pennsylvania); 1931
Christmas (Los Angeles, California); 1924
Christmas (San Diego, California); 1921–22
Delta (Memphis, Tennessee); 1948–49
Dixie Classic (Dallas, Texas); 1922 and 1925
Fort Worth Classic (Fort Worth, Texas); 1922
Garden State (East Rutherford, New Jersey); 1978–81
Gotham (New York); 1961–62
Grape (Lodi, California); 1947–48
Great Lakes (Cleveland, Ohio); 1947
Harbor (San Diego, California); 1947–49
Mercy (Los Angeles, California); 1961
Oil (Houston, Texas); 1946–47
Pasadena (Pasadena, California); 1967 and 1969–70
Presidential Cup (College Park, Maryland); 1950
Raisin (Fresno, California); 1946–49
Salad (Phoenix, Arizona); 1948–52
Shrine (Little Rock, Arkansas); 1948

Most Bowl Appearances
Alabama 38
Texas 32
USC 29
Tennessee 27
Oklahoma 26
Georgia 25
Louisiana State 25

Best Bowl Record
USC with 21 wins, 8 losses in 29 appearances

Worst Bowl Record
Iowa State and Utah State with 4 defeats in 4 appearances.

Rick Fenney, Washington Huskie's fullback.

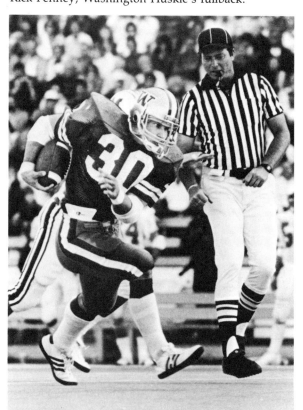

National Champions from 1936

1936 Minnesota	1961 Alabama
1937 Pittsburgh	1962 USC
1938 Texas Christian	1963 Texas
1939 Texas A&M	1964 Alabama
1940 Minnesota	1965 Alabama
1941 Minnesota (UP)	1966 Notre Dame
1942 Ohio State (UP)	1967 USC
1943 Notre Dame (UP)	1968 Ohio State
1944 Army (UP)	1969 Texas
1945 Army (UP)	1970 Nebraska
1946 Notre Dame (NFF)	1971 Nebraska
1947 Notre Dame (NFF)	1972 USC
1948 Michigan (NFF)	1973 Notre Dame
1949 Notre Dame (NFF)	1974 Oklahoma
1950 Oklahoma	1975 Oklahoma
1951 Tennessee	1976 Pittsburgh
1952 Michigan State	1977 Notre Dame
1953 Maryland	1978 Alabama
1954 Ohio State	1979 Alabama
1955 Oklahoma	1980 Georgia
1956 Oklahoma	1981 Clemson
1957 Auburn	1982 Penn State
1958 Louisiana State	1983 Miami, Florida
1959 Syracuse	1984 Brigham Young
1960 Minnesota	1985 Oklahoma
	1986 Penn State

National Champions

Every season all the newspapers and journalists throughout the land hold their own weekly polls to see which college is given top rating. At the end of the season, usually sometime in late December, the sportswriters get together in a national poll organized by the Associated Press and vote for their top team of the year.

Occasionally this poll will be put off until after the New Year's Day Bowl games and sometimes the results of these games will determine who carries the mantle of America's No 1 college.

The first poll took place way back in 1936, when Minnesota won the crown. During the war years (1941–45), the United Press took a poll of football coaches to determine the winners and from 1946–49 the National Football Foundation undertook the role. These bodies have in recent years revived their ballots but the Associated Press poll still stands as the best guide to the National Champions.

The Heisman Trophy

The John W. Heisman Memorial Trophy is presented each year to the outstanding college football player by the Downtown Athletic Club of New York.

Originally known as the DAC Trophy, the award was renamed in 1936 after John W.

Heisman, the first athletic director of the Downtown Athletic Club, a football player for Penn State and Brown University, and a coach for 36 years at Auburn, Oberlin, Clemson, Akron, Penn State, Rice, Washington and Jefferson and Georgia Tech.

The bronze trophy was sculpted by Frank Eliscu, with the advice of one of Notre Dame's famous 'Four Horsemen', Jim Crowley, by then coaching at Fordham University in New York.

The first winner of the prized award was Chicago University's halfback Jay Berwanger in 1935. A year later it was Berwanger who again wrote his name into the record books by being selected as the first choice in the NFL's inaugural draft.

The award is made to college football's player of the year, but it is interesting to note that only twice has the prize gone to a lineman, and then not an interior one. In 1936 Yale's end Larry Kelley won and in 1949 Notre Dame's star end Leon Hart was chosen.

Boston College's talented quarterback Doug Flutie became the fiftieth recipient in 1984, but only 14 quarterbacks have ever won the award, the majority of triumphs belonging to running backs.

Since its inception Notre Dame players have won the award more times than any other

1986 Heisman Trophy winner, Vinny Testaverde.

college with six winners: quarterback Angelo Bertelli in 1943, quarterback John Lujack in 1947, end Leon Hart in 1949, halfback John Lattner in 1953, quarterback Paul Hornung in 1956 (Hornung later went on to become a star

Winners of the Heisman Trophy

Year	Player	Position	College
1935	Jay Berwanger	Halfback	Chicago
1936	Larry Kelley	End	Yale
1937	Clint Frank	Halfback	Yale
1938	Davey O'Brien	Quarterback	Texas Christian
1939	Nile Kinnick	Halfback	Iowa
1940	Tom Harmon	Halfback	Michigan
1941	Bruce Smith	Halfback	Minnesota
1942	Frank Sinkwich	Halfback	Georgia
1943	Angelo Bertelli	Quarterback	Notre Dame
1944	Les Horvath	Halfback	Ohio State
1945	Doc Blanchard	Fullback	Army
1946	Glenn Davis	Halfback	Army
1947	John Lujack	Quarterback	Notre Dame
1948	Doak Walker	Halfback	Southern Methodist
1949	Leon Hart	End	Notre Dame
1950	Vic Janowicz	Halfback	Ohio State
1951	Dick Kazmaier	Halfback	Princeton
1952	Billy Vessels	Halfback	Oklahoma
1953	John Lattner	Halfback	Notre Dame
1954	Alan Ameche	Fullback	Wisconsin
1955	Howard Cassady	Halfback	Ohio State
1956	Paul Hornung	Quarterback	Notre Dame
1957	John Crow	Halfback	Texas A&M
1958	Pete Dawkins	Halfback	Army
1959	Billy Cannon	Halfback	Louisiana State
1960	Joe Bellino	Halfback	Navy
1961	Ernie Davis	Halfback	Syracuse
1962	Terry Baker	Quarterback	Oregon State
1963	Roger Staubach	Quarterback	Navy
1964	John Huarte	Quarterback	Notre Dame
1965	Mike Garrett	Tailback	USC
1966	Steve Spurrier	Quarterback	Florida
1967	Gary Beban	Quarterback	UCLA
1968	O. J. Simpson	Tailback	USC
1969	Steve Owens	Halfback	Oklahoma
1970	Jim Plunkett	Quarterback	Stanford
1971	Pat Sullivan	Quarterback	Auburn
1972	Johnny Rodgers	Flanker	Nebraska
1973	John Cappelletti	Halfback	Penn State
1974	Archie Griffin	Halfback	Ohio State
1975	Archie Griffin	Halfback	Ohio State
1976	Tony Dorsett	Tailback	Pittsburgh
1977	Earl Campbell	Tailback	Texas
1978	Billy Sims	Halfback	Oklahoma
1979	Charles White	Tailback	USC
1980	George Rogers	Halfback	South Carolina
1981	Marcus Allen	Tailback	USC
1982	Herschel Walker	Tailback	Georgia
1983	Mike Rozier	Tailback	Nebraska
1984	Doug Flutie	Quarterback	Boston College
1985	Bo Jackson	Halfback	Auburn
1986	Vinny Testaverde	Quarterback	Miami, Florida

running back with the Green Bay Packers), and John Huarte, the Fighting Irish quarterback of 1964, who was their last winner.

The college with the next highest number of winners is the University of Southern California who are represented by some of the best known names in football today: Mike Garrett, O. J. Simpson, Charles White and Marcus Allen in 1965, 1968, 1979, and 1981 respectively.

The Heisman Trophy is without doubt the biggest single award a college player can receive, and as multi-million dollar contracts are offered to the winners, the announcement of the results every December is awaited with bated breath.

The Outland Trophy

The Outland Trophy is presented each year to the outstanding interior lineman in collegiate football by the Football Writers' Association of America.

The award was first presented in 1946 to Notre Dame's talented tackle George Connor, and has been greatly prized by the 40 footballers who have won it since.

Because of its similarity to the Lombardi Award many winners have won both in the same year, but nevertheless the Outland Trophy is one of the highest honours in college football a lineman can receive.

Winners have included: Merlin Olsen, who later starred for the Los Angeles Rams and after retiring from football became a movie star and sports TV presenter; Randy White, Dallas Cowboys' defensive tackle who won the Super Bowl XII MVP award as part of the now famous 'Doomsday II' defense; and Tommy Nobis, the Texas All-American who won it for his play both ways—as a guard and a middle linebacker.

The Lombardi Award

The Lombardi Award was instituted in 1970 by the Rotary Club of Houston. It was set up as a memorial to the legendary Vince Lombardi who played as guard for Fordham University from 1934 to 1936.

The Lombardi Award is presented annually to the country's best lineman and, like the Heisman, it is of vital importance, as the winners can almost guarantee themselves a money-spinning career in professional football.

Winners of the Outland Trophy

1946	George Connor	Tackle	Notre Dame
1947	Joe Steffy	Guard	Army
1948	Bill Fischer	Guard	Notre Dame
1949	Ed Badgon	Guard	Michigan State
1950	Bob Gain	Tackle	Kentucky
1951	Jim Weatherall	Tackle	Oklahoma
1952	Dick Modzelewski	Tackle	Maryland
1953	J. D. Roberts	Guard	Arkansas
1954	Bill Brooks	Guard	Arkansas
1955	Calvin Jones	Guard	Iowa
1956	Jim Parker	Guard	Ohio State
1957	Alex Karras	Tackle	Iowa
1958	Zeke Smith	Guard	Auburn
1959	Mike McGhee	Tackle	Duke
1960	Tom Brown	Guard	Minnesota
1961	Merlin Olsen	Tackle	Utah State
1962	Bobby Bell	Tackle	Minnesota
1963	Scott Appleton	Tackle	Texas
1964	Steve DeLong	Tackle	Tennessee
1965	Tommy Nobis	Linebacker	Texas
1966	Lloyd Phillips	Defensive Tackle	Arkansas
1967	Ron Yary	Offensive Tackle	USC
1968	Bill Stanfill	Defensive Tackle	Georgia
1969	Mike Reid	Defensive Tackle	Penn State
1970	Jim Stillwagon	Middle Guard	Ohio State
1971	Larry Jacobsen	Defensive Tackle	Nebraska
1972	Rich Glover	Middle Guard	Nebraska
1973	John Hicks	Offensive Tackle	Ohio State
1974	Randy White	Defensive Tackle	Maryland
1975	Leroy Selmon	Defensive Tackle	Oklahoma
1976	Ross Browner	Defensive End	Notre Dame
1977	Brad Shearer	Defensive Tackle	Texas
1978	Greg Roberts	Guard	Oklahoma
1979	Jim Richter	Center	North Carolina State
1980	Mark May	Offensive Tackle	Pittsburgh
1981	Dave Rimington	Center	Nebraska
1982	Dave Rimington	Center	Nebraska
1983	Dean Steinkuhler	Offensive Guard	Nebraska
1984	Bruce Smith	Defensive End	Virginia Tech.
1985	Mike Ruth	Defensive Tackle	Boston College
1986	Jason Buck	Defensive Tackle	Brighan Young

Winners of the Lombardi Award

1970	Jim Stillwagon	Middle Guard	Ohio State
1971	Walt Patulski	Defensive End	Notre Dame
1972	Rich Glover	Middle Guard	Nebraska
1973	John Hicks	Offensive Tackle	Ohio State
1974	Randy White	Defensive Tackle	Maryland
1975	Leroy Selmon	Defensive Tackle	Oklahoma
1976	Wilson Whitley	Defensive Tackle	Houston
1977	Ross Browner	Defensive End	Notre Dame
1978	Bruce Clark	Defensive Tackle	Penn State
1979	Brad Budde	Offensive Guard	USC
1980	Hugh Green	Defensive End	Pittsburgh
1981	Kenneth Sims	Defensive Tackle	Texas
1982	Dave Rimington	Center	Nebraska
1983	Dean Steinkuhler	Offensive Guard	Nebraska
1984	Tony Dregate	Defensive Tackle	Texas
1985	Tony Castillas	Defensive Tackle	Oklahoma
1986	Cornelius Bennett	Linebacker	Alabama

'Football is like committee meetings, called huddles, separated by outbursts of violence.'
George Will

MERLIN OLSEN

Late in 1967, the Los Angeles Rams found themselves in a crucial game with Green Bay, trailing 24–20 with less than two minutes to play and with the Packers in possession.

The Rams' devastating defensive line renowned as the 'Fearsome Foursome' took over. For three straight plays they stopped the Packers cold and then blocked the fourth down punt at the Packers five-yard line. The Los Angeles team then took over the ball and scored the winning touchdown on the next play.

A week later in the divisional championship game against Baltimore, the Fearsome Foursome sacked Johnny Unitas seven times and forced two interceptions as the Rams went on to win 34–10.

Throughout those years the leader of the gang was a quiet, unpretentious but deadly effective defensive tackle, Merlin Olsen.

In a career that spanned 15 years, the All-American from Utah State was one of the most widely lauded defensive stars. His reputation for excellence did not die with his retirement in 1976. Proof enough today in the fact that he is now one of the anchormen for NBC TV sport and presented Super Bowl XX from New Orleans in January 1986.

George Allen, who coached the Rams between 1966–70, summarized his star tackle's contribution when he said, 'We never had a bad game from Merlin Olsen. You always got a good game from Oly and more often than not you got a great one.'

Allen's opinion was shared by all who saw him play. The league's coaches named him to the Pro Bowl a record 14 straight years. He was a unanimous All-NFL selection for five consecutive years during the heyday of the fearsome foursome act from 1966–70. Then as if to prove he could excel on his own, he earned universal All-NFC acclaim in 1973.

Olsen's selection in the first round of the draft of 1962 proved to be an instant hit. He won the starting tackle's job in the third week of the season and never looked back.

Early in his rookie season Olsen found that sheer brute strength was not as important as in high school or in college football. 'A good defensive lineman has to be part charging buffalo and part ballet dancer,' he once explained. 'And he has to know when to be which. It's more an emotional state and an ability to concentrate. If you haven't those, you can't generate the horsepower to make the right things happen.'

When Merlin Olsen was around though, things did happen. The Fearsome Foursome

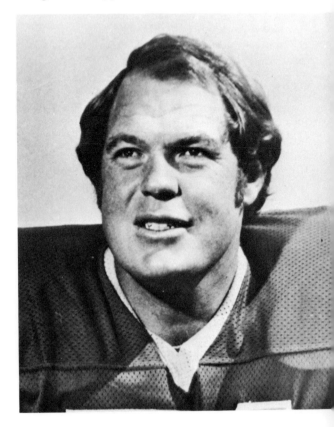

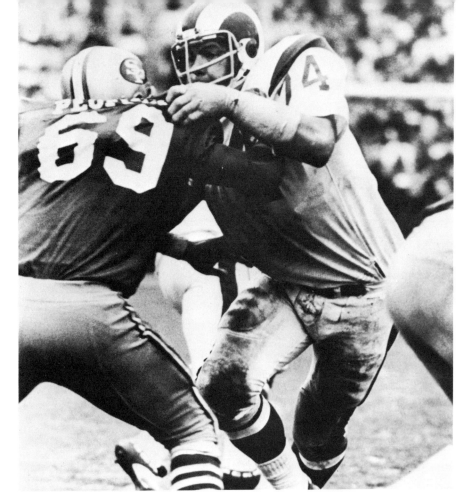

was not yet formed when Merlin joined the Rams in 1962 but, within two years, the components of one of history's finest defensive units were on hand. David (Deacon) Jones, who preceded Olsen into the Pro Football Hall of Fame in 1980, was at left end with Rosie Grier at right tackle and Lamar Lundy at right end. And it was Merlin who accepted the responsibility of forming all of these talents into one frighteningly devastating team.

Olsen and Jones became firm friends both on and off the field, despite their different backgrounds—Jones a southern black and Olsen a Mormon from Utah. Jones was noisy, Olsen quiet. Jones was the spectacular one, Olsen steady, but they made a great team. 'I think one of the reasons that Deacon and I played so well together was that we were close personally,' Olsen reminisced years later. 'He knew what to expect from me and I from him.'

At high school, Olsen was one of the biggest, so to take advantage of his size, his coach made him a tackle and that is where the legend began. He could have played for virtually any college, but opted to stay in his home state and with the hometown school, Utah State. In spite of the college's little known football programme, Merlin's reputation soon spread. He made some All-America teams as a junior and most of them as a senior, winning the 1961 Outland Trophy that goes to the nation's top lineman. A grand slam of appearances followed in the East-West Shrine game, the Hula Bowl and the Chicago College All-Star Game.

It was to the Rams that the young Olsen went and made a name for himself and throughout his career merged his superb physical talents with a thinking man's approach to the games—an ideal that is evident today on NBC TV. Once he took umbrage when a vice presidential candidate likened the incumbent president's financial advisers to a 'big, slow, dull-witted lineman.'

With a masters degree in finance, Merlin Olsen was a far cry from such a description. He was big, but never slow or dull-witted. He was mentally and physically one of the finest defensive tackles ever to play professional football.

117

4   Canada

If you had not already been told, you wouldn't know whether you were watching Canadian or the United States version of football.

One team is lined up against the other, one has a football, the other is trying to take it away. The crushing of players' heavy bodies contrasts with the quick dancing feet of others; the football is flung into the air by one player and caught by another; a heap of bodies, then an orderly line-up again.

Soon it dawns on you. Each team has 12 players on the field; the punter comes on to the field in a third-down situation; an opponent catches the punted ball; he is tackled in the endzone and the referee signals one point for the punting team.

This is Canadian football: 12 men on the field; 3 downs instead of four; 1 yard between the teams on the line of scrimmage instead of their being nose to nose; 25-yard endzones instead of 10; backfielders in motion in any direction before the ball is snapped; each quarter ending with a play instead of running down the clock; no scrimmaging of the ball within a yard of either goal; a single point or rouge scorable on a punt, a missed field goal or a kickoff.

Tacklers may not go within five yards of a punt returner until he has touched the ball, and there is no such thing as a 'fair catch', except that a returner may ground the ball in his own endzone to concede a single point.

One of the main differences between Canadian and American football is apparent at first glance. The Canadian field is huge by comparison, measuring 10 400 sq. yd, compared to the 6400 sq. yd that make up a field in the USA. About half of the 40 000 sq. yd difference is made up in the two end-zones. In Canada the endzone is 25yd deep. Overall, a Canadian football field measures 110yd from goal line to goal line, whilst its American counterpart is only 100yd long. The Canadian field is 65yd wide whilst the US version is 53yd 1ft wide.

Because players love to corner a larger area, speed and agility are the prerequisite of the Canadian game, particularly in defensive players who have an additional 11yd 2ft to cover on wide sweeps.

In Canadian football the hashmarkings are placed 24yd from each side-line, leaving a 17-yd gap down the middle of the field. In American football the hashmarks are placed directly in line with the goalposts. For field goal kickers this means that in the USA the kicker has an almost straight kick, but in Canada the kicker could be up to five yards outside the goalposts.

Origins

The Canadian Football League, as it is today, broke loose from the amateur Canadian Rugby Union (CRU) in 1958 to shape its own destiny. But the true history of the game in maple leaf country can be traced back as far as the American version. It could even be said that the American game derived from Canada.

On 15 May 1874 students from Montreal's McGill University travelled over the border to play a friendly game with the students of Harvard. Until then both colleges had been practising a version of rugby union, but because four members of the Canadian team were ill and didn't travel, the scheduled 15-a-side game became a match between teams of

British Columbia Lions were the last team to join the CFL in 1954. Winnipeg, Saskatchewan and Calgary began life in 1933, whilst the eastern division teams first played together as a league in 1907.

11 men. If those four Chinooks had travelled to Harvard, the game as we know it today might have been played with 15 men.

In 1891 the CRU became the sport's first governing body and set about drawing up the rules of the game. Teams in Quebec and Ontario had been playing according to rules which were slightly different from those of other provinces, and the CRU had a tough time sorting the matter out. Ontario actually left the Union from 1886–91 in protest.

In 1907 the first league was set up in the east of the country when Montreal, Ottawa, Toronto and Hamilton formed the Interprovincial Rugby Football Union. The Governor General of Canada, Earl Grey, donated a cup to the fledgling league in 1909. The Grey Cup was open to all amateur rugby clubs and the first to win it in that year was the University of Toronto.

In 1921 a major change in the rules radically altered the face of Canadian football. Until then 14 players had been used by both teams on the field of play, but the number was now reduced to 12, one more than in American football, the extra player being in the backfield. Until this date the ball had been heeled back to the quarterback in rugby league style, but in accordance with another new rule the center now had to snap the ball backwards in the style known today.

The year 1921 also saw the emergence, albeit briefly, of the western teams. The Edmonton Eskimos became the first western team to compete in the Grey Cup final. The Eskimos lost 23–0 to the powerful Toronto Argonauts but the match was a clear indication that football, Canadian style, was spreading.

The forward pass was adopted in western Canada in 1929 and throughout the nation in 1931.

With the growth of the American game south of the border, more and more teams began to import players. The limit to the numbers allowed at the end of the Second World War was five per team, although nowadays up to 15 are allowed in a total squad of 34.

The Montreal Concordes were originally called the 'Alouettes' (Larks).

It was Calgary's Jerry Sieberling who threw the first legal forward pass in Canadian football in 1929.

1986 Grey Cup offensive star Mike Kerrigan.

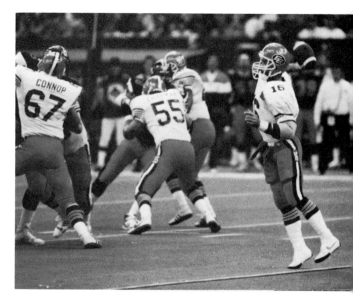
Edmonton quarterback Matt Dunigan.

Football in Canada was becoming more of a national game. The teams in the west, whose history can be traced back to the 1920s and 1930s, were beginning to catch up with their eastern giants. Winnipeg Blue Bombers became the first western team to win the Grey Cup in 1935.

By 1954 the members of the western division had risen to five with the inclusion of the British Columbia Lions from Vancouver.

In 1956 the Canadian Football Council (CFL) was formed to amalgamate the three different leagues: the western, the eastern, and the pirate Ontario Rugby Football Union. Two years later the Canadian Football League was born and since then football north of the 49th parallel has grown into one of the top spectator sports with huge crowds and national TV coverage.

Canadian football begins its season in the first weekend in July and runs through to the end of November when the Grey Cup final is contested. Each team in the nine-club, two-division league plays the others twice to find the four participants for the playoff semi-finals.

The CFL at last came of age in 1983 when football was rated the country's second most popular sport behind ice hockey, a total of 3 million people buying tickets for games.

Canadian football is certainly progressing. After giving birth to the American version, the CFL's rather unique brand of football is at last catching up with the more universally acclaimed NFL game.

The Immigrants

In today's very professional CFL nearly half of every team's squad is made up of American players. The CFL allows 15 of a team's 34-man squad to be American players. The other 19 players must be of Canadian origin.

This level has fluctuated over the years, but Canada has seen many top players use their league as a launching pad to further success and stardom in the richer playgrounds of the NFL.

One such player who is now known throughout the football world, but began his pro career in the CFL, is Washington Redskins' quarterback Joe Theismann. Theismann graduated from Notre Dame in 1971 and moved north to play for the Toronto Argonauts. Other ex-Argonauts are Ohio State's Outland Trophy winner Jim Stillwagon, and quarterback Bernie Faloney from Maryland.

The Edmonton Eskimos have in recent years been a force to be reckoned with, mainly because of a coach and a quarterback now making their mark in the NFL with Houston Oilers. The coach in question is Hugh Campbell, and the quarterback is Warren Moon. With their assistance the Eskimos won the coveted Grey Cup in 1978, 1979, 1980, 1981 and 1982.

Another American legend in the coaching field made his mark in Canada, and entered its folklore long before his theories were tried and tested in Minnesota. Bud Grant spent ten years in charge of the Winnipeg Blue Bombers before moving over the border. In those ten

Hamilton's defense stop quarterback Matt Dunigan.

Paul Osbaldiston tied a CFL record with 6 field goals in the 1986 Grey Cup game.

years he won them four Grey Cups and numerous other awards, as well as being inducted into the CFL Hall of Fame. Every year the CFL unearths a future star for the NFL of the USA.

The famed University of Texas coach Darrell Royal began his head coaching career in Edmonton, Canada.

What's the difference

	America	Canada
No of players	11 men on the field, 45 kitted and ready to play	12 men on the field, 34 kitted and ready to play
Size of field	100yd × 53yd 1 ft plut two 10-yd end-zones	110yd × 65yd plus two 24-yd end zones

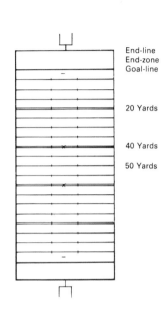

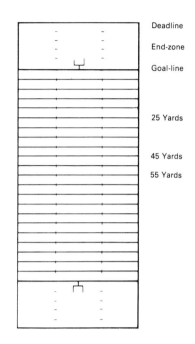

Downs	Four downs to make 10 yards	Three downs to make 10 yards
Scoring	Touchdown 6 pts, field goal 3 pts, safety 2 pts, conversion 1 pt	Touchdowns, safeties and field goals all the same. Conversions are one point but are worth two with a pass or run. A single scores one point
Single score	No such thing	One point score when a punt or missed field goal goes into the endzone, is recovered by a defender who is tackled. Also when a punt or missed field goal goes out of bounds through the endzone.
Timing	Four quarters of 15 minutes. Teams get 30 seconds to put ball back in play	Four quarters of 15 minutes. Teams given only 20 seconds between plays but officials allow for more time
Time outs	Each team has three per half	One only is permitted per team per half and must be taken in the last three minutes of that half
Backfield motion	At the snap only one back in the offense can move either backwards or sideways	All backfield players can move in any direction before the snap
Line of scrimmage	The lines should be separated by the length of the ball	The lines must be one yard apart
Kick-offs	From the 35-yard line to start each half	From 45-yard line to start each half or after a touchdown. After conceding a field goal, a team can either kick-off, scrimmage from their 35 or even receive
Punt returning	Punts may roll dead or be received with a fair catch or returned. The ball can't be recovered by the kicking team unless touched by the receiving team. A punt through the endzone is a touchback at the receiving team's 20-yard line	There is no fair catch, all punts must be run back. A returner tackled in the endzone concedes a single. Tacklers must remain five yards away from the receiver until he touches the ball unless they are played 'onside' by the kicker
Penalties	Range from 5 to 15 yards	Start at 5 yards but rise to 25

5 UK and The Rest of The World

Who did actually play the first ever game of football in the UK?

That is a distinction many footballing folk lay claim to. The London Ravens are probably the first 'British' team but 74 years before their historic game against the USAF Chicksands in 1983, two US battleships fought out a bitter battle in front of over 4000 bemused Kentish people at the Stonebridge sports ground, in Northfleet, Kent.

A player called Levy, whose christian name we are never likely to know, was the game's MVP, if there was ever such an award in those early days, as the USS *Georgia* stormed to a convincing 12–0 victory over the USS *Rhode Island*.

After the game, it was reported in the local *Gravesend and Dartford Reporter* (24 December 1910) that over 220 sailors from both ships were entertained by local civic dignitaries.

And, as far as history shows, nothing really happened in this country until after the Second World War.

In the late 1940s and 1950s there were still many thousands of US servicemen stationed in this country and games between army and air force units were commonplace.

Modern football, the stuff we all drool over today, didn't happen until 1982 when the nation's newest TV channel, Channel 4, announced that it was to screen a weekly programme. Public reaction exceeded all expectations and, without doubt, because of the weekly TV diet, the first of many British-based teams began to form.

In London's Hyde Park a team calling themselves the London Ravens practised on a make-shift pitch as, once again, bemused locals walked by. Little did any of them realize that in three years they would be British champions. By the summer of 1983 they had acquired some kit from the USA and the first

WEMBLEY · LONDON · AUGUST 3, 1986

game between a British team and an American one took place at Stamford Bridge, home of Chelsea FC, in July. The Brits' won a moral victory that was to awaken the whole nation. In fact they lost the game 8–0 but their performance encouraged other teams—Birmingham, Manchester and Glasgow—to form.

By the end of the first year there were at least a dozen known teams in existence, and throughout the winter months of 1983 attempts were made to form a national league, but most foundered.

In February 1984 at a meeting at the Post House Hotel, Bedford, 35 teams met to discuss the formation of an association. It was decided at that meeting to reconvene in two weeks time in London where, it was hoped, the first wheels would be set in motion.

At that meeting at the world headquarters at the Boy Scouts movement on 3 March, not one but two leagues were formed. A total of 26 clubs were represented and after a stormy debate seven clubs broke away to form the British American Football Federation (BAFF),

Nottingham quarterback Tony Cope (now with Leicester) hands off to runningback Andy Smith.

with the remaining 19 becoming the American Football League United Kingdom (AFLUK).

That opening season proved interesting. There was no proper league structure and teams played an *ad hoc* schedule with no championship at the season's end. In fact the season never really ended—many teams carried on playing through the winter trying desperately to gain more experience.

Milton Keynes attracted over 7000 paying fans to watch their clash with local rivals, Northampton, in June. A missed field goal with only two seconds left on the clock gave the Bucks victory and cost the Stormbringers their unbeaten record. And, as with any new sport, there were teething problems. Teams couldn't find enough officials, the national press were not interested, unless someone broke a leg, and most likened it to the short-lived skateboard craze of a decade before. A conference in Birmingham, aimed at forming a national sporting body, failed. Unity was a word we all used in theory. Sadly, then, it was never put into practice.

Mike Sheppard, a local Birmingham council official met with AFL's Gerry Hartman and BAFF's Mike Lytton in the Digbeth Halls in Birmingham. The only outcome of the meeting was a third league—UKAFA—with Sheppard as its head.

After one of those meetings, on a dark and dreary day in the Midlands, several members of the AFL and BAFF reconvened to a run-down cafe on the edge of the city's Bull Ring shopping centre to try and find a solution. Drinking mugs of tea and munching bacon sandwiches, they talked for over two hours. The meeting came to an end when the cafe owner decided that he wanted to close. Both sides departed by shaking hands and promising to get together again soon. Sadly it was never to happen.

At the beginning of the 1985 season the AFL had 40 members, all fully equipped to play tackle football and ready to start a gruelling 16-week campaign, while BAFF's membership stood at some 20 clubs, many of which had no equipment at all.

One team, the Heathrow Jets, had tried to cut the exorbitant cost of equipment by manufacturing their own helmets. They immediately gained the dubious nickname of the 'Motor Bike Kids'.

If there was a winner in this ridiculous war of words, it was the AFL. They had more teams and perhaps more importantly better teams with the calibre of the London Ravens who ran through their opposition with the precision of a butcher's knife.

The Ravens were assured a playoff berth as early as week 10. They hadn't been defeated and they weren't going to be. After seeing off Oxford in the quarterfinals they came up against Leicester in the second semifinal of the day. Earlier in the day Streatham had emerged victorious against Birmingham by a narrow 13–12 scoreline.

Many of the fans who had watched that game had sped with haste up the motorway to watch the Panthers–Ravens clash. The small Saffron Lane stadium was packed to the rafters to see the Big Black Shadow rally in the third quarter to win the tie.

Ravens coach that day was Lance Cone, now one of the most respected coaches in British football. 'Leicester gave us one hell of a fright that night,' recalled Cone later. 'It was our toughest game ever, despite the scoreline at the end.'

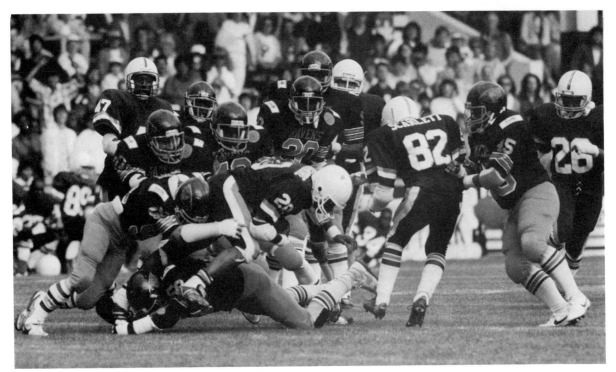

London Ravens vs. Streatham Olympians in the first British championship game held at Aston Villa FC, August 1985.

The final was to be played at Villa Park in Birmingham, but before either team could set foot on the hallowed turf, more renowned for stirring FA Cup semifinals than American football, there was a lot of work to be done.

Thanks to the efforts of a sponsor the final would go ahead. But the league wanted to call it the UK Super Bowl and the NFL in New York gave a polite, 'No'. Eventually, over coffee one morning, the name Summerbowl was agreed upon, and Summerbowl it became.

The game never really lived up to its expectation. The Ravens stormed to a superb 45–7 victory in front of 10 000 fans. Joe St Louis, a London disc jockey, won the MVP award after a 70-yard waltz that left a trail of Olympian players in his wake. All in all, as many who were there can testify, the event was the best yet seen in British football. (The fact that it took six league officials almost eight weeks to stage the event, working day and night, was never reported.)

A month later in London, Rockingham Rebels won the only BAFF championship beating the Croydon Coyotes 13–0. Both BAFF and Croydon have since folded but the Rebels are still out there somewhere. The final was not a good game. The only good outcome of the afternoon was the announcement at the game's end by BAFF's president Mike Lytton and the AFL's new chairman Terry Clark of a merger. The new league was to be called BAFL but members were not known because on the horizon loomed another league—the Budweiser League.

American brewers Anheuser Busch had decided months earlier that they wanted to sponsor a league. A series of meetings took place but personal differences marred any development.

In October of 1985 European Sales Director Harry Drnec declared defiantly: 'We are going to play football next year'. They did. Budweiser held their first meeting a week later, an open event for anyone interested in football. Most of the country's top teams attended.

When the London Ravens and Streatham announced their intention to join Budweiser a vicious war of words erupted that, at one stage, threatened the whole of football. The sport was in total disarray.

Budweiser appointed Chris Childs as its first commissioner and BAFL's Radcliffe Phillips embarked on a propaganda campaign the likes of which we had never seen before.

The war hotted up even more when the EFL, the sport's governing body in Europe, ruled that it would only recognize BAFL teams.

Birmingham's Mark Williams helped the club to a Summerbowl championship in 1986. (Fotosports International).

Open hostilities were declared when the Streatham Olympians were told that an attractive fixture against the top German team, Dusseldorf Panther, could not go ahead. They had already been snubbed once, in December, when Manchester Allstars took their place against a French team in Boulogne.

Such childish arguments about the right and wrong league quietened considerably in April when the regular season got underway.

For many people, 1986 was a season to consolidate. Teams were still springing up at an alarming rate. Radcliffe Phillips, still in the hot-seat at BAFL, announced that 'nearly every team was born pregnant'. Maybe they were but there was no way to stop the enthusiasm. If someone wanted to play football who had the right to stop them? Certainly not Phillips.

Birmingham, who had beaten Leicester in a Euro-Bowl preliminary cup tie in February, was the pre-season favourite to lift the Summer Bowl trophy.

In Budweiser, the Ravens were once again the team to beat.

Birmingham recieved a couple of jolts on their way to the championship—from Nottingham and Leicester—and in September gained much respect for the demolition of Glasgow Lions in the final.

The Ravens, meanwhile, had gone all season unbeaten before they came up against their old adversaries—Streatham—in the Budweiser Bowl at Crystal Palace two weeks earlier. A half-time lead of 20 points was nearly not enough as the Olympians came storming back in the fourth quarter. In the end Lance Cone was thankful for a 20–12 scoreline.

Cone was also thankful three months later when, after almost two years of bitter war, football was united. BAFL folded with debts of around £40 000, and a new-style Budweiser League with teams having control took over.

Much of the credit for uniting football must go, in future years, to David Gill, the chairman of the Budweiser League and owner of the Bournemouth Bobcats.

Gill travelled to every corner of the country cajoling and persuading teams to join his crusade.

It worked. For 1987, 106 teams were united. Some 40 others are members of the newly-formed BAFA—the sport's overall governing body.

A long way in a very short space of time. And that skateboard question—the answer is there for all to see!

European football

Italy
Football in Italy is probably the most advanced in Europe.

The Italian league (AIFA) was set up six years ago and has since grown into a formidable commercial set-up.

In 1986 Bologna Warriors defeated the Pesaro Angels in front of over 20 000 gridiron-hungry fans.

The Italian league is split into three divisions. The first, being the major league, has 20 clubs playing in regional leagues which culminate in the Super Bowl every July.

The Italian second and third divisions play their football in the autumn with the top clubs being promoted to the higher leagues the following spring.

Like most of Europe, AIFA rules that only two Americans can play in each team. But Italy also operates a non-American rule as well, although most clubs sign an American fullback who is then legally able to throw a pass once he has received the ball from an Italian quarterback.

Bologna Doves American running back Garry Pearson.

German star Marcus Becker.

Football in Italy has also benefited, largely because of its longer history, from major sponsorships, with one team, Bologna Doves, being owned by the giant Stiassi paperworks.

Germany

Like Italy, football in Germany has also been in existence for a long time. But that is where any similarity ends. There is no NFL football on TV in Germany so the game has not taken quite the same hold.

Nevertheless there are about 80 teams playing regular football in three divisions of excellence from April to October.

Dusseldorf Panther won the 1986 final beating out '85 winners Ansbach Grizzlies.

Other teams to watch out for include Hanau Hawks, Cologne Crocodiles and the Munich Cowboys.

France

Football in France has had a rather spasmodic existence. Crowds have varied considerably and, although the country is a great rugby playing nation, American football has yet to take a firm grip. Like Germany, NFL games are few and far between. Teams and growing

although the main bulk are centred in the north, especially around Paris. Top teams include Paris Jets and Paris Spartacus.

Holland

The Dutch are relative newcomers to the sport. However they did stage the last Euro-Bowl competition in their country last summer and their top team the Amsterdam Rams have been playing football for a number of years having played in the German third division before the Dutch association (NAFF) was born.

The Rams lost their top spot in 1986 when they were surprisingly beaten by the Hague Raiders in the final.

Finland

Few would have thought that this country, geographically out on a limb, could boast both national and club champions of Europe, but Finland can.

From a small city some 50 miles from Helsinki, TAFT (Terrikulen American Football Team), swept the board in last summer's Euro-Bowl beating the mighty Italians in the final.

The year before, the Finnish national team had shocked the football world with an equally surprising win over Italy in the Euro Nations Cup.

London Ravens' Victor Ebubedike. (*Fotosports International*)

Football in Finland has been thriving for a number of years and in summer 1987 the country staged the third European championships. Top teams include the Helsinki Rooster and, of course, TAFT.

Rest of Europe

Switzerland and Austria, landlocked in the middle of Europe, have been steadily growing in football terms over the past two seasons. Both countries were represented at the recent Euro-Bowl event with Salzburg Lions and Lugano Seagulls, the respective national champions.

Recent newcomers to the game include Ireland where the All-Ireland federation has 10 teams, the champions being the Dublin Celts.

The Rest of the World

Apart from Canada and Europe, football is also played in many other countries.

In Mexico the game has been growing since its introduction over half a century ago. But soccer is still No 1 and American football, because of its high cost to play, will probably only stay confined to some of the larger colleges.

In Japan the most popular team sport is baseball, so it comes as no surprise to learn that American football is also growing. In 1934 a group of American university professors visited Japan to study the education system, and left behind a legacy of their own game. It soon began to flourish, and by the end of the decade was becoming an accepted part of student life for many Japanese studying at universities. However, during the Second World War, because of the anti-American feeling in Japan, epitomized by the events at Pearl Harbor, football became one of the first things to be banned. As soon as the war was over, though, baseball and football began to pick up the pieces, but the foundations of the sport were lost and it took over 20 years to regain its status.

In 1970, a Japanese journalist, Sadao Goto, who was hooked on the game decided to publish a magazine, *Touchdown*, and many think that this helped to spark a genuine revival. Before this publication there were only 19 colleges playing the game, but today there are over 150 college teams, 500 highschool teams and in excess of 50 clubs organized mainly by some of the large Japanese manufacturing companies.

The NFL and the NCAA have not been slow to recognize the potential of football in the Orient. In 1975 the St Louis Cardinals and the San Diego Chargers played one of their pre-season games in Tokyo before a crowd of about 38 000. Every year since then top college teams have played an exhibition game in Japan, and the Mirage or Japan Bowl attracts crowds in excess of 70 000.

Most of the clubs are based around the cities of Tokyo or Osaka, although teams have been known to have started in some of the smaller islands off the southern mainland.

In 1986 Super Bowl III, as it was unofficially called, was played in Tokyo when Nihon University won the title in a bruising battle with Renown Rovers.

One Japanese player even tried out for an NFL team–but only as a kicker. Kyoji Matsui tried out for the San Diego Chargers in 1981, but didn't make the final squad.

Football is also spreading into the Antipodes with Australia now receiving regular NFL coverage. Teams are known to have formed in both Australia and New Zealand and there is already talk of a test series between Australia and Britain in 1989.

And although it has yet to be played there, the Super Bowl is now screened every year in China, where an estimated 40 million watched highlights of Super Bowl XXI some three months after the game.

6 Equipment

The sight of a 280lb lineman standing barefoot in nothing but his athletic support is awesome. With his rippling muscles, thighs and biceps like tree trunks, he is the epitome of athletic prowess.

But, before entering the arena to participate in the day's gladiatorial battle, a player must first don some 18 pieces of protective equipment. This will add a further 15lb or so to his weight, and will instantly turn him into a fearsome beast of enormous magnitude.

Some say that an American footballer is more protected than an astronaut, but, considering the very violent nature of his profession, every piece of equipment is necessary.

After donning a thick cotton T-shirt and a pair of elasticated ankle socks the player will undergo a process that is almost unique to American sports. Nearly all college and professional teams insist that their players' ankles are taped by the training staff. Taping, when done properly, can eliminate sprains and decrease the severity of other injuries, thus cutting down the period a player might be out of action.

It is said that up to 130 miles of tape are used every season by each NFL team. The NFL is rated as the world's largest consumer of elastic tape. Up to 10 yards of tape may be used just to wrap two ankles, these being parts of the body where the most work is done. Years ago players would first shave their legs so that the adhesive would not stick, but

Pittsburgh University's Troy Benson, a modern day warrior ready for battle – warpaint and all! (University of Pittsburgh).

nowadays with the invention of various types of pre-wrapping this is not necessary. Each team will employ a squad of trainers specifically to do this job.

First a spray of undercoat is administered over the ankles to prevent them from itching and to make the post-game removal process easier. Then special heel and lace pads are fitted to the foot. A light rubbery 'pre-wrap' comes next followed by the tape itself.

Shoes are often taped to the foot as well, with the aim of further decreasing the likelihood of silly knocks and sprains. The taping of ankles and feet is done an hour or so before the kick-off. After the players have returned from their pre-game warm-up the trainers will then get to work on other parts of the body: hands, shoulders, elbows, etc. The amount of tape used on the arms and hands depends

The New York Titans, of the old AFL, were the last team to use leather helmets in 1960.

Cleveland coach Paul Brown introduced the first cages for helmets in 1950.

129

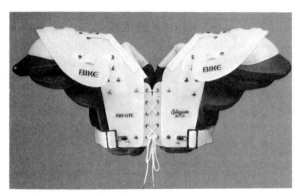
Shoulder pads.

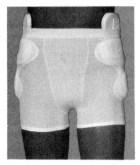
Girdle worn underneath pants.

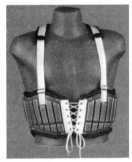
Rib protector.

Arm and hand pads.

entirely on the player's position. An offensive lineman will tape just his thumbs. Guards and tackles will often tape their entire forearms forming a rigid battering ram. Centers, who need more flexibility because of the snap of the ball will tape their forearms, but not as rigidly as other linemen.

Quarterbacks use the least tape of all. Because of their position, they need more mobility and flexibility than anyone else, so they only tape their ankles and wrists.

A running back will tape his wrists and forearms to a point just below the elbow, as will wide receivers and defensive backs. This gives the latter a certain amount of stickiness, which is an obvious advantage in pass receiving. The use of a substance known as 'stickum' (a sticky adhesive in which a receiver's hands and arms

could be smothered) has long since been banned.

Knee injuries account for about 25 per cent of all serious football knocks. Players with a history of such complaints are specially adorned with knee braces and supports. Special team players also have their own taping processes. Kickers are often taped in a manner that will lock the toes in an upright position, which helps to increase the height at which the football can be kicked and is especially used if the opposition employ a quick rushing blitz against the kick.

After the taping process the next piece of equipment to be placed upon the body is the pants. Made of nylon they are designed to be close-fitting and are made with special pockets so that foam thigh and knee pads can be inserted. It is now a mandatory requirement that players also wear a girdle under their pants which is fitted with foam cushioning hip and spine pads.

Back in football's pioneering days, when man-made fibres like nylon and plastic were unheard of, the players' equipment would be manufactured from cotton and wool. Taping, while used in some areas, was certainly not as common and thorough as it is today, so injuries happened more often and were invariably of a far more serious nature.

The players' pants were made originally from either cotton or thick wool. It was not until the 1920s that the Notre Dame head coach Knute Rockne designed a pair made from silk. These were cut very tight and less baggy-looking than the older designs. Shoulder pads, too, were made of more traditional materials, most commonly leather, which was often soaked and toughened in such a way as to become rock hard. The cumbersome padding built into the shoulder pads was made of horsehair, and such was their weight and awkwardness that players found it virtually impossible to throw long passes, or indeed even to catch them, so the game remained a mainly rushing affair.

After the Second World War came the invention of nylons and plastics. As with everything else, football changed much because of these new materials. Various designs of shoulder pads were made to suit the needs of players in each position. Those of a quarterback would be slim to enable him to move his arms freely and effect the pass of the ball. Linemen, on the other hand, would wear enormous

Injuries to players are treated as soon as possible, even on the sidelines. Note the knee brace. (All-Sport).

shoulder pads with huge epaulettes over the shoulders and deltoids. The weight of a modern pair of shoulder pads varies, but the average pair weighs around 6 lb. Nowadays they are made from nylon, plastics, rubber and other man-made fibres and afford the maximum protection to a player's upper body and shoulder area.

For injured players, various pieces of equipment have been used over the years, but the best design dates from 1978 when Byron Donzis invented an inflatable flak jacket to protect the injured ribs of Houston quarterback Dan Pastorini. The Donzis jacket weighed only 7 oz and soon other quarterbacks were copying it. The original design has since been further modified and very lightweight rib protectors that will enable even the most maimed and aching player to continue in the game are often used today. Attached to the main-frame of the shoulder pads are bicep pads, worn by some players, notably linemen, to protect the upper part of the arm, where so much of the hard hitting by the opposition line will be absorbed. Players who wish further to protect their necks (or those with a history of neck injuries) wear a neck roll, a soft piece of foam padding, which

attaches quite easily to the top of the shoulder pad.

The player's jersey identifies him by his number, and is made from tough nylon with overstitched seams.

In the early days of football, however, jerseys were made from wool and carried none of the striped and numbered patterns seen today.

It was not until 1921 that the Green Bay club became the first team to wear a distinctive marking on their game tops. The Indian packing company which owned the team paid $500 to purchase jerseys with the words 'Acme Packers' boldly emblazoned on them.

The first uniform bearing a team's identification came in 1926 when the Duluth Eskimos wore jerseys with a black and white igloo on the front. Until the 1930s numbers were not to be seen. They were then first worn on the front of the jerseys only, but the difficulty of recognizing players from only one angle resulted in their being placed on the back as well. Players' names were not placed on their jerseys until the AFL and the NFL merged in the season of 1970.

A player's footwear was probably the first piece of standard equipment used when football became a dominant force in the mid-60s. Originally the first shoes used were modified baseball shoes. They were high-topped boots, whose metal heels and sole plats were removed because they were considered too dangerous for a contact sport. In the 1890s shoes were developed with permanent cleats or studs and by 1921 the interchangeable cone-shaped stud was in use. Shoes of the 1920s and 1930s were very like those worn by European soccer players, large, heavy 'pit-type' boots made of leather. Over the years, as in most other sports, these shoes have become slim-lined and are now almost 'slipper' like. Until the mid-60s the colour of a player's shoes was always black. In 1966 New York Jets' quarterback Joe Namath sported a dashing pair of white ones, and a new trend was born. Players were quick to follow Namath's lead and nowadays almost all footballers wear what has become the traditional white. However, Baltimore's Alvin Haymond, quick to see the publicity gained by the Jets' player with his white shoes, decided to go one better and wore green ones!

A professional player today can have as many as four or five different types of shoes in his locker. The traditional grass shoe has seven rubberized cleats (two in the heel and five in the front); whilst the artificial turf shoe can have as many as 100 cleats which are shorter and smaller than for grass and give more grip on an unnatural surface. A shoe known as the Canadian Broomhall has become very popular in recent seasons. When stadiums switch from natural turf to a synthetic surface, teams can have many problems, and the Broomhall with four rubber cleats on the heel and up to a dozen on the front can be a great help.

A running back may use a spiked shoe, similar to that of an athlete, which improves his grip when running at high speed. Kickers also need special shoes. Some use a square-toed shoe to help give the football a better flight-path. Many others, like high jumpers, for instance, will use one type of shoe for the non-kicking foot, to get a good grip and balance from a sound footing, and a different shoe often of another colour, for kicking.

Other useful pieces of equipment used by players are thermal underwear, shin guards, wrist and elbow braces, and of course socks, which were made a mandatory item in 1945.

To a non-American the most distinguishing piece of equipment is without doubt the helmet. Because of the ferocity of the sport the helmet is probably the most important item in a player's kit. However, the helmet of today with its air-powered cushioning is a far cry from that used some 50 years ago.

As late as 1937 helmets were little more than flimsy pieces of leather, much like those used by Second World War fighter pilots. Many players found them distasteful, preferring to use a bushy head of hair as protection. It was felt by most that the use of a helmet was a slur on a player's manhood. Broken noses and disfigured faces were seen as noble battle scars with which to woo girlfriends. One famous battle-scarred face is that of actor Charlton Heston, who broke his nose twice whilst playing football at college.

After the war, players were required to wear headgear and, as with other pieces of equipment, helmets became more sophisticated.

The John T. Riddell Company which had manufactured pilots' helmets during the war years developed a plastic shell that became standard equipment in the league. It was initially rather weird in shape, but after more than a decade's development the modern-style teardrop-shaped helmet evolved. Face guards and cages, like helmets, were first shunned by the players. They were considered a slight to a player's masculinity. The Cleveland Browns' coach Paul Brown introduced the first cages in the early 1950s. Face guards had been around in various primitive forms as early as the 1930s, but as players suffered more and more facial injuries varying types of guards and cages were used. One and two bar masks became standard issue for backs and receivers whilst the linemen began wearing a multiple crossed bar version known as the birdcage. Nowadays there are about eight or nine different types of guard, which can be screwed to the helmet itself.

All clubs playing professional football today, with the exception of the Cleveland Browns, have their own distinctive logo emblazoned on the sides of the helmet. The tradition originated in 1948, when Fred Gehrke, the Los Angeles Rams' running back, took his helmet home and painted two yellow rams horns on it.

In later years Gehrke used to say that he had been scared of getting the sack when he took his helmet into the club. But much to his amazement the management liked his design, and soon all the Los Angeles Rams' helmets were laid out in Gehrke's garage being similarly decorated.

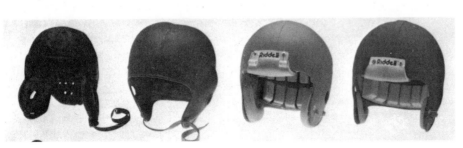

From left to right helmets through the ages.

132

It was not long before the rest of the football world took up the idea and now, of course, every team except for Cleveland have their own logo painted on their headgear. Attempts to put bull-eyes on helmets have foundered, however, as the NFL regards them as too obvious a target, and therefore potentially dangerous. The helmet of today is a far cry from that used during the Gehrke era. What is now seen is a highly sophisticated piece of equipment. The modern helmet weighs about 3lb and is made up of polycarbonate vinyl-foam, styrene and leather with an ingenious interior. Until recently, helmets were fitted with a honeycomb of pockets filled with liquid to fit a certain head size, but most of today's players wear helmets with air-filled pockets which are inflated to their full when placed on a player's head. Because all players' heads are of differing sizes this development has been extremely useful.

Twenty years ago when O. J. Simpson began playing college football these air-powered toppers had not even been invented. As Simpson's head was the oddest of shapes, when he joined the Buffalo Bills in 1969 he put the Bills' equipment manager into something of a spin. He told the Bills that he was unable to wear the conventional suspension types of helmet because of his unusually elongated face. A quick phone call was put through to his old college, USC in Los Angeles, and his hydraulic helmet was flown to Buffalo for him to use until a new one could be made.

A football helmet is not designed for use as a weapon. Each helmet bears the words: 'WARNING—Do not use this helmet to butt, ram, or spear an opposing player. This is in violation of football rules and can cause paralysis or death.'

A football helmet is worn as a protective measure, and the amount of battering it has to endure whilst protecting a player's cranium throughout a season is truly phenomenal. In 1962 a university professor sent Detroit line-backer Joe Schmidt out to play in the Pro Bowl with a specially wired-up helmet designed to measure the amount of stress the player was subjected to during a game. The test revealed some staggering facts. During the game Schmidt's helmet had had to withstand blows many times the force of gravity. To put this into perspective, an astronaut at blast-off is only subjected to 6gs, and a fighter pilot, faced with a force of 20gs will often black out.

A 'hot-seat' bench warmer sited in New York's Giants Stadium during the Jets–Bills fixture on a cold day in the big apple. (All-Sport).

Other pieces of equipment used in conjunction with the helmet are mouth-guards and chin-straps. Mouth-guards were originally modelled on those used by boxers, but at most clubs today a wax impression of a player's mouth is taken and a perfectly fitting guard is made for him. Quarterbacks usually dislike wearing mouth-guards because they cause speech problems when a player is trying to call plays, but as most have found to their cost it is better to put up with this than to lose three or four teeth.

The chin-strap usually has a four-point hook up and keeps the helmet firmly in place on the player's head. It is illegal for a player to go on to the field of play without having his chin-strap hooked up, and the penalty for doing so is the loss of a time-out, which in an extremely tight game could be very costly indeed.

Odds and Ends

There are various bits and pieces that players can and sometimes cannot use. The NFL requires all teams to have oxygen equipment and instant X-ray sets available within the confines of their stadiums. Oxygen is normally placed on the side-lines and often a TV viewer can see a player with the mask placed firmly over his face regaining some lost air after a long run.

During the winter months, and especially in the cold northern states, many teams wear women's tights for warmth. The Minnesota Vikings had theirs specially tested by a party of Everest mountaineers. Other little warming devices commonly in use are chemical bag hand warmers; battery-powered heaters which are taken on to the field during time-outs to warm up frozen fingers; electric blankets installed under the benches on the side-lines to keep feet warm; and pouch pockets, which are specially sewn-in pockets on game uniforms to enable the quarterbacks and also the receivers to keep their hands warm during play.

On rainy days ladies' hair spray can be seen on the sidelines for this is a good water repellent and can be used on shoes to keep players' feet dry. The St Louis Cardinals have a special ball dryer, a heated drum which keeps up to seven balls dry on wet days.

On days of sweltering hot weather, many teams use air-conditioning units on the sidelines to keep players cool. The first team to use such a device was the University of Southern California in 1977 whilst playing a game in steamy Alabama.

The Cost

The cost of kitting out an entire squad of 50 or so players and their coaches is colossal. Including such odds and ends as belts, shoelaces, practice pants and jerseys, sideline jackets, a bill for a professional team can be as high as $250 000. A major college team can expect to pay almost as much, whilst the newer developing teams in Europe do not have such a high price to pay. They still have to conform to standards governing the quality of their equipment, but they do without many of the extras used by the American professional teams. A typical British team would be faced with a bill in the region of £20 000 per annum.

The Name Game

Like any sport, football has its fair share of oddly-named characters. One of the funniest named players ever must be former pro quarterback Yelberton Abraham Tittle. Other names from the past that stick in one's mind are, Elmer Bighead, Fair Hooker and T. Truxton Hare.

Not to be outdone by the old timers, modern players also have an assortment of amusing names. The defunct USFL's Orlando Renegades offensive tackle Chuck Slaughter must have one of football's most apt surnames, whilst the Renegades, whose home is arguably the 'playground of America' (with Disney World and the futuristic Epcot centre on its doorstep), was owned by a certain Donald R. Disney!

In terms of family networks the Zendejas boys must rate highly. Tony Zendejas was the place-kicker for Los Angeles Express, cousin Luis kicked for the Arizona Outlaws after a record-breaking career at Arizona State University; Luis's brother Max kicker for the nearby University of Arizona; another brother, Joaquin, was place-kicker for the NFL's New England Patriots, and Martin Zendejas, brother of Tony and cousin of Luis, Max and Joaquin kicked for the University of Nevada at Reno.

Another kicker with a claim to fame is Obed Chuckwuma Ariri. Ariri was on Tampa Bay Buccaneers' books in 1984, and must have the most apt name of all time for a kicker. His middle name of Chuckwuma translated literally from his native Nigerian tongue means, 'God Only Knows!'

7 A Basic Guide To The Rules

American football has been described as scrappy, competitive, physical, pragmatic, yet in its own unique way it is very much like a game of chess played with human beings.

Often referred to as the 'gridiron', the 100 yards by 53 yards 1 foot playing area is further divided by chalk stripes marked horizontally across the field at 5-yard intervals. At either end are the end-zones or scoring areas which are a further 10 yards deep.

At the back of the end zones are the goalposts, one upright with a crossbar 18 ft wide, 10 ft above the ground. At either end of the crossbar are two uprights extending some 30 ft into the air. Rugby-type goalposts are still used in college football and here in the UK, but the new Y-shaped posts were adopted by the NFL in 1967.

Marked on the pitch itself are broken lines known as hashmarkings. These are placed 70 ft inside the side-lines and show the central playing area where all plays begin from. No matter where the play stops, the ball will always be resited within these lines.

The object of the game is to advance the ball by a series of plays, or 'downs' as they are called, into the opposition's end zone for which one is awarded a touchdown worth six points.

The team in possession of the ball will have four attempts or downs to advance the ball a minimum of 10 yards. After each attempt the game will stop, the officials will measure the distance gained or lost, and spot the football parallel to the yardage advanced.

The two teams will go into a group, or 'huddle' as it is known in football, and the next play will be planned.

With this information we can see that the phrase 'second and seven' means the team has moved three yards forward and is making its second attempt with seven yards to go.

'Third and long' or 'third and short' mean exactly what they sound like—the former means that the yardage needed to gain a first-down is more than 10 yards, and the latter means that there is under 3 yards to go to reach the required distance and get another first down, and four more attempts.

If the attacking team, known in American football as the offense, reaches the 10 yards mark within the four downs allowed to them, they will then be allotted another four downs to advance further. If they fail, the opposition gains possession of the ball and attempts to do the same thing towards the other end-zone.

Unlike soccer, where both the offense and defense are on the field at all times, American football has 11 men on the field to attack, and another 11 to defend, and a further squad of specialist players who are interchanged at various times throughout the game as tactics are altered either to gain or to stop the progress of the ball.

If a team's offensive unit loses possession they will leave the field and be replaced by their defensive team. Similarly a team gaining possession of the football on defense will swap their defensive unit for their offensive team.

A 'touchdown' does *not* have to be touched down in the end zone. As long as any part of the ball-carrier's body breaks the plane of the goal line, six points will be awarded. The forward pass is legal so a player can position himself actually in the end zone and receive a pass to score a 'TD' as the American commentators call it.

When a touchdown has been scored the offensive team will have a chance to score another point by kicking the ball between the uprights of the goal posts. In college football the team will also have the chance to score two points if they can return the football by rushing or passing back into the end zone. This two-point rule also applied in the USFL and the British game.

Apart from the touchdown and the extra points that can be derived from it, there are two other ways that points can be scored. A field goal, which is similar to a penalty kick in rugby, can be attempted at any time by the offensive team. A specialist kicker will come on to the field and if he can kick the ball between the uprights three points will be awarded. The other score is called a safety. If a player is caught inside his own end zone by a player from the opposing team, and brought to the ground, two points will be awarded to the opposition.

The playing time in American football is divided into four quarters of 15 minutes. Unlike soccer, however, when the ball is not in play the clock is stopped. This is the reason why a game can last anything up to three hours.

As in basketball each team is permitted six time-outs (three per half). After the first and third quarters the teams will immediately change ends, and only at half-time do they leave the field for a break.

The continual changing of ends is designed to give neither team any distinct advantage from any adverse weather conditions.

In cases where the score is level at full time, a 15-minute period of overtime is played and the first team to score is declared the winner. In regular season games in the NFL a tie or draw is declared if after this extra time the scores are still level. In the championship games at the end of the season further periods of extra time are played until a winner is found.

The offense or attacking team consists of five linemen: the center, who passes the ball between his legs to the quarterback; two guards either side of the center; and on either side of the guards, two tackles. This is the engine room of the team, pushing and blocking to protect their quarterback from marauding defensive players, or creating openings for running backs to run through.

Also on the offensive line is a tight end, whose position is close to the other linemen at the end of the line of scrimmage, and a split end, who, as his name suggests, is split further out.

Behind the offensive line are one or two backs. They can be positioned in many ways, the most favoured one in today's game being the 'pro set'. The No 1 back is the quarterback who is the most important player on the field, for it is his job to set up a play that will gain yards. By passing the ball to a powerful running back or throwing a long pass to a receiver he will orchestrate the attack of the team.

Depending on the play there will be a variety of formations used by the running backs. Fullbacks, tailbacks, flankerbacks and receivers make up the backfield along with the field general, the quarterback. On one play the quarterback may use two running backs and one wide receiver, in another only one running back and two wide receivers who will sprint down the field expecting to receive a pass.

The specialist men such as the kickers and the punters will be positioned on the sidelines awaiting their chance of glory. They will only come on to the field if required. A punter will be brought into the game if after three attempts a team has not made their required ten yards, and still has a long way to go. Instead of simply giving the ball to the opposition at that spot, the punter will kick the ball as far away from his own goals as possible, thus giving the opposition that much more ground to cover when their offensive drive begins.

On the defensive unit the first line of defense is made up of the linemen. The defensive tackles and defensive ends form the front line troops. The number of these players on a team can vary. Some teams will employ a four-man front with two tackles and two ends, whilst others might use only three men: two tackles flanking a nose-tackle.

The number of interior linemen also depends on how many linebackers are used. If four linemen are used, then only three linebackers will be employed. But if three linemen are positioned then four linebackers, two inside linebackers and two outside linebackers, will be in the formation. The linebackers are the roughest and toughest of all players; it is said to be a bad idea to allow your daughter to be dated by a linebacker! They are strong, fleet-footed players, whose main job is to stop the rush; they have to be mobile, agile and very, very hostile. It is usually the task of one of the middle linebackers to be the defensive team captain. He will be able to tell in an instant what the offense is doing and direct his troops to the danger zones.

Behind the linebackers, the last line of defense is made up of the cornerbacks and

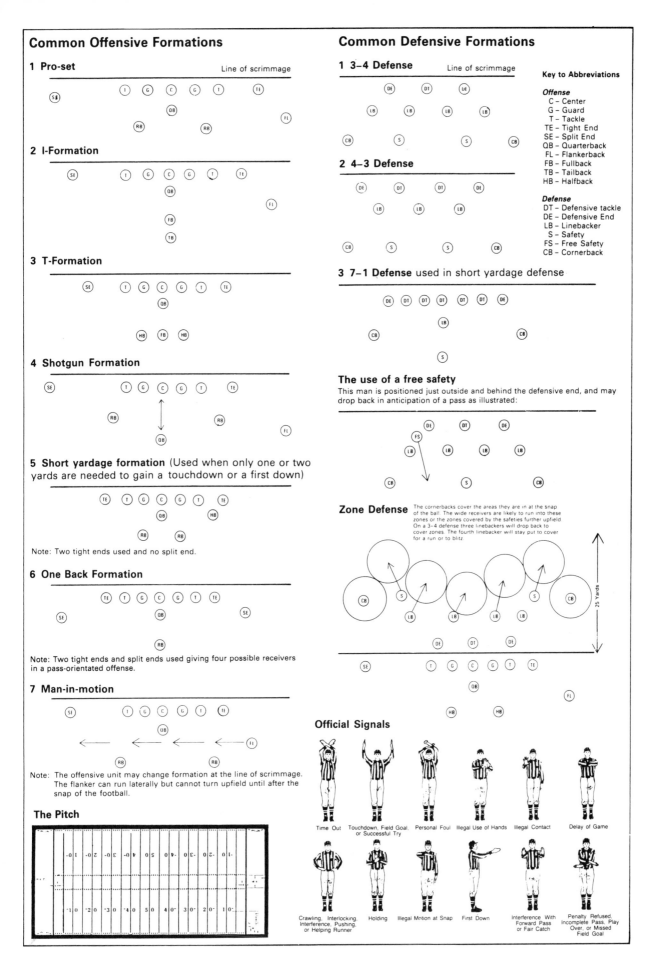

Common Offensive Formations

1 Pro-set
Line of scrimmage

2 I-Formation

3 T-Formation

4 Shotgun Formation

5 Short yardage formation (Used when only one or two yards are needed to gain a touchdown or a first down)

Note: Two tight ends used and no split end.

6 One Back Formation

Note: Two tight ends and split ends used giving four possible receivers in a pass-orientated offense.

7 Man-in-motion

Note: The offensive unit may change formation at the line of scrimmage. The flanker can run laterally but cannot turn upfield until after the snap of the football.

The Pitch

Common Defensive Formations

1 3–4 Defense
Line of scrimmage

2 4–3 Defense

3 7–1 Defense used in short yardage defense

The use of a free safety
This man is positioned just outside and behind the defensive end, and may drop back in anticipation of a pass as illustrated:

Zone Defense
The cornerbacks cover the areas they are in at the snap of the ball. The wide receivers are likely to run into these zones or the zones covered by the safeties further upfield. On a 3–4 defense three linebackers will drop back to cover zones. The fourth linebacker will stay put to cover for a run or to blitz.

25 Yards

Key to Abbreviations

Offense
C – Center
G – Guard
T – Tackle
TE – Tight End
SE – Split End
QB – Quarterback
FL – Flankerback
FB – Fullback
TB – Tailback
HB – Halfback

Defense
DT – Defensive tackle
DE – Defensive End
LB – Linebacker
S – Safety
FS – Free Safety
CB – Cornerback

Official Signals

Time Out | Touchdown, Field Goal, or Successful Try | Personal Foul | Illegal Use of Hands | Illegal Contact | Delay of Game

Crawling, Interlocking, Interference, Pushing, or Helping Runner | Holding | Illegal Motion at Snap | First Down | Interference With Forward Pass or Fair Catch | Penalty Refused, Incomplete Pass, Play Over, or Missed Field Goal

safeties, often called the secondary or umbrella. The secondary consists normally of four men: a strong safety, a free safety and two cornerbacks. The strong safety will line up on the opposition's tight end and will attempt to tackle him should he receive a pass. If the ball goes elsewhere then the strong safety will act as a back-up to the other defensive players. The free safety, who is often called a rover, acts as a sweeper and will move to wherever the action is. The job of the two cornerbacks is to mark the wide receivers. They will turn to intercept the ball and create a 'turnover'; or, if the intended receiver completes the pass, to halt his path towards the end zone immediately.

Each player's number denotes the position he plays, for only the tight ends, split ends, wide receivers, quarterbacks and runningbacks can receive a pass, in the right conditions. The only time one of the giant linemen can legally carry the ball is if the ball has been dropped by the opposition, and then the term 'fumble' is used.

The substitution of players is allowed at any time, when the ball is not in play, and teams will have at least three players for every position on the bench ready to go into action should a tactical change be necessary. Only 11 players are allowed on the field at any one time, but clubs are allowed to have a maximum of 45 kitted players ready on the sideline.

The main rule as the players prepare to make the play is that, once in the down position on the line of scrimmage, offensive linemen are not allowed to move until the ball has been passed from the center to the quarterback. As soon as the center moves the football, all sorts of things happen as linemen on both sides of the field hit each other with ferocious speed, each trying to outdo the other.

Although the offensive players cannot move once they are in a 'set' position, defensive players are allowed to move around, provided that they do not cross the line of scrimmage. The defense will try and make the offense jittery and cause them to move too soon, thus giving away a penalty.

The offensive players will block, using their forearms, and can only use their hands when forming a pocket to protect the quarterback while he is attempting to pass the ball. Then they cannot grab at an opponent, they will just use their hands to fend off attacking defenders as they retreat into their pocket.

The defense on the other hand can make greater use of their forearms and hands. They can use their hands in an attempt to get past offensive linemen, pulling or pushing them out of their path. For this reason, it is often said that defense comes naturally, whilst the finer points of offense have to be taught.

At various times during a game, a foul may be called by one of the seven officials on the field. If a foul is spotted, a yellow weighted duster will be thrown to the ground. As soon as the play comes to an end, the officials will meet and decide if the foul call should stand, or if an advantage has been gained already by the team against whom the foul was committed. A small discussion will take place between the referee and his other officials and a ruling will be made. The captains of the teams will then be called forward and they will be told the options that are open to them. Sometimes there can be many options open to a captain, but it is a general rule that a referee will give the best option first.

The penalties for fouls are either the loss of yards, which the referee will mark by moving the ball forward or backwards to the new starting spot, or the loss of a down. Thus a penalty committed on a first down might result in the play having to begin again as a second down from exactly the same position. Sometimes, as a penalty for serious fouls, a loss of yards and the loss of a down will be imposed together.

American football is a territorial game played with finely-tuned athletic bodies. It is without doubt one of the toughest games in the world, where players literally go through the pain barrier to ensure victory. The players' protective padding is often inadequate when two 20 stone, 6ft 6in Goliaths collide at breakneck speed. However, despite what is sometimes said, gridiron is one of the most strictly-controlled games in existence, as a result of rules that have evolved over a century of play. In recent years they have been modified to increase the excitement of the spectator, thus keeping the fans on the edge of their seats for the entire game.

'Nothing funny ever happens in football.' Tom Landry

---

8 Glossary

Pro football teams have their own language. It is different from the language of the sports page or the television booth. It is strange, even bizarre. And it may be the single most complex aspect of the sport.

The following terms are authentic. Coaches and players actually speak them to each other. Terms such as these and others that teams adopt for a season make up the jargon they speak—the secret language of their meetings, practices, and games. But if coaches and players can understand pro football language, others can, too. In doing so, it is possible to gain greater insight into the true nature of the game and how its people think.

A 1. The halfback on the left side. 2. The onside guard pulling and blocking a cornerback or safety.

ace A formation with two wide receivers on one side, a third wide receiver or back on the other side out wide, and one back in the backfield.

alley The area between the hashmarks and the field numbers, from the line of scrimmage to 15 yards downfield.

audible A call changing the offensive at the line of scrimmage.

away The remaining back going away from the point of attack.

ax Knocking down a receiver.

B The back on the right side.

back A call to change the defense from a called front to a four-three front.

backer A linebacker.

Ben A block by a back on a defensive end.

blast Pass rush by defensive tackles.

blitz An all-out rush by the defense.

Bob A block by a back on a backer.

bomb A long pass.

bomber Force by a backer, same as bronco.

bootleg The quarterback moving with the ball away from the flow.

boss A block by the near back on the first defensive back to show.

both near A formation with both X and Z one to three yards from the offensive tackles.

bronco Force by a backer; same as bomber.

brown A formation with the fullback behind the quarterback and the halfback on the weakside; same as far, four right, and opposite.

Buck The backside or weakside linebacker; same as Wanda and Willie.

Buck ax Buck knocking down a receiver.

Buck I Buck dogging.

buzz A linebacker covering passes; same as drop.

call A command.

check with me A call by the quarterback in the huddle telling the team he will audible a play at the line of scrimmage.

Cleo 1. Force by a cornerback; same as cloud and crash. 2. A block by a wide receiver on a cornerback.

close The alignment of a slot receiver in tight less than three yards from the tackle.

cloud Force by a cornerback; same as Cleo and crash.

club A block by a tackle on a middle linebacker.

combo Combination pass coverage by Jill and Sam on Y and the strongside back.

corner The deep outside zone of the field.

counter A play in which one or more backs move away from the point of attack.

crackback A block by a wide receiver on a linebacker. Illegal.

crash Force by a cornerback; same as Cleo and cloud.

cross A call alerting the defense that a receiver is crossing shallow.

cutback Maintaining inside position on a running back and tackling him when he turns inside; same as fill.

deep middle The middle one-third of the field from 15 yards from the line of scrimmage to the goal line; same as post.

delayed sweep A sweep with backfield deception and which develops late.

dog Pass rush by defensive players other than linemen.

double wing A formation with two wide receivers on each side and only the halfback in the backfield behind the quarterback; same as dual, deuce, and duce.

down A block by the tight end and tackle one man farther in than usual, the tight end now blocking the defensive end and the tackle blocking the defensive tackle.

draw A running play with a delayed handoff and delayed blocking off an initial action that shows pass.

drop A linebacker covering passes; same as buzz.

dual Same as double wing.

duce Same as double wing and dual.

eat A double team block by a tight end and tackle on a defensive end.

even 1. A defensive front with tackles head on the offensive guards and ends head on the offensive tackle. 2. Ordinary run blocking with each lineman responsible for the defender in front of him. 3. A block by the onside guard pulling and blocking a cornerback or safety, with the tackle going through on the middle linebacker and the center cut-blocks.

F 1. A series or family of running plays in which the fullback hits over the onside guard as a blocker, faker, or ball carrier. 2. A replacement block by a back on a defensive tackle.

fan The areas of the field between the flats and the corners.

far 1. A formation with the fullback behind the quarterback and the halfback on the weakside; same as brown, four right, and opposite. 2. A position of the weakside back more than three yards from the tackle.

fill Maintaining inside position on a running back and tackling him when he turns inside; same as cutback.

fire A call by a defensive player as soon as he has made an interception; same as oskie.

five-three A defense with five linemen and three linebackers.

flanker Z.

flare action The coordinated movement of running backs to block dogging linebackers, or if there are none, to go out for passes.

flat The area of the field from the line of scrimmage to a point eight yards downfield and, horizontally, from two yards outside the field numbers on each side of the side-lines.

flex 1. A defense with the linemen staggered on and off the line of scrimmage. 2. The alignment of X only three to six yards from the tackle.

flip 1. A quick lateral pass to a back in the two or four position. 2. A series or family of plays built around that play. 3. A block by the onside tackle on the cornerback or safety.

float Alignment of Z three to six yards from Y; same as X in flex.

flood Putting more than one receiver in a zone so the defender playing that zone can't cover them all.

flop Change sides.

flow 1. The direction of play. 2. Movement of the remaining back or backs to the side of the point of attack. 3. A series or family of plays with the backs moving toward the same side.

flux A formation with X flexed and Z floating.

fly A back in motion to the weakside.

fold A combination block by the center and a guard against an even front, the center blocking on the defensive tackle and the guard pulling through and blocking the middle linebacker.

force Turning a running play inside; same as support.

four position Behind the right offensive tackle.

four I A formation with the tight end and the two running backs in a line behind the quarterback.

four right Early name for formation in which the back in the four position moves out to become the flanker; same as brown, far, and opposite.

four-three A defense with four linemen and three linebackers.

front The defensive line and linebackers.

full 1. A formation with the running backs behind the tackles and the fullback in the four position; same as red and split right. 2. A series or family of plays in which attack as a blocker, faker, or ball carrier. 3. A block by a back or a defensive tackle or a defensive tackle or linebacker after the guard has pulled.

G A block by the onside guard, pulling and blocking the outside man on the line of scrimmage, usually the outside linebacker.

gadget A trick play.

gap 1. The space between two offensive linemen. 2. A defense with a man in every gap.

gap over A defense with the weakside defensive tackle moving into the weakside guard-center gap.

gap under A defense with the strongside defensive tackle moving into the strongside guard-center gap.

gas A double-team block by the center and a guard on a defensive tackle.

go A back in motion to the strongside.

gob A block by a guard on a backer; same as G.

gone A defense without a middle linebacker.

green A formation with the running backs behind the tackles and the halfback in the four position; same as half and split left.

gut A cross block by the onside guard and tackle, the guard going first.

half A formation with the running backs behind the tackles and the halfback in the four position; same as green and split left.

half zoom Z in motion toward the ball and the ball snapped before he reaches the tight end.

hole The area of the field between the hooks.

hook 1. A block by a tight end on a linebacker, preventing him from going outside. 2. The area of the field extending from the Y position to points 15 to 18 yards upfield.

I 1. A formation with two running backs in a line behind the quarterback. 2. A series or family of plays from the I formation.

I man A defensive tackle.

Influence Deception by the offensive line, denying keys to the defense and leading it away from the play.

isolation block A block by a back on a defensive lineman who has been influenced.

Jack A combination block with the guard blocking the middle linebacker

Jerry A charge by a defensive tackle to the inside gap.

Jill The weakside or free safety.

jumbo A defense with six or more linemen.

key An alignment or movement telling a defensive player where the ball is going or what blocks to expect.

lead A block by a running back, preceding the other running back into the line and blocking the first defender in his path.

Les The left safety, who could be Jill or Sam.

Lex A stunt by Lon and Lin, crossing at the snap of the ball.

Lin The left I man or defensive tackle.

Linda Zone rotation left.

Link The left linebacker, who might be Stub or Buck.

Linki Link inside his normal position.

Linko Link outside his normal position.

lion A slant by both defensive tackles to the left.

log A block by pulling linemen, hooking the defender to the inside.

Lon The left O man or defensive end.

Lou The left cornerback.

Mac The middle linebacker.

Mac I Mac dogging.

mad dog Mac, Stub, and Buck dogging.

man-for-man Pass coverage in which each defender is assigned to a specific receiver for the entire play.

Mike A nose tackle.

misdirection Deception by the offensive backfield, denying keys to the defense and leading it away from the play.

mix A stunt by Mac and a defensive tackle.

mombo Combination pass coverage by Mac and the outside linebacker on Y and the first back out of the backfield.

near 1. A formation with the fullback behind the quarterback and the halfback on the strongside; same as blue, strong, two left, and wing. 2. Alignment of X only one to three yards from the tackle.

nickel A defense with five defensive backs.

nose tackle A lineman head on the center.

O A block by the offside guard, pulling to the onside and leading the back through the hole.

odd A defense that is not even, i.e. an over or under.

offside The side away from the play.

Okie A three-four defense.

O man A defensive end.

onside The side to which the play goes.

opposite A formation with the fullback behind the quarterback and the halfback on the weakside; same as brown, far, and four right.

option 1. Running without predetermining the hole in the line where the ball carrier must go, allowing him to run wherever he sees open space; same as running to daylight. 2. A running play in which the quarterback moves down the line and has the option to hand off, pitch, or run. 3. A play in which the runner has the option to run or pass. 4. Blocking in which the lineman carries the defender in the direction his own movement is taking him rather than in a predetermined direction.

oskie A call by a defensive player as soon as he has made an interception; same as fire.

over A defense with the weakside defensive tackle head on the center and Mac head on the weakside guard.

peel A dogging linebacker or defensive back stopping his rush and covering an offensive back who releases for a pass.

pick A screen by a receiver on a defensive back to take him out of coverage.

pinch A charge by the defensive linemen to the inside.

pix Y when he is the only receiver on his side.

play action Plays in which the quarterback fakes a handoff and passes; same as play pass.

play pass Same as play action.

poc Alignment of Y one to three yards from the tackle.

port Early name for left defensive halfback.

post 1. The middle one-third of the field from a point 15 yards from the line of scrimmage to the goal line; same as deep middle. 2. The outside receiver on the two-receiver side of a slot formation. 3. A call by defenders to team mates that a receiver has broken for the deep middle.

power 1. Any formation with three running backs in the backfield. 2. Double-team blocking at the point of attack.

prevent Any defense designed specifically to stop long passes.

pro A four-three defense.

queen A combination block with the tackle blocking the middle linebacker.

Rat A right linebacker farther in than Ripi.

read See a key and interpret it.

red A formation with the running backs behind the tackles and the fullback in the four position; same as full and split right.

red dog Stub and Buck dogging.

replacement block A back filling the space left when a lineman pulls, blocking the defender.

Rex A stunt by Ric and Roy, crossing the snap of the ball.

Ric The right I man or defensive tackle.

Rip 1. The right linebacker, who could be Stub or Buck. 2. A charge by Mike to the right.

Ripi Rip inside his normal position.

Ripo Rip outside his normal position

Roger Zone rotation right.

Rose The right cornerback.

rotation Shifting zone coverage left or right.

Roy The right O man or defensive end.

rule blocking The coordinated action by which offensive linemen know substitute blocking assignments if the defense changes its alignment.

run to daylight Running without predetermining the hole in the line where the ball carrier must go, allowing him to run wherever he sees open space; same as option running.

Russ The right safety, who could be Jill or Sam.

Sam The strongside safety.

Sara The strongside linebacker; same as Stub.

scissors Cross-blocking.

scoop A block by an offside lineman toward the onside, usually against an odd front.

scramble screen A screen pass in which the tackles pass protect and the guards and center fake a roll or cut-block and scramble to set up a blocking wall left or right.

scrape Charge by a linebacker off the position of a defensive lineman.

screen A pass that develops behind the line of scrimmage, in which the rushers are allowed to penetrate while the offensive linemen fake blocks and then set up a wall for the receiver.

shield A block by a wide receiver on a cornerback.

shotgun A red formation with the quarterback seven to nine yards behind and taking a long snap from center.

shovel pass A pass behind the line of scrimmage to a receiver who then runs in a designated hole.

Sid The middle safety of a three-deep defense.

sky 1. Force by a safety; same as stone. 2. A block by a wide receiver on a safety.

slam The strongside defensive end charging to the inside.

slant 1. A planned charge by a defensive lineman to the left or right instead of straight ahead. 2. A running play hitting sharply off guard or tackle. 3. A series or family of plays built around that play.

slash A shield block by a wide receiver on a linebacker.

Slot 1. A formation with both wide receivers on the same side; same as twin. 2. The inside receiver on the side. 3. The area between X and his tackle end, on the other side, between Z and Y, to points eight yards downfield.

split left A formation with the running backs behind the tackles and the halfback in the four position; same as green and half.

split right A formation with the running backs behind the tackles and the fullback in the four position; same as full and red.

split end X.

spread A formation with no running backs at all in the backfield with the quarterback.

spy Restrained pass rush by a defensive lineman as he watches for draw plays or screens.

stack 1. A linebacker behind the linemen. 2. A defense with the line shifting to the tight end and the linebackers behind the linemen.

starboard Early name for the right defensive halfback.

stone Force by a safety; same as sky.

strong A formation with the fullback behind the quarterback and the halfback on the strongside; same as blue, near, and wing.

strong dog and cat Mac and Stub dogging.

strongside The side of the offensive formation with Y and Z, the tight end or flanker, or if slot formation, the side with the two wide receivers.

strong zone Zone rotated to the strongside.

Stub The strongside linebacker, same as Sara.

Stub ax Stub knocking down a receiver.

stunt An unusual change by linebackers and linemen, or by linemen alone, in which they loop around each other instead of charging straight ahead.

sucker play A play in which the back runs into the hole left when the defensive lineman is lured away chasing a pulling guard.

tag A double team block by a tackle and a guard on a defensive tackle.

three I A formation with a wide receiver and the two running backs in a line behind the quarterback.

three position In the backfield directly behind the quarterback.

tight end Y.

toss A pitchout.

trap A block by an offside guard pulling to the onside and driving the defender out.

trey A formation with three receivers on one side and only the fullback behind the quarterback.

triple Same as trey.

twin A formation with both wide receivers on the same side; same as slot.

two position Behind the left offensive tackle.

two left Early name for formation in which the back in the two position moves out to become the flanker; same as blue, near, strong, and wing.

unbalanced A line with both tackles lined up beside each other, creating four linemen on one side and two on the other.

under A defense with the strongside defensive tackle head on the center and Mac head on the strongside guard.

Viking A charge by a nose man straight into the center and controlling both gaps to the left and right of him.

waggle The quarterback moving with the ball away from the flow with protection.

Wanda The weakside linebacker; same as Buck or Willie.

weakside The side of the offensive formation with only one receiver.

weak dog and cat Mac and Buck dogging.

weak zone Zone rotated to the weakside.

wedge Double-team blocking; shoulder-to-shoulder, straight ahead.

wham The weakside defensive end charging to the inside.

Willie The weakside linebacker; same as Buck or Wanda.

wing 1. A formation with the fullback behind the quarterback and the halfback on the strongside; same as blue, near, strong, and two left. 2. Z aligned one to three yards from Y.

X The split end.

Y The tight end.

yoyo Double coverage on the tight end.

Z The flanker.

zone Pass coverage in which defenders are assigned specific areas to cover, not specific receivers.

zoom Z going in motion.

Index

Page numbers in italics refer to illustrations, those in bold to continuous treatment of a subject; *col* refers to colour pages. Players and teams mentioned only in tables, and non-US/Canadian teams mentioned only in pp 125–7 are not indexed. University teams are suffixed 'U'. The American system of compressed page references has been used, thus '22–7' means references will be found on each page.

A
Acme Packers [later Green Bay Packers] *14*, 22
Adams, K S 'Bud' Jr 63
Adderley, Herb 43, 51
Akron Pros 11–12, 22
Alabama U 108, 112–13
Albert, Frankie 98
All-America Football Conference [AAFC, later NFL] 17, 24
Allegheny Athletic Association 8, 22
Allen, George 89, 100–1, 116
Allen, Marcus *col12*, 20, 46, 48, 114–15
Alworth, Lance 51, 77
Ameche, Alan 18, 25, 65, 114
American Football Conference [AFC] 27–30, 33; 1986 statistics 101–2; teams 59–80
American Football League [AFL] 19, 23, 25–7, 31–3
American Professional Football Association [later NFL] 11–12, 22
Amos Alonzo Stagg Bowl 112
Arbanas, Fred 66
Ariri, Obed Chuckwuma 134
Arizona State U 106, 108, 110
Arnspager, Bill 92
Atkins, Doug 51
Atlanta Falcons 26, 32, 58, **80–1**
Auer, Joe 69
Austin, Bill 76
Austria 127

B
babysitters 39
Bach, Joe 74–5
Badgro, Morris 'Red' 51
Balanda, George 51
Baltimore Colts [later Indianapolis Colts] 18, 25–7, 33, 44
Barber, Red 24
Barni, Roy 100
Battles, Cliff 51
Baugh, Sammy 50–1, 63, 72, 100, **104–5**, *105*
Bavaro, Mark 47
Baylor U 107–8
Becker, Marcus *126*
Bednarik, Chuck 42, 51
Bell, Bert 14–15, *15*, 23–5, 30–1, 38, 50–1, 65, 74, 93–4
Bell, Bobby 51, 115
Bell, Upton 61
Bennett, Leeman 81, 99
Bennigsen, Ray 96
Benson, Tom 91
Benson, Troy *129*
Berry, Raymond *col11*, *19*, 51, 72
Berwanger, Jay 15, 23, 38, 42, 114
Bettis, Tom 67
Bidwill, Charles 'Stormy' Jr 27, 96–7
Bidwill, Charles W Snr 51, 96
Bidwill, William V 27, 96–7
Big Ten [Western Athletic Conference] 10, 106, 108, 111
Biles, Ed 64
Biletnikoff, Fred 48
Bishop, Keith 51
Blanchard, Doc 'Mr Inside' 17, 107, 114
Blanda, George 63, 68
Bleier, Rocky 76
Blood, Johnny *see* McNally, Johnny 'Blood'
Blount, Alvin *108*
Boston Patriots [later New England Patriots] 25–7, 31, 34
Boston Redskins [formerly Braves, later Washington Redskins] 15–16, 23
Boston Shamrocks 23

Boston Yanks [later New York Bulldogs] 24
Bowl Games, college 109–13
Bowlen, Patrick 29, 45
Bradley, Lee 95
Bradshaw, Terry 35, 42, 45, 48, 76–7, 82
Braman, Norman 30
Britain 122–5, 127–8
British Columbia Lions 118–9
Brooker, Tommy 26, 32
Brooklyn Tigers [formerly Dodgers, later Boston Yanks, NY Bulldogs] 23–4
Brown, Charlie 45
Brown, Jim 18–19, 25, 51, 61
Brown, Paul 17, 19, 26, 31, 51, 60–1, 129, 132
Brown, Roger *25*
Brown, Roosevelt 36, 51
Brown U 108, 110
Brown, Willie 51
Bryant, Paul 'Bear' 7, 106
Budweiser League 124–5
Buffalo All-Americans 22
Buffalo Bills 25–6, 30–1, **59–60**
Bullough, Hank 60
Buncom, Frank 78
Butkus, Duck 51
Butler, Keith *76*
Byars, Keith *94*

C
Calhoun, George 22
California U 10, 106, 108
Camp, Walter 7
Campbell, Hugh 64
Campbell, Joe 120
Campbell, Marion 81, 95
Canadeo, Tony 51
Canadian football 118–21
Cannon, Billy 42, 63, 114
Canton Bulldogs 9–11, *12*, 22–3
Card–Pitts 24, 74, 96
Carr, Joe 12, 22–3, 30, 50–1
Center U 108, 110
Chamberlin, Guy 51
Chandler, Chris *col8*
Chandler, Don 26, 43, 87
Chicago Bears [formerly Decatur, Chicago Staleys] 12–13, *col13*, 15–16, 23–6, 30, 38, 46, 58, **80–4**
Chicago Cardinals [formerly Normals, later St Louis Cardinals] 22–3, 25
Chicago Rockets 22
Chicago Staleys 22
Chicago U 8
Childs, Chris 124
Christiansen, Jack 51, 98
chronology 22–30
Cincinnati Bengals 26, 28–9, 33, 37, 45, 60
Clair, John E 22, 86
Clark, Dwight 83
Clark, Earl 'Dutch' 50–1, 85
Clark, James P 24, 93–4
Clark, Monte 98
Clark, Terry 124
Cleveland Browns 17–19, 24–5, 46, 60–2
Cleveland Rams [formerly Indians, later Los Angeles Rams] 17, 22–4, 33
clothing 129–34
Cofall, Stan 22
College Football Conferences 108–9
Collier, Blanton 26, 61
Collins, Ted 24–5
Columbia U 7, 108
Columbus Panhandlers 22
Cone, Lance 123, 125
Conkright, Bill 'Red' 67–8
Conlan, Shane *106*
Connor, George 51, 115
Conzelman, Jimmy 51, 96
Cooper, Earl 45
Cope, Tony *123*
Copley, James 78
Coryell, Don 79, 96
Cotton Bowl 111–2
Cox, Steve *col10*
Craig, Roger 46
Cribbs, Joe *col6*
Crowley, Jim 14, 114

Csonka, Larry 20, *34*, 44–5, 48, 70
Culverhouse, Hugh F 36, 99
Cuozzo, Gary 65

D
Dallas Cowboys 25–8, 30, 33–34, 36, 38, 40, 44–5, 58, **84**
Dallas Texans [1959–63, later Kansas City Chiefs] 26, 32
Dallas Texans [1952 Colts, formerly Baltimore, later Indianapolis] 25
Daugherty, Duffy 107
Davis, Al 26, 32, 67–8
Davis, Ernie 42, 61, 100, 114
Davis, Glenn 'Mr Outside' 17, 107, 114
Davis, Willie 51
Dawson, Len 44, 47–8, 50
Dayton Triangles 22
DeBartolo, Edward J Jr 28, 98
Decatur Staleys [later Chicago Bears] 11, 22
Dempsey, Tom, 27, 90
Denver Broncos 25–6, 28–9, 32–4, 36, 46–7, **62–3**
Dethman, Bob 111
Detroit Lions, [formerly Portsmouth Spartans] 25–7, 33, **85–6**
Detroit Panthers 23
Detroit Tigers 22
Devine, Dan 88
Devore, Hugh 94
Dewveall, Willard 25
Dickerson, Eric *89*
Dietz, Will 'Lone Star' 99
DiMelio, Luby 74
Ditka, Mike 84
Donelli, Buff 74–5
Donovan, Art 52
Donzis, Byron 131
Douds, Forrest 'Jap' 74
Dowhower, Rod 66
Dowler, Boyd 43
draft system 15, 23, 30, **38–9**; number one choices 42
Dreyfuss, Barney 22
Driscoll, John 'Paddy' 23, 52, 95–6
Dudley, Bill 'Bullet' 42, 52, 75
Duke U 108, 111
Dunigan, Matt *119*, *120*

E
Eason, Tony *col9*, *col11*
Ebubidike, Victor *127*
Edmonton Eskimos 119–20
Edwards, Glenn 'Turk' 52
Eisenhower, Dwight D 110
Elway, John *col4*, 42, 46, *62*, 63
equipment 129–34
Erdelatz, Eddie 67
Erhardt, Ron 72
European football 125–7
Everett, Jim *col1*
Ewbank, Wilbur C 'Weeb' 25, 27, 52, 65, 72

F
Fairbanks, Chuck 61, 72
Faison, Earl 78
Faloney, Bernie 120
Faulkner, Jack 62
Fears, Tom 17, 52
Feathers, Beattie 84
Feldman, Marty 67
Fenney, Rick *113*
Filchock, Frank 24, 62, 74, 91
Finland 126, 128
Flaherty, Ray 16, 52, 100
Flores, Tom 68
footwear 129–34
Ford, Gerald 110
Ford, Henry 80
Ford, Len 52
Ford, William Clay 86
Fordham U 107–8
formations 137, 139–42
Fortmann, Dan 52
Foss, Joe 25–6, 69
Fouts, Dan *col5*, 78–9
France 126
Frankford Yellowjackets [later Philadelphia Eagles] 23
Frontiere, Georgia 89

Fuqua, John 'Frenchy' 76

G
Gabriel, Roman 42, 89, 95
Garrett, Mike 66, 114–5
Gator Bowl 112
Gatski, Frank *30*, 52
Gault, Willie *81*
Gehrke, Fred 24, 132
George, Bill 52
Georgia Tech 108, 110–12
Germany 126
Gibbs, Joe 45, 101
Gibson, Billy 23
Gifford, Frank 52, 92
Gilchrist, Cookie 59, 62
Gill, David 125
Gilliam, John 90
Gillman, Sid 52, 56, 64, 77–8, 88–9
Gipp, George 10–11, 110
Glanville, Jerry 64
Gogolak, Peter 26
Gordon, Richard F Jr 90
Gouka, Larry 50
Graham, Otto 25, 52, 60–1, 100
Grange, Harold 'Red' 10, 12–13, 23, 50, 52, 81, 91, 107
Grant, Bud 20, 120
Gray, Earnest 97
Gray, Gene 111
Green Bay Packers [formerly Acme Packers] *14*, 16, 23–4, 26–9, 33, 35, 43–4, 48, **86–8**
Greene, 'Mean' Joe 20, 45, 50
Gregg, Forrest 52, 60–1, 88
Grier, Roosevelt 'Rosie' 89, 117
Griese, Bob 45, 70
Griesedieck, Joseph 96
Grigas, Johnny 75
Grogan, Steve 61
Groza, Lou 17, 52
Gunsel, Austin 25, 31
Guyon, Joe 52

H
Hadl, John 77
Halas, George 12–13, 16, *19*, 22–5, 27, 50, 52, 81, 84, 110
Hall of Fame, members **51–5**
Ham, Jack 45
Hammond Pros 22
Hanifan, Jim 96
Hapes, Merle 24, 91
Harris, Franco **20–1**, *21*, 27, 48, 76–7
Harris, James 89
Hartman, Gerry 123
Harvard U 7, 108, 110, 118–9
Haymond, Alvin 131
Healey, Ed 52
Hecker, Norb 80
Heffelfinger, William 'Pudge' 8, 19, 22
Hein, Mel 50, 52
Heisman Trophy 113–5
Henry, Wilbur 'Pete' 50, 52
Herber, Arnie 52
Herschberger, Clarence 8
Hess, Leon 72–3
Heston, Willie 'The Wisp' 107
Hewitt, Bill 52
Hickey, Howard 'Red' 98
Hill, King 42, 94
Hilton, Conrad and Barron 77–8
Hinckle, Clarke 53
Hirsch, Elroy 'Crazy Legs' 17, 53, 88
Hirt, Al 90
Hoak, Dick 20
Holland 126
Holovak, Mike 61
Holtz, Lou 73
Hope, Bob 89
Hornung, Paul 26, 42, 53, 87, 114
Horween, Arnold 'McMahon' 95
Houston, Ken 53
Houston Oilers 25–6, 30, 32, **63–4**
Howell, Jim Lee 92
Howley, Chuck 44, 48
Howsam, Bob and Lee 62
Hubbard, Cal 23, 50, 53
Huff, Sam 18, 53
Hughes, Chuck 86
Hughes, Ed 64
Hunnington, Hollis 110
Hunt, Lamar 25–6, 31–2, 43, 53, 66
Hutson, Don 16, 50, 53